Praise For

Pursued

Michael Heil's book is the best example of God's effectual calling of anyone I have met or heard about. In spite of Michael's resisting God's love and grace with his rebellion and seeking meaning and purpose in life through all the ways the world offers, our Heavenly Father reached down and marvelously saved Michael. This book will capture your heart as you see the steadfast love of our Lord Jesus overcoming all of Michael's resistance and claiming Michael for His own. In this book, we see the beauty of the heart of Jesus as His love and grace are greater than all our sin—no matter the depths of sin to which we have descended. Michael's book will encourage anyone who is seeking real meaning & purpose in life to turn to Jesus and find what matters most in life—life eternal. I highly recommend this book for those who already know Jesus & those seeking Him.

—James Stewart, South Region Coordinator for Evangelism Explosion International

***

This book is vulnerable, extensive, articulate, and engaging through invigorating and adventurous personal experiences that help the reader to see the redemptive power of the living God. Through the writer's journey, I was reminded how God pays attention to every detail of our lives and will use it to reveal his glory. I was taken on a journey of tears, laughter, and raw truth. I recommend this book to youth pastors, leaders, and missionaries. And anyone who struggles to see the power of God at work.

—Mpumi Maweni, Director of Mobilization, Operation Mobilization, Canada

***

Michael Heil's memoir tells us a real-life, modern-day retelling of the Prodigal Son parable. The details of his life describe how the wayward human mind can move away from God's loving and caring, beautiful plans for each of us.

As with the original Prodigal Son, the blessings of living in the Father's house eventually make every prodigal child wonder why they are not living under God's will for their lives. It is delightful to see the changes in a spiritually, physically, and emotionally transformed life by the love and lordship of Jesus Christ.

—Harold Viana, Youth With A Mission Asia and Pacific Region

***

Wow! Some might think Michael Heil's story and the miracles he experienced on his journey are almost unbelievable. Knowing Mike personally allows me to express that I believe his story is true. If you're a parent dealing with a wayward child, this book will bless you and provide you with some hope. If you're a high school or college student, this book may be the light at the end of a dark tunnel you desperately need. I really hope a lot of people read it and discover the power of God's love!

—Rev. Greg Johnson, President of Standing Together

***

Now and then, The Lord raises up a Nehemiah. He has been preparing him to lead a great work. Often these servants have experiences that are there to prepare them for a great work. I believe that's what the Lord has done with Brother Michael Heil. His story is very powerful & compelling, redemption at its best. What a tangible example of the blessing of responding to God's call in one's life.

—Pastor Dewayne Rembert, Founder of Flatline Movement

Pursued

God's relentless pursuit and a drug addict's journey to finding purpose

Michael J. Heil

Published by KHARIS PUBLISHING, an imprint of

KHARIS MEDIA LLC.

Copyright © 2023 Michael J. Heil.

ISBN-13: 978-1-63746-208-9

ISBN-10: 1-63746-208-5

Library of Congress Control Number: 2023931991

Cover Design Illustrated by Denise Heil

Disclaimer: This book is a memoir. It reflects the author's present recollections of real experiences and events that have happened over time. Some names and characteristics have been changed, some events have been compressed, and some dialogue has been recreated.

All KHARIS PUBLISHING products are available at special quantity discounts for bulk purchase for sales promotions, premiums, fund-raising, and educational needs. For details, contact:

Kharis Media LLC
Tel: 1-479-599-8657
support@kharispublishing.com
www.kharispublishing.com

Contents

Acknowledgements

I am so grateful for my God who refused to give up on me and loved me through to the end, for my parents who stood by me even as I put them through hell on earth, for my wife who worked extra to pay the bills so I could spend three years working on this book full-time, for my sister whose friendship and faithfulness has never wavered, and for my dear friend Edward for his unending prayers, support, and encouragement. May this book be a testament of love and hope for others as each of you have been for me.

Free Discussion Guide

If you would like to download a free discussion guide to go along with this book please visit www.michaeljheil.com/campanion-guide. This guide can be used personally or in group settings whether it is for personal growth, a book club, a study group, for rehab or counseling purposes, within a family, or between a parent and their child.

Prologue

As I lay on the cliff's edge, the medics held my body and shook me incessantly to keep me from losing consciousness. They knew, if I blacked out, I'd likely never make it back. I had been cascading down a cliff in the back country when I crashed into a boulder as tall and impervious as the heavens themselves. It was March 22, 2011.

The medics weren't sure if I was going to make it or not. When they cut off my pants to assess the damage, they saw that my leg was detached from the rest of my body. My femur was cut in half from my hip downward. The skin was still connected, and the bone hadn't protruded through my flesh yet, but my leg dangled, hanging limply. By the time they finally got me down the mountain and into an ambulance, all the fentanyl and dilaudid in the world couldn't shut me up. I screamed until they pumped so many narcotics in me, I passed out.

Before this accident, my motto in life had been: Live life to its fullest while you can because you only get to live it once. I had abided by that motto, packing my life so chock-full of adventure it was hard for people to believe that all my stories were real. The only problem was, none of it satisfied. Partying, sex, drugs, rebellion, success… These were the things people told me would satisfy, yet even at their very best none of them seemed to hit the mark.

Some people change when they hit rock bottom; I couldn't. Some people change when they've reached all their goals and realize they're still dissatisfied; I couldn't change then either. I could only change when hitting that stupid rock made me face the prospect of my existence coming to an abrupt, unforeseeable, and unalterable termination. When that happened, I realized my utter impermanence. I realized that everyone who lives will die. Try as we might to evade it, death is inevitable. Sooner or later, this life will be gone forever.

How will we choose to spend it while we still can?

Is the greatest pursuit in life to satisfy our lusts with as many fleeting pleasures as humanly possible before we die? Is life's greatest purpose to acquire material possessions and reach ambitious goals? Is it to build a family, to acquire status and wealth, to enjoy life's luxuries? What happens when we die and all of our memories are remembered no more, or when all the treasures we've stored up are permanently left behind?

What do we do when the path we've taken and the things we fervently believe in are the very cause of our demise? When the things we thought would add meaning to our lives have only led us into captivity? When our bad habits have given way to addiction, our own minds work against us, our consciences are mangled, and our beliefs keep us repeating the same mistakes, how are we supposed to change?

As much as that accident was one of the worst things I could've imagined happening in my life, it also is something I'm now grateful for. It took several surgeries in which titanium rods, screws, and bolts were drilled through my bones, and months of healing, before I could get out of bed and start learning to walk again. Yet, I rose from that bed a new man. That tragic accident was exactly what I needed to wake up from my self-indulgent, self-imposed slumber. When I sat at the edge of death, I realized everything I'd ever worked for and accomplished in life was utterly meaningless. So… a rock battered me; it broke me open and exposed what was inside.

"A rock?" you may ask. "A literal, physical, bulbous chunk of earth?"

Yes, but it was something much more than that, much deeper. It was also the Rock of Ages.

***

I ran from God for years, but despite my mockery and defiance, He busted me out of jail. He pursued me with such relentless love and persistence that I couldn't shake Him. When I got in trouble, He would step in and let me off the hook; a spiritual being I did not believe in kept intervening in my life in concrete, tangible ways. I repeatedly rejected Him because I was convinced He had nothing of value to offer me.

I had decided the only thing worth living for was to please myself and make a name for myself, like everybody else seemed to do. Sex, drugs, partying, wealth, status, and opportunity were my gods, yet the Rock of Ages would not stop pursuing me. Each time He picked up the pieces of my crumbling existence and glued them back together, I destroyed them again, not because I wanted to see my life disintegrate, but because I didn't know how to do anything else. I believed the more success, more drugs, more sex, more money, more pleasure, and more free time were the formula to create a meaningful life.

I was wrong.

Chapter One

YOLO, Why Not Try Drugs?

When I was a kid, I loved playing sports. I wasn't really that good at any of them, but I always gave my best effort. I sprinted full speed with my little arms flailing. I hustled for all I was worth, running and panting and heaving. Even during practice, I gave my all. One year, Coach McGuire drew my name out of a hat to be on one of his teams. After that, he drafted me each year to join both his basketball and baseball teams. He was a great coach and almost every year our team won first, second, or third place trophies.

At some point, I couldn't help asking him why he kept choosing me, since I considered myself to be one of the worst players on the teams. He said it was because I always hustled, I never did anything halfhearted, and always gave 100% effort to the task I set my mind on doing. He said it was an inspiration for the rest of the team to see someone giving their all and encouraged them to do likewise. I lived my whole life like this, figuring if I was going to do something, I might as well do it to the best of my ability. When I was young, that attitude was applied toward adventuring and any sport or activity that could get my adrenaline pumping. Over time, it applied to my relationship with drugs.

I'm not sure where the belief came from, but I remember, as kids, we would shout "YOLO" (you only live once) or "DGAF" (I don't give a f***) right before committing acts of fortuitous stupidity. One of my friends would shout "YOLO" and then crap on the doorstep of the scout leader's tent. Another would break into his neighbor's car and steal their iPod and, when asked about the act, respond with a nonchalant DGAF. We would shout these words before jumping off a cliff at Lake Powell, before combining copious amounts of drugs into potentially lethal combinations, or before driving drunk to yet another party.

My life philosophy went something like this: If I really only "Live once," shouldn't I "Live once" in a way worth living? My primary focus was enjoying myself and having fun. You only live once; why not get turnt, get savage, get lit, get blazed? It never occurred to me to ask if we indeed only live once, so wouldn't it benefit us to live in a way that lengthens our lifespan or increases its quality rather than decreases it? I was so set on feeling good and experiencing pleasure that even after I started feeling the consequences of my actions, I still couldn't change the belief that this lifestyle was ultimate. Even after getting arrested, after getting addicted, after the pleasure started to fade and the pain set in, even then I was insistent that this path was superior to all else.

Before I ever tried drugs both of my best friends were hooked on pot. We used to skate and longboard everywhere we went, and we prided ourselves in being able to longboard at the same speed as the cars traveling down our precipitous mountain roads. Our most skillful act was the way in which we crashed. Yes, you read that correctly, we prided ourselves most in how we crashed. As soon as our wheel hit a sizable divot or rock, our boards would immediately stop while our bodies were launched forward at whatever speed we had been traveling.

We would fly face-first through the air looking like Buzz Lightyear shooting for the stars, and then we would tuck and roll right before we hit the asphalt. This roll, if done correctly, would spread out the scrapes across our backs rather than the entirety of the impact directly crippling our hands, arms, or legs. During this season of our lives, there didn't seem to ever be a point in time when at least one of us did not have a mean road rash on one part of our body or another.

CD, bless his soul, had trouble learning this trick successfully. One time he catapulted himself down what was unanimously labeled "dead man's hill." After hitting the asphalt, he slid on all four of his appendages like a penguin sliding down an arctic cap. The bloodied mess of the boy that stood up from that fall was appalling to the naked eye. A woman witnessed it from her window and came running to his aid with medical supplies. She insisted on calling an ambulance, or at least our parents, but good old CD took it like a champ. There was more than a little bit of peer pressure as we shouted at him from the bottom of the hill to man up and learn how to skate so we could meet up with our girlfriends. He got a lot of sympathy from that crash, and he milked it. With one girl under each arm, he happily endured the Valley Grove Carnival with his bruises and scrapes and his quirky little smile.

He always did wear that silly smile of his, like there was always something to laugh or joke about. He became my best friend in no time. His family adopted me as a pseudo child and even once checked me out of school for a family vacation to Colorado. Little did I know that vacation would change both of our lives. Upon returning from that short trip, his family announced they'd be moving soon. We would have a few more weeks together, and then my best friend would be gone.

Graham was almost like a big brother to me; we did everything together. We became best friends going through Boy Scouts together. After that, we were inseparable. He was a grade older than me and was in high school while I was still in junior high. He introduced me to all the older kids, and he was the one who suggested that I try out for the high school wrestling team.

When I made the team, my life changed, and I'm not just talking about the workout routine. I started taking half my classes at the high school and got connected with all Graham's friends who were older and cooler than me. I'll never forget the day he introduced me to Cat, who constantly talked about drugs, and as he did, he made them seem like the most wonderful thing on earth. He was a mystical character who reminded me of the caterpillar from *Alice in Wonderland*, hence the name Cat. He'd sit and hum as he plucked various strings on his knockoff guitar. Later, when I started getting high and listening to him, it always seemed like his head was twirling around on a stick.

He was a drug guru. You could ask him about any drug and he would spout information like an encyclopedia. He dressed and acted like a guru, too, with baggy, wonderful, colorful shirts that drooped from his skeletal body. He had fluffy hair that curled up into a wannabe afro. He spoke with that hippie drawl where he lengthened each of his vowels. I didn't realize at the time that it was the sound of being perpetually stoned, I just thought he was so cool. He said drugs were a quick fix that made you confident and melted your insecurities away. The perm fried way in which he conducted himself made it seem as if he were perpetually floating on a cloud of hookah smoke.

This was his normal state of being. He spoke as the caterpillar did as well, in quirky strums of unintelligible introspection. He spoke about floating outside his body. He spoke about seeing duplicates of everything, as if he had entered a world in which fantasy and clones and flying were all real. He spoke of alternate realities and the trips he had taken to visit such places. He spoke invitingly, drawing us in. It was almost an art, the way he drew out our curiosity and left us wanting and wondering.

Until that point, I had never really entertained the thought of drugs, but Cat got my mind wandering, racing off in different directions. It wasn't just that the cool kids were doing them, and that my friends were doing them. Now there was personal intrigue. I wanted to sit outside my body and look at it. I had always wanted to fly; maybe floating would feel sort of similar. *Maybe I did want to get high?* Cat said it was only cold medicine after all, and he'd shown me the research which instructed us on safe dosages. As tempting as it was, I had to say no. I was not ready nor willing to try drugs. But Graham kept bringing it up, and when CD, my second closest friend, started using as well, I was constantly surrounded by it.

We used to have sleepovers, and my home was everybody's favorite place to crash and my mom was everybody's favorite person to hang out with. To this day, I swear some of my girlfriends only dated me because they liked her so much. We had a projector, surround sound, and just about every gaming system on the market. Sometimes we would stay up all night playing video games. During the summer, we could sometimes finagle our parents into letting us have week-long sleepovers, or longer by bouncing from house to house. It was at one such sleepover that I finally caved to the peer pressure. I didn't know the drugs would end this season of our lives and launch us into a new one, that drugs would end these innocent and hysterical nights of gaming, laughter, and fun.

CD and I got the pills at the local grocery store and voraciously consumed thirty each, a moderate dose, according to Cat. I'm not sure how many hours passed. We spent the time talking until we were too tripped up to speak sensibly any longer, and then CD got sick and puked. We sat on couches across from one another until the blood slowly began boiling in our veins, more so mine than his. I flipped off of the couch, doing somersaults at what I was certain was light speed. I started rolling around the floor, shooting back and forth across the room, bouncing off the couches and walls.

After a while, I was convinced I was Super Mario. In time, CD joined me in humming the tune. We both waged war against semi-invisible mushroom creatures. This occupied us until I realized that not only was CD no longer with me in the epic battle against these creatures, but in fact, he was himself collaborating with them. He was pointing his phone at me and taking a video. It was a mockery. I pounced on him. He was siding with the little creatures, and as Mario, it was my duty to either jump on his head or throw stuff at him. I gave him a quick tackle and smacked the side of his head. He retaliated with fury, and we scrambled on the floor until a resounding, eerie voice shot out of the darkness around us.

"Michael! What the heck do you think you're doing!?"

We almost jumped out of our skin with terror as we looked in every direction for the source of the voice. For a moment, we thought God had broken through, and it was all over for the two of us. But as our eyes scoured the darkness, we saw the outline of my mom standing in the hallway.

"Your father has to work at 6 a.m. tomorrow, and you are making so much noise that neither of us can sleep."

After she left, we sat whispering for a time until we found ourselves being carried away again. We were yelled at three times that night. The fourth time someone came down, it was my dad coming down in the morning to put on his shoes for work. We were still up but feigned sleep to avoid trouble.

My brain felt like a watermelon that had been split open, sliced up, jumbled around, and spat out. CD and I just sat there, slowly recuperating, trying to catch up on lost sleep and sanity. We had slept late into the afternoon when we were awakened by Graham. He told us that he and Cat were going to trip out together later that night and that they wanted us to join them. I felt sick, even disgusting inside, but I wanted to look tough in front of my older friend, so I agreed. Graham stole enough pills for all of us, doubled the dose from what we had taken the night before, and arranged for us to meet at the house of a neighbor whose parents were out of town. CD puked again, and we made fun of him for not being able to stomach the stuff. He seemed to have some sort of allergic reaction. I, on the other hand, was not so fortunate.

My older sister always told me that drugs drilled holes in your brain. The weird thing was that I knew she was doing drugs even when she told me that. I figured she just told me to scare me off, so I wouldn't do them too. She told a story about this guy who took so much acid that he thought he was the Kool-Aid Man (a walking, talking pitcher of Kool-Aid). From that point on, he sat upright and was afraid to lie down in case his brains spilled out. He'd been a cool kid, but after that, he went to the nuthouse, never to return to sanity.

Cat and I could hardly move, let alone think. It was our second night in a row taking mass quantities of this same drug and its effects seemed to be compounding. We both kept nodding out as we rested incoherently on the floor. CD and Graham seemed to be just fine, as both of them had puked before the drugs could fully set in. For this reason, they felt like they were missing out on the fun. They wanted to get high too, so they decided to go and get a bag of weed, except neither of them had any money. They kept trying to wake me up to ask me if they could borrow fifty bucks; I was the only one with money because I was the only one who wasn't a druggy yet. Whenever they woke me, I would merely mumble something and then fade back out of consciousness.

It felt like a Tasmanian devil was running around my brain, wreaking havoc with a jackhammer. I didn't think they were missing out on anything. I was so incoherent, I didn't know what was happening around me. I only knew we were at the house of a fat kid who hated me. I had nicknamed him "Twinkie" at scout camp when he wore a giant yellow Spongebob t-shirt. I found it funny at the time, but now I was in the perfect state of being for him to exact revenge upon. Twinkie's best friend Waylon was there, too. He was the weirdest person we knew.

After a few hours, they were able to rationalize with me. I didn't want to try weed, let alone spend fifty bucks on it. I'd never spent that much of my own money in a single purchase before, and I wasn't about to throw that much away for a drug I didn't even want. But by now, they were begging. CD was spending the last part of the summer with my family as his parents were in Colorado. They had just bought a home there, and he was moving away soon. He told me this would make his stay with me complete, that it would be the best gift I could give him before he left. I kept complaining about it, but quietly resolved to give him the money —the biggest purchase for the best friend— it made sense.

When CD and Graham came back with the weed, they found us even more comatose than before and could hardly wake us up. Eventually, they decided to grab Waylon, hoping he might be able to pull us out of our incoherent stupor. He was drunk, raging, and rambunctious. He popped into the room with his thick spectacles dangling off his face. Before his head hardly had time to peep through the door, his body came scrambling in, arms flailing, knees twerking. In rhythm with the song he was singing, his body dangled as he made his way towards us. Without missing a beat, he jumped on top of the bed and began bouncing up and down between us.

It took us a while before we realized that Waylon, in his erratic dancing, was stark naked. When we saw his nakedness, he began screaming and giggling like a maniac before running out of the room. The next time I opened my eyes, the naked figure was leaping through my field of vision again. He rocketed over me and landed squarely on Cat. The moment he decided to spread his naked body across that bed, it was game over. Up until that point, I lay sick, zoning in and out of reality, but homeboy took it too far. His craziness pulled me back to the present moment.

Cat started moaning; it was his best attempt to shout for help. Even though the jumbled-up noise didn't make any sense, I clearly understood his message. Without needing further incentive, I hurtled a lopsided fist into the head of his naked assailant.

Whack!

"Ow, wtf, who the hell hit me?!"

Whack!

"Wtf guys, stop that!"

Whack!

Waylon scrambled out of the room like a spider fleeing its crushed web. Blacked out and incognizant, he cried uproariously.

When Waylon finally reappeared, CD and Graham were following him. He was rambling now about how he'd tried to wake us up like they'd asked him to.

I overheard him say, "He hit me, can you believe it? He freaking hit me, right in the face! Broke my glasses, damn it... Make them tell me right now, who the heck hit me?"

I was aware enough now to smirk, and Cat also responded for the first time in hours; smiles crept across our faces.

Some people have an internal monitor that allows them to analyze when they have taken something too far, but not Waylon. No, Waylon was something else entirely. We endured his absurdities because the laughter that he brought about through them could turn anyone's day around for the better. He was always dancing, twerking, singing a song, or rapping, his butt was always jiggling in your face, doing some grotesquely personal dance move.

He was always doing something erratic and unpredictable, like leaking giant Tootsie Rolls in the swimming pool or atop someone's vehicle. He was as white as a cracker and acted as gangster as he could. He was so boisterous and hysterical that he took even the real gangsters by surprise and won his way into their entourage as a mascot of sorts. He wore deep Vs and skinny jeans, a beanie always perched atop his dome. For a while he lived in the dumpster behind the local church; he would shower at our place and couch surf occasionally to keep decent hygiene. It was simply who he was.

By the time they reached our room, CD and Graham had managed to pacify Waylon by promising to get to the root of things. In the end, it didn't matter. He ran and hid in the bathroom, where he spent the next several hours puking. We thought he had drunk too much, but that wasn't the case at all. I mumbled to them how much my stomach hurt and how I wished that I could puke, too. The group urged me to smoke some weed, promising that it would help my stomach. I didn't want it, I didn't want to do real drugs. Cough medicine was one thing, but... I had to draw the line somewhere.

I looked up and saw CD smoking weed with a glint of crazed infatuation in his eyes, taking hit after hit. I stopped him.

"CD, do you really think it will help me?"

He looked at me and said, "It feels good, just trust me. Plus, you're already high. Just try it, man, it's just a plant."

I saw my hand slowly outstretch to take the bong they had crafted. They lit it for me and showed me what to do.

As I inhaled, the weed and cough medicine fused together in my brain. Everything slowed to an echoing pulse. I tried to stand up but it seemed to take days. People's voices lowered in frequency, as if they were operating inside a slow-motion recording. I couldn't figure out how to balance the weight of my torso on top of my legs, so I looked much like a bobblehead on the dashboard of a crazy man's car as I stumbled in every direction. Eventually, I landed on a trampoline outside, but only had the strength to lie there while the rest of the crew bounced around me. Eventually, they went inside, and I sat there looking up at the stars spinning in circles above me. After an indeterminable time looking up at the vast starry expanse, my friends retrieved me.

They pulled me into a back room and told me to rest up. My gaze fixed blankly upon the ceiling until dawn broke and we were rushed out of the kid's house. I hadn't sobered up a single bit. My vision was still blurred, and my two-word monosyllabic responses made me feel as if my intellect had been degraded to that of a caveman. I wondered if my ability to think and speak clearly would ever return, or if this storm cloud of incoherency had found itself a new permanent dwelling. We slowly worked our way back to my house, relieved to find that my parents were working. When we finally made it home, I slept for twenty-four-hours straight.

It took me two weeks before I started feeling normal again. I couldn't speak or think right during this time. For two weeks, I feared I might end up like the Kool-Aid man.

Many of us turn to drugs for a variety of reasons. The real question is, are they capable of doing for us what we hope they will do? I convinced myself that despite the chaos I left in my wake, I always had a good heart. I didn't harbor ill-will towards anyone. I wasn't acting in malice, but I could not deny that my "good heart" continually led me to do selfishly destructive things.

"The heart *is* deceitful above all *things,* and desperately wicked; Who can know it"
—*Jeremiah 17:9.* (NKJV)

Chapter Two

The Forest Fire

After my twenty-four-hour slumber, I remember awaking to a flurry of activity and CD urging me to get in my parents' truck. We were headed to Redding, California, on our annual family road trip to visit Grandma. Since CD's family had already moved to Colorado and he was spending his last summer in Utah with us, he got to come too. I'm not sure who packed my bag or if I even brought one. I just remember flinging myself across the back seat and squirming restlessly for the majority of the twelve-hour drive.

When we finally arrived, CD urged me to go and smoke with him. It was all he could talk or think about.

"Why are you being so lame? Why won't you just smoke with me? Come on, man. If you're not going to smoke, at least let me go have some."

Since I had bought the weed with my money, and bought it mainly for him, I was in possession of it. At that moment I felt miserable and was having a hard time distinguishing how much of that was due to weed and how much was due to the cough medicine and other over-the-counter drugs Cat had fed us.

After almost two days of recovery, I was just beginning to come to grips with what was going on around me, and now CD was telling me to once again increase that dreadful grogginess that made me feel more animal than human.

"It's not the weed," he said. "It's all that other stuff that's making you sick. Just try it out. I promise it will make you feel better."

In that brief moment of clarity, I had a second chance to say no to drugs. I hesitated and then, after remembering how much money I'd spent on the bag, I decided to finish it.

With eagerness, CD made a makeshift pipe and taught me how to ingest the substance once again. This time it was different; it did ease my pain, and it made me feel alive.

CD looked at me with pride. "I told you you'd like it. It's good stuff."

From that point on, I lived in a perpetual state of grogginess and inebriation.

Weed made life seem remarkable when I was on it. Over time, I came to need pot in order to have fun and appreciate life; when I was not high, life became barely tolerable. While other non-smokers were able to enjoy life without it, I grew increasingly dependent on weed for my joy.

The next day, CD nudged me again. "C'mon, man, let's go smoke."

I told him we'd have to wait until nightfall, but as it began to grow dark, I caved, and we slipped out of the house. We quietly crept out into the forest behind my grandmother's house, seeking a pleasure that would soon, without my consent, take total control of my life.

We smoked a bowl, and then two. It was growing on me. The forest spanned for miles in every direction. It was so large, in fact, that a train ran through the middle of it. As kids, my sister and I would tape pennies to the train track and collect the flattened disks after the train passed over them. In my early days, I boasted, "My grandma's backyard is *so* big she has a train running through it." I didn't realize it was public land until much later. In my mind, it was always Grandma's train in Grandma's forest.

After stumbling around for an hour or two, to my dismay, CD realized he had lost the bag of weed. I was furious. *What kind of friend convinces their buddy to spend $50 on a gift and then goes and loses the dang thing?!* I was so angry that I lost my cool. Along with calling him a flurry of derogatory terms, I remember demanding —in all seriousness— that he either find the bag or pay me back.

We started searching frantically, but the sun soon set, and darkness fell over the forest. Determined to find what we had set out to find, we continued searching. Our primitive minds scrambled to find a method for creating light.

We held our small lighters in the air, using them to search as best we could, but they were not enough. The light they shed was hardly enough to see our own toes, let alone a small, dark bag lost somewhere in the deep, wide span of the shrubby forest growth. Both agitated, we continued our search. Suddenly, from behind me, an orange glow seemed to consume the darkness. Its light burst out in a circle, up and over my shoulder, and briefly lit the ground before my eyes. I turned quickly to see what it was, only to discover my best friend holding a torch in the air, looking like a caveman, proud and dense. Thinking we'd surely found a way to succeed, we both rustled through the brush, gathering the most flammable material available to us, which seemed to be just about everything we laid our hands on. The California forest was parched dry after having endured the endless heat of summer for several months in a row. Everything but the trees around us was brown and sagging with thirst.

Holding up our torches, we smugly grinned at one another and reached out to light up. Sadly, the torches lasted only a few seconds before they extinguished, but our hope was reignited when their embers fell to the ground and instantly lit up. Through our failure, we discovered that the tall dead grass which surrounded us lit easily. With this infinite source of light, we were sure we would be able to recover our lost treasure. We scoured through the forest, igniting circle after circle of dead, dry ground into stardust. After what seemed like a long time of having no success whatsoever, we got a little bit bolder and our circles of flame grew.

We found that letting the fire expand into circles about three feet in diameter before we put it out was not too risky and that once it got to this point, we could easily extinguish it. The dilemma was that after only a few seconds of being lit, the fire would consume everything around it and create a flaming front that spread rapidly from the point of ignition. This gave us only a few seconds of light and then a moderately-sized fire we needed to swiftly put out. Since we were high out of our minds, our logic was as rudimentary as it gets: More fire equals more light, more light equals a higher chance of finding our weed.

Our meticulous scheming worked for a while, but as our circles of flame grew bigger, something happened. At some point, I tried stomping out the fire. This had always worked before, but this time, as my foot came down, instead of putting the fire out, the momentum of the force funneled wind into the flames. Contrary to my intended purpose, each stomp only fueled the flames and accentuated their trajectory, pushing them outward in a circle around my foot. To my dismay, my most desperate attempts to stomp out the fire only made it stronger.

In a last-ditch effort, I realized the only thing that could combat a fire of this magnitude was water, of which I had none. And then, as if having stumbled upon the most ingenious revelation, I looked around hesitantly and pulled down my shorts. It wasn't a firehose, but it was all I had, and it would have to do. The fire sizzled and popped, almost as if mocking my paltry efforts, and then it raged on, unimpressed and unimpeded. I turned to CD, despair glinting through my hazed eyes, and shouted for help. He was pointing at me with his outstretched index finger while rolling on the ground in hysterics.

And then it struck me. This was what we had been drilled for since the time we were children: "Stop, drop, and roll." *That was it,* I thought. *CD, you're a genius!* But as I prepared to dive into the flames, I looked at the boiled pee, glistening as it dripped from the dead, dry grass in front of me. I hesitated, and as I dove into the raunchy mess, my nose filled with fumes of burnt hair and piss. I rolled around in the wet ashes, shouting for CD to help me, but this last feat had sent him over the edge with laughter.

By the time he finally regained his composure, the fire had grown immensely. If we didn't stop it soon, it would become a forest fire. We tried everything, and nothing seemed to help. I asked CD how much pee he had, hoping, just hoping, he had access to deeper reserves than I did. Despite our strenuous efforts, we made no progress in diminishing the strength of the fire. We shouted back and forth over the growing flame that was beginning to roar with ferocity. I shouted at CD, telling him to run to the nearest house and bring back buckets of water. In the meantime, I would stand face-to-face with the mess we had created.

Through trial and error, I discovered that after the fire had thoroughly burned a section of land, I could then kick the flame back into the already burned area and it would have nothing more to light. This would slow the fire for a short while, at least until the rest of the flaming front would mold back together and close in the gap. It was as if this thing were alive; there was nothing we could do to stop or even slow it down. Suddenly, the sound of a train came funneling toward me, loud and strong.

I looked down to see a train conductor hanging out the window of the train, gazing up at me. Beneath the roar of the raging fire, I faintly heard a frantic holler boom up from the tracks below. "HOOOOLLLY $#!@." The train then screeched as if the man were trying to stop, but to no avail. It continued blitzing past until it faded into the distance. Now I was getting concerned; what if this conductor called the cops on us? What would we do? I was tempted in that moment to run away and hide in Grandma's house. Inside, I would wish it all away, just pretend none of it ever happened, but I was afraid that if I left the fire would keep going and by morning Grandma wouldn't have a home to hide in.

Suddenly, I had one last idea, this one being the most brilliant of them all. The reason this fire was spreading so quickly was because of the type of grass we were in; it was thin, dead, dry, and extremely flammable, but that also meant it would be easy to dig up. I ran ahead of the fire and started pawing at the dirt with my hands. Digging like a savage mutt, I sent fragments of dirt and grime flailing through the air behind me. CD finally came back with a small bowl of water in his hands; it was big enough for cereal, but this was not the time for that.

I shouted at him, explaining the method I'd discovered about kicking the flames back into the area that had already burned. I explained how the flames were most fierce in the direction the wind was blowing. I directed him to cut off the left and right flanks while pointing out how the flaming front was headed toward the line I was digging. I told him our goal was to ensure that it would have no fuel to burn when it got to me. When I finally finished digging the ditch, I looked up with increasing confidence that we would be able to extinguish the fire without anyone else, other than the conductor, finding out about it.

As I knelt there on the ground, I watched my endeavors turn to ash and fly away, melting my hopes into fantasy. My ditch would've worked to prevent the grass fire from spreading past it, but as I watched, the grass set fire to a shrub, the shrub set fire to a bush, the bush set fire to a tree, and the fire roared mockingly over my ditch. For a moment, it almost seemed as if the burning beast stopped to glare at me, before smirking with condescension at my petty ditch, and trampling it.

My glower was shadowed only by the flames that burned around me. A crazed look danced across my eyes as the flames flickered in the twilight.

Despite my fear and sorrow for accidentally creating such an abysmal mess, adrenaline pumped through my body in endless waves. Maybe there would be consequences, but at least I felt alive.

I did not know it then, but the fire that small bag of weed would ignite inside of me was going to be much bigger and much more difficult to put out than the fire we started in Redding, California. Starting with that one small bag of weed, hit by hit, bowl by bowl, I would build a dependency so strong that I would not find my way back to sobriety for years. After trying weed, normal life lost its luster. I started to need weed in order to have a good time. It became the light that illuminated my life. When I tried weed, it was just like lighting a forest on fire and watching it burn—only that forest was my brain and life. At first, the fire served a purpose, but the longer it burned, the more evident was the scarring.

Our last option for conquering the fire had failed, which meant one of two things: We either needed to run, hide, and pretend we'd had no part in this mess, or we needed to own up to what we'd done. Reluctantly, we ran back through the forest to Grandma's house. If we let the fire take over, it would surely take a dozen houses with it and maybe even more. The quicker we could get help, the quicker we could put this thing out, but getting help would also frame us for arson.

Immediately upon entering the home, we detoured into the kitchen, scrambling for a quick snack. Fighting fires was exhausting work, plus we had the munchies. We were relieved when the first person we saw was my sister. Of all people, surely she would understand.

Despite our mouths being full of food, we managed to mumble, "We... umm... we started a fire."

As if she couldn't already tell from the smell. She glanced at the food in our hands, back up to our bloodshot eyes, and down again.

After a slight pause, she shouted something like, "You f***ing stoners!"

She looked out the window, and in the deep distance saw an orange glow. She picked up the phone and hit the dial with three quick strokes while we became overwhelmed with a sense of doom.

We had lit a forest on fire...

We were stoned as crap...

My sister was calling 9-1-1...

Our weed was still out there; we had forgotten to keep looking for it when the forest lit on fire. We couldn't believe it. Out of everyone, we thought that my sister would cover for us, or maybe even pick up a bucket and run out there to the frontlines. This, however, was as bad as if we were to dance around the flames flailing our arms while chanting, "We lit this fire, blame it all on us!" to the beat of parading drums. As she stood there on hold, she explained that we did not understand the gravity of our situation and that putting out a fire of this size was impossible on our own. When they picked up again she gave them her own name, our address, and the estimated size of the fire. After she hung up, CD and I ran back to the fire, still hoping we could put it out before the fire crew arrived. We struggled with it until we heard sirens in the distance. As they approached, we dove into the thick of the forest where we were out of sight and slowly worked our way back home through the darkness.

From the brush, we saw three fire trucks, two police cars, and an ambulance driving down the dirt road, through the forest, and into the clearing that our fire had blazed. They parked their vehicles in a well-practiced semicircle. As they did so, we ran back to the house. We figured we were in the clear since none of their lights were pointed outward or seemed to be searching for culprits. They were focused on the fire, and we had successfully escaped the premises. We snuck through the back and crept quietly into the living room. I froze.

There stood my little grandma with a large, suited fireman hovering over her in the doorway. We were convinced he was here for us. Diving behind the couch, we crawled along the floor until we made it to the back room, where all was calm and dark. We were afraid to turn on the light for fear that someone would spot us, and as we sat there in the darkness, the fear-striking realization of what we had done set in.

As both of us sat there filled with terror, thoughts of potential headlines were brimming in our minds: "Two Kids Light Forest on Fire." "Stoners Try to Burn Down Neighborhood." "Charged with Arson, Sentenced for Life." Although both of us were too tough to admit it, we started crying. We were scared for our lives. We were convinced that life as we knew it was going to end before it had even begun. As young teenagers, we would get locked up for arson and spend our adolescences locked away. We didn't know what would happen to us; we'd never lit a forest on fire before, nor had we known anyone else who'd ever done it. We felt like we needed a miracle.

CD looked at me. "Do you believe in God?"

"I don't know," I responded. "I don't really like Christians or religion, but I think He might be out there. I hope He is. We could use some help right now. Do you think He would help someone like us, CD?"

We got down on our knees, and with trembling voices, we volleyed one-sentence prayers up towards the heavens, hoping that Someone was listening.

"God, if You exist, we need Your help."

"Please get us out of this."

"Make them let us go. Please don't let them charge us for this."

"Please give us a second chance."

"My sister and mom are gone. Please don't let them rat on us. Please use them to protect us instead."

This was the first time I had prayed since I was a small child. It would be the last time that I prayed for many years. Not because the prayer wasn't answered, but simply because when everything unfolded exactly as we'd prayed, I didn't believe there was some invisible force guiding things. I chose to believe it was just chance, a series of uncanny coincidences. Nonetheless, He showed up.

We sat, and cried, and prayed, and feared for our lives, and after we had exhausted ourselves, I told CD I felt like we were supposed to go back outside. Although it went against all my intuitions, something greater than my intuitions was telling me to man-up to what I'd done. We stood up with renewed courage and faced the task ahead of us. As we hiked back down the trail, we saw two dark figures approaching us. We quickly jumped into the bushes, hoping we'd not been spotted. As they passed, we realized it was my mom and sister.

Once again, a premonition urged me to go talk with them. We came out of the dark and asked them if the firemen had been able to put out the fire and whether they knew who started it.

My mother told me, "Well, they know that 'someone' lit the fire, and they're inclined to think that it was two certain young teenage boys."

We were stiff with terror and then filled with anger. "Why did you rat on us? Are you trying to ruin our lives?"

She continued calmly, "I think the firemen will honor it if you step up and tell them about your part in this whole mess. The fire chief is very nice, and I think if you just do the right thing, everything will be alright."

Our intuition told us to run, to flee responsibility, to turn around and bolt back into the safety of Grandma's back room. If we'd had our choice, we would have hidden and fled and not come out, but from what my mom said, it seemed like she'd already hammered out a deal with the fire chief in our stead. So we trudged ahead, eventually reaching the clearing that was now covered with ash and shriveled black clumps where bushes and trees had been. We crept out of the darkness, slowly stepping forward, preparing to face the consequences of our actions.

As we approached the circle of emergency vehicles, we saw something that made us freeze in our tracks. Our gazes drifted upward toward one another, looks of awe on both our faces. As soon as we made eye contact, our gawking eyes fell back to the circle of police cars, fire trucks, and ambulances, and what was lying on the ground at its center. There, in plain view of all the police and firemen around us, sat our bag of weed! Lights beamed brightly, highlighting the bag like a star player in a stadium lit up for game night. Promptly, I weighed the options. If we were caught with this weed, we would surely get in more trouble than we were already destined to be in. But if we left it there, with every light from each of the emergency vehicles shining straight on it, it would be found once the frenzy died down and the officers returned to their vehicles.

I nodded to CD, signaling that after all this hassle, we were going to retrieve what we intended to. We walked awkwardly to the center of the circle and stood there a moment, looming over the bag of weed.

"Hey CD, your shoe is untied," I beckoned loudly.

He picked up on my signal and stooped down as if to tie his shoe. His hand loosely grasped the bag and quickly flung it upward. I snatched it from him and stepped behind him, using his body to block the view. In the same motion, I stuck the weed down my pants and hoped to God that I'd not be found out. With hearts pounding, our eyes slowly scanned the surroundings, dreading what we were about to see.

At least a dozen officers of the law —police, firemen, and rescue workers— were standing there. While most of them were dispersed throughout the immediate surroundings, working hard at putting out the fire, we were in the center of the crime scene, and some of them were glancing our direction. We stood frozen like statues, but when my friend finally finished tying his shoe, we proceeded, breathing heavy sighs of relief when no one shouted at us or made inquiries as to what we'd just picked up.

We signaled the first worker we caught eye contact with and asked him if he could get us the chief. We felt extraordinarily out of place as we waited. Two kids in the midst of a workforce of heavy-laden and tattered men, dressed head to toe in protective gear and foreboding weaponry. We stood there awkwardly for what seemed like an eternity. When the chief finally arrived, we were so afraid that neither of us could talk right.

Eventually, we broke down, and after crying for a bit, we confessed. We didn't know what else to do. We were just kids; we didn't mean to do it. We spared all the details, but we told him about our torches and our fire circles. We confessed that we had created this mess, and when he asked us what we were searching for, we lied and told him we were looking for my cell phone and that its battery was dead. I'm not sure he bought the story, but when he looked down, compassion filled his eyes. Maybe he noticed my melted flip-flops, ash-covered clothes, and singed leg hairs, or maybe he'd seen the ditch I'd dug, and the dirt under my fingernails and in my hair.

We knew that if this man felt like prosecuting us, he could, and he had the full right to do so. They could fine us an amount that, at this point in our lives, would have been hard for us to conceive of, let alone pay. We stood there, the high wearing off, confessing what we'd done, and awaiting our punishment. As we did so, a sense of compassion came over the chief.

He looked deep into our bloodshot eyes and said, "You know what? I was a kid once, too. It's okay. We are going to let you go. Your mother and your sister took the right action. They saved you, kid. Because they took the right steps, we were able to put this thing out before it could do any real harm."

We stood there trying to digest what we'd just heard, and then we clumsily confirmed it with him.

"So just to double-check, are we free to go?"

He contemplated for a moment, then said, "We need to write some reports, but I have most of the information I need, and I have your mom's number, just in case. I'm giving you a second chance. You're free to go, kids. We're not charging you or even writing you a citation."

On our way back up to Grandma's house, both CD and I took note of how almost everything we'd prayed for came to pass.

"But now... listen to the Lord who created you... the one who formed you says, 'Do not be afraid, for I have ransomed you. I have called you by name; you are mine. When you walk through the fire... you will not be burned up; the flames will not consume you.'" —*Isaiah 43:1-2.* (NLT)

Though I turned my back on Him, He had not given up on me. God in His mercy was trying to reach CD and me before our problems ignited and became altogether unmanageable. Though we did not deserve it, He sent us help in our most desperate moments. He didn't just spare us from the penalty of our actions, but He also spared my grandma's house, and perhaps the entire neighborhood.

"Who is a God like You, who pardons wrongdoing and passes over a rebellious act... He does not retain His anger forever, Because He delights in mercy." —*Micah 7:18.* (NASB)

***

There is something insidious about the way drugs slowly grab control over your life. Their first appearance can be a delightful, consequence-free indulgence, lighting up your mind and body with incomparable euphoria. The first time you use drugs, it can feel like they're adding something to your life, giving you something you've been missing or have longed for, but that first moment is the only time drugs will give you anything; what they give is merely a façade.

I didn't know about the longitudinal research on pot smoking which shows while short-term use of weed delivers euphoria, long-term use is linked to mental illnesses like depression, anxiety, schizophrenia, fatigue, mood changes, memory problems and impaired planning and decision-making [25]. While short-term marijuana use increases dopamine levels (which is what creates that euphoria), long-term use lowers dopamine levels and has been found to have complex, diverse, negative effects on the dopamine system [24]. Studies have found that those who frequently use marijuana report "lower life satisfaction, poorer mental and physical health, less academic and career success, and more relationship problems [32]." Up to thirty percent of those who use the drug may develop some degree of marijuana use disorder and those who begin using it before age eighteen are four to seven times more likely to develop a use disorder [34]. In other words, many people who use marijuana "medicinally" not only decrease their quality of life, but make themselves sick.

Without knowing it, I had exchanged long term wellbeing for short term euphoria. When weed releases dopamine to the parts of the brain that deal with pleasure and awe, it temporarily makes the menial seem remarkable. Normal sights, sounds, tastes, and smells become less and less attractive in contrast to their weed-enhanced alternatives. Over time, weed becomes more essential for appreciating anything at all, and we lose the ability to appreciate normal "unenhanced" life. The longer we force the doors of our brains to open and repeatedly dump out dopamine, the more difficult it is for those doors to function; they begin to rust, creak and break. The adverse effects can span decades after one stops using [33].

Chapter Three

I Don't Wanna Be a Clone Trooper

" And so the Lord says, 'These people say they are mine. They honor me with their lips, but their hearts are far from me. And their worship of me is nothing but man-made rules learned by rote.' " —*Isaiah 29:13*. (NLT)

When I was 11 and first watched *Star Wars: Episode II—Attack of the Clones*, I felt like someone finally understood what my world was like. It was full of people who had been engineered for optimal performance and then drilled to feign perfection and trained to hide their faults, struggles, and insecurities behind a mask when they fell short. They were remarkable. They were clone troopers. In their presence, I felt insignificant.

Trying to explain the culture that I grew up in is difficult. I grew up in the heart of Utah County, the most religious metropolitan area in the United States [11]. There was no fragment of that society unaffected by the predominant religion: school, work, social life, friendships, activities, neighborhood gatherings, sports, relationships —everything was connected to and influenced by religion...a religion to which I did not belong. I trained ruthlessly to fit in, drilling myself for optimal adherence and minimal interference. You would think one kid striving with all his might to march in step wouldn't stick out among thousands, but I stuck out like whack-a-mole.

When I grew up in the Nineties, 80% of the people in my county were Mormon, and most of them were active. There were rules: No swimming on Sundays; the devil was in the waters. No shopping, no playing, no going to visit friends. Everything was closed; to buy beer you'd have to drive all the way to Salt Lake County where 40% of the people were non-Mormon. It was a different world up there. Where we lived, in the heart of it all, there was no tea drinking, coffee drinking, smoking or alcohol consumption. There were no franchise coffee joints.

I cannot emphasize how much our valley has changed over the past 30 years, but when I was growing up, it was like stepping through a portal into a twilight zone. It wasn't as obvious as going to Colorado City or one of the other polygamist hubs where people wear old pilgrims' garments, but there was a palpable difference. The culture was so concentrated and unique that people called it "the Utah County bubble." The missionaries visited us frequently. On our doorstep, we found letters expressing heartfelt sentiments for us to turn from our misdirected ways and join "the one true church." We were "the non-members," and every neighbor within a mile knew it. We were the only family in our neighborhood that didn't go to the local ward each week. While all the other kids got to meet up, hang out, play games, and learn the rules of our culture, I remained oblivious and obsolete.

When I was invited to a neighborhood gathering, the other kids usually smiled to my face but talked about me behind my back. One time, one of the most honest, forthright kids told me, "Mike, I had a dream, and the world was ending. Everyone lived, except you. You died because you're not Mormon." I never knew how to face such reproaches, so I shut my mouth and bottled it up, just feeling awful inside. I knew my friends wouldn't rebuke me this way, but I also knew they were undergoing the same religious teachings that gave rise to these beliefs and statements in others. At times, even their kindness felt duplicitous. My sweet, sincere friends learned from their religion that there was only one way to live, think, and act. I did not fit in that box.

On seeing the coffeepot in our home, some kids' eyes would widen, and they would slowly back out the door, as if they'd come face-to-face with a prowling lion. If they ran home and told their parents, we'd get a phone call from them. I became self-conscious about everything. Every time I drank coffee, or tea, or used the wrong type of vocabulary, or accidently suggested doing something on a Sunday, I felt like a reprobate bound for the pits of hell. Although I was fairly certain there were health benefits to drinking coffee, and I didn't believe it was a sin, the social pressure was so intense that I felt awful about myself whenever I drank it. Meanwhile, everyone around me seemed to be hooked on sodas and colas; for some reason, caffeine was acceptable when it was aerated with copious amounts of sugar and carbonation.

It was baffling. My friends' religion taught that coffee, tea, alcohol, and cigarettes were bad and not to be consumed, yet prescription drugs were totally permissible. I always accredited the inconsistencies to the fact that the Word of Wisdom, the document which mandated these various laws and prohibitions, was written before prescription drugs existed and the man who wrote it couldn't foresee the future. That belief merited even greater ridicule.

As I grew up, it seemed impossible to keep track of all the contradictions. The continual awareness of right and wrong created a sense of guilt and unworthiness that accompanied me wherever I went. I kept trying to do and be better, but it never seemed to be enough. One day I realized it didn't matter if I white-washed my vocabulary, scrutinized all my actions, and changed the way I dressed. Until I bore their same religious label, I would never truly fit in.

I carried the weight and sadness of this reality for many years. I experienced this feeling as shame, as something fundamentally wrong with who I was, and I blamed religion for this deep feeling of inadequacy. I never realized that Mormonism didn't represent the whole of Christianity. I never realized that people are people; we all do stupid things whether we're religious or non-religious. I never realized it's not fair to judge a religion based on the actions of its teenagers, who are fallible and riddled with hormones and inconsistencies. Instead, I judged and rejected God, religion, and all of Christianity based on the sum of a few bad childhood experiences.

I never knew then that Christianity was based on the idea that the God of the universe saw through me to my reprobate's core, and still loved me enough to give His life for mine. I didn't know that Jesus was the creator of the universe and that He came for the sick and sinners, the lost and broken, the outcasts, the immoral, the failures, and that by coming He willingly surrendered His eternal safety and security to rescue flawed people like me. Or that He does not require perfection, but accepts anyone, with the single condition that they believe in Him. While other religions require people to perform certain rituals and maintain a certain level of morality in order to merit acceptance with God, Christianity is the most inclusive belief system on earth because it includes those who are morally bankrupt and destitute as much as it includes the disciplined and the upright. The God of the Bible fully understands our crooked desires, our insidious nature, and our pursuit of that which benefits self at the expense of others. He understands that we cannot change ourselves in any significant or lasting manner, and despite our depravity, He loves us.

When I was growing up, I only saw religion, I did not see Christianity. I did not see Jesus. I did not hear or understand the gospel. I thought Christianity was just a rat race in which people strived to maintain a pretense of perfection, then lied about it when they fell short. This religion was the opposite of Christianity, but it was my only point of reference. So, I rejected everything to do with God.

I did not know my decision to resist religion would involve my decision to conform to drug use and addiction. I didn't know that in throwing out religion, I was tossing away the protocols, boundaries, and safety mechanisms that could have prevented decades of trauma, or that by throwing out God, I was annihilating the source of affirmation, care, and encouragement that my soul desperately longed for. I didn't know my decision to resist the social pressures of religion would leave me solely in the company of other wounded souls sedating their lives with substances. The drugs seemed so much less tyrannical, so much less monopolizing, but how wrong I was. The drugs were enough of a mystery to keep me enticed, enough of a high to keep me unworried about whether I fit in or not, and enough of a habit to give me an identity and a social group —all the ingredients necessary to effectively take control of one's life. Rejecting religion, I found no purpose in conforming to any form of morality. Licentiousness, pleasure, addiction, and self-indulgence freely subsumed me.

Out of over 2,000 in my school, only a handful of us weren't Mormon. During my childhood, I knew of only one non-Mormon Christian church within 20 miles of my home. My parents often attended this church, but it was so insignificant that it made me feel like more of a loser and outcast when they forced me to join. Although we didn't have a common label for it back then, I was a "None." I didn't buy into any religious teachings. Yet, in Valley

Grove, even those of us who weren't actively religious felt the pressures to conform, to be a certain way, to live a certain life, and to hide our faults. The masks we wore helped us survive the system's pressures without dropping under the weight of it all. The masks —no matter how much we hated them— were our lifelines.

I remember in school one day they showed us a documentary about the drug problem in our valley. It taught us that our state was consistently ranked the fifth to seventh worst state for drug abuse problems in the nation, and that our valley was the heart of drug activity in our state. I thought it must have been a lie because everyone and everything in my valley was perfect or appeared to be. The documentary exposed the community around me in a way that made me uncomfortable and seemed to contradict everything I knew about my home. A staggering number of people in our valley were doing drugs. Most of them started by innocently taking pills their doctor prescribed, but a huge percentage had become heroin and meth addicts, after getting addicted to various scripts.

That film showed that the number of antidepressant drugs prescribed in my state was double that of the national average, which meant that behind all the big smiles were a lot of broken hearts. Where I grew up was, and still is, a place of inherent contradictions, an incarnation of inconsistencies. This video confirmed that I wasn't crazy and I wasn't alone. It showed me that a significant percentage of the people around me also struggled and had problems, even if they never showed it. At the same time, it confirmed my suspicions that religion was a hoax or, at the very least, endlessly superficial.

Although I couldn't articulate any of these thoughts at the time, I think the final straw was when they taught us about evolution in school. Since evolution told me where I came from and why I existed, it was a comprehensive alternative to religion, but it was better than religion because it didn't come with any do's, don'ts, demands, or requirements. It also didn't come with the negative stigma. It was a socially acceptable belief system, and I was granted social esteem for believing it. Believing it gave me a sense of superiority over those who held to traditional religious accounts. It not only enabled me to dismiss religion, but also to mock it.

Looking back, I realize how inconsistent it was to listen to the science that enabled me to dismiss God, while denying the science that proved drugs were harmful for my life, health, and future. I was simply willing to believe anything that allowed me to dismiss God and do what I wanted, even if my beliefs didn't stack up.

If we really did come from animals that originated out of a series of indeterminable coincidences, why strive to be "good"? If, at our core, we are animals, why not act like them? It all made so much sense to me. If we're just animals, no wonder so many of us just want to hump. This theory also made sense of school and the education system for me. If I was an animal, of course they must confine me to my cage until they've taught me obedience and whatever else they've determined I must know. They must lock me in until I've learned to be a good boy. And yet, if I'm an animal, why should I not be disruptive? Shouldn't I be out running around, mating, and having a grand old time?

I couldn't understand why my teachers taught that I came from a monkey and then got mad at me when I acted like one. If there was no big guy upstairs, then there would be no consequences for doing whatever the heck I wanted. If natural selection got me here by being tougher and meaner than all the other foul creatures out there, why stop?

Survival of the fittest meant that other humans were my competition, not my family; I was to compete with them, not love them. The reason I was here now was because my ancestors beat theirs. The most dubious issue to me was how my teachers could teach me this stuff and go on believing in their religion. The two seemed mutually exclusive. Yet everyone seemed to be taking little fragments of each and combining them. Natural selection, survival of the fittest, and evolution left no room for morality or loving others. This worldview excused me from both and obliged me to neither. If I was an animal, I didn't need to think about anything but my own well-being, and maybe that of my direct family.

I chose drugs because they looked fun. I chose to push religion away because it didn't. I figured most of the normal world —outside of Valley Grove— was evolving past religion anyway. I figured I might as well do the same. It would take me years before I found out that drugs and sex were their own sorry version of the rat race of endless marathons of promises that failed to deliver.

After fifteen years of trying to fit in, I finally admitted I did not know how to fit into a world like this, so I joined the rebellion. My personal glory and pleasure were ultimate, and the entire idea of God was stopping me from getting it. So, I ignored Him, amplified my doubts, and allowed my vision to become clouded by all the things I desired most.

"Yes, they knew God, but they wouldn't worship him as God or even give him thanks. And they began to think up foolish ideas of what God was like. As a result, their minds became dark and confused." —*Romans 1:21.* (NLT)

Chapter Four

Feeling Alive

"Focusing on the self is the opposite of focusing on God. Anyone completely absorbed in self ignores God, ends up thinking more about self than God. That person ignores who God is and what he is doing. And God isn't pleased at being ignored." —*Romans 8:7-8*. (MSG)

The same summer when I first tried weed, pills, and forest fires, I made the high school wrestling team. These two feats were enough to launch me up the social ladder to a place of tolerable decency. That same year, Graham introduced me to all the stoners he knew, all the cool kids who were older than me, could drive, and had hot girlfriends. They didn't know I was an outcast. They seemed willing to accept me based solely on the fact that I was willing to smoke weed with them. During wrestling we would work out two-to-five hours every day and finally started drawing attention from girls. When I landed a short brunette named Denny, I felt like the luckiest guy in the world. It wasn't just because she was a grade above me and way out of my league, it was the fact she had accepted me, someone pretty and fun had chosen me. That summer, my entire life changed, and I believed every bit of positive transformation was the result of weed in my life.

We skipped class together and smoked weed in the mountains, in various parks, forests, shrubs, and overgrowths, going on adventures and staying out late at night. We smoked cigarettes and got buzzed. The cool kids taught me about porn and masturbation, a quick fix of dopamine to send any deprived soul soaring. I had never seen, experienced, or imagined so many forms of instant pleasure and self-gratification. It was like ramen noodles for the soul, instant, easy, tasty, fun. I didn't understand how each of these things was rewiring my brain, how pornography would lead me to objectify women and distort the way I saw and interacted with them. I did not understand that these pursuits were causing me to abandon a stage of innocence that I wouldn't ever be able to recreate or recover. I was an impervious teenager; I didn't have time to think about how these things were affecting me.

I wish I would've known that 198 million people in the US struggle with, and are in bondage to pornography, or that most people who engage in it long-term are ashamed of it, enslaved to it, and completely incapable of stopping. Porn sites receive more web traffic in the US than Twitter, Instagram, Netflix, Pinterest, and LinkedIn combined, even though watching pornography has devastating effects on self-esteem and mental health [19].

I felt dirty and ashamed, but also thrilled to have found a way to make myself feel so good, so easily. As badly as I needed someone to sit with me and walk me through the ramifications of my actions, I know I would have mocked them if they had. It was no one's fault but my own that I kept drifting. As I acted on all these fleeting pleasures, I was training my mind to require drugs, women, and acceptance from others. Over time I steadily put more trust and emphasis on these things. Eventually they came to determine my wellbeing. We noticed pretty quickly that relationships filled a gap that drugs couldn't. While drugs numbed us and helped us to not care about what others thought, relationships met our deeper needs for approval, at least temporarily. The two fueled each other as anvil and hammer; these two things forged our social existence, defining and outlining how we saw ourselves and what we lived for. But they were not enough for me; I needed more.

Unwittingly, I clung to friendships in the same way that I clung to relationships, expecting them both to meet my deepest needs. The more I put my hope in popularity and other people, the more I developed a need for a sort of fan club. It was almost always about quantity rather than quality. I was always going out of my way to create surface-level relationships. Weed gave me courage and helped unlock parts of my personality that had laid dormant under fear. By nature, I was a raging goofball, full of quirkiness and spontaneity. My goal was always to make people laugh, and each time I did, I felt like I was making their life and mine just a little more meaningful.

The more people who knew my name, the better I felt about myself. The crazier the feats I pulled off, the more people who knew my name. My character was cockiness on the outside, but an endless cycle of insecurity on the inside. Although weed numbed me and helped me temporarily forget about my insecurities, it never made them go away. Instead, they grew steadily, like a fungus in the dark. Based on appearances, no one would've ever guessed. With my long brown hair that folded down around my face in waves, my hazel eyes that always changed color with my mood and the seasons, my skinny jeans, my skateboard, and my toned muscular body, I was the image of confidence.

On weekdays, Graham and I hung out until ten or so, extracting every minute of time our parents allowed us to spend together. Throughout the week we'd spend hours together working out, wrestling, and honing our skills. On the weekend, we would lay comatose on the couch playing video games nonstop. If someone picked on one of us, they'd have to deal with the other as well, but the bond extended to less positive attributes. As one became more dependent on drugs, so did the other. Sports weren't our only extracurricular activity; we also were Boy Scouts together. Every week we'd learn various tools and trades, learning about trust and learning to lead as we acquired merit badges of every imaginable kind.

We acted like our drug use and our healthy activities were parallel lines, never bound to intersect or interfere with one another. We went along haplessly, enjoying Scouts or church activities just as much as we enjoyed smoking weed afterward, unable to discern how the two did not mesh. We hid our decisions from the nerds, the kids we thought were not mature enough to understand our choices, but they were really the mature ones. It wasn't just that they had thought about and planned for their futures, it was that when we finally got off drugs years later, we had to start doing all the things they had already accomplished years before.

All our life goals and objectives became steadily wrapped up in the simple task of getting and staying high. We prided ourselves in creating secret meeting spots that were strategically positioned so that wherever we were and whoever we were with, we could always get away to smoke. We labelled our favorite spots: the Gnome Garden, Narnia, The Circle of Trees, The Bunker, The Rabbit Hole, Dry Canyon, and Adalynn's Shed. We had spots close to school and in each of the neighborhoods where we lived so we could get lit between classes as easily as we could after school. The mountains provided refuge when we got totally plastered and needed time away to balance out. At night, the valley below us would light up like a bonfire, teeming with activity.

In the fall, from our perch in the mountains, we could hear the announcer from the high school football games. That is where the normal kids dwelt. We just didn't fit in with them, we just didn't belong down there. I say "we" but it was more me than the others. I went to school, played sports, and joined in extracurriculars like the normal kids, but I was still an anomaly. My crazy feats and attention-seeking quirks could draw attention from others but I would've been delusional to think I actually fit in with any of the cliques: not the jocks, nerds, goths, emos, troublemakers, peacekeepers, or the hipsters. In a lot of ways, I didn't even fit in with the stoners.

It's not that they weren't welcoming or even kind; heck, everyone was kind in Valley Grove, smiles always plastered across their faces. It was something else, something deeper. I could not fit into these groups because I did not adhere to the religious majority and everyone else did, to varying degrees. All of these cliques, despite their differences, were adulterated with religion. Since I didn't have it, I didn't fit. I drifted from one clique to the next, acting cool and pretending like I fit in, but it was mostly my drugs, my stories, my connections, and my looks they tolerated.

Since all the other stoners were raised in the predominant religion, they knew the right lingo, and could at least pretend that they were active members. Because of this, they fit in with the other kids in a way that made me envious. I couldn't fit in with the religious firebrands who controlled the school. I was a misnomer, unquantifiable, and subject to scrutiny. At least the other stoners would join me in criticizing the religion behind the backs of those they were trying to impress and fit in with. I would joyfully clink glasses with any critic, any sceptic, any cynic. All who could see through the deceptive schemes of religion and its associated rat races had a friend in me. More than that, what mattered more than anything was getting high.

I loved that feeling of arising when I finished smoking and climbed out of the shed, bushes, basement, or attic, and emerged into a world completely transformed in front of me. There was that unquenchable giggle that would make even a child blush and the stoned musings and ponderings so deep and so reflective that they seemed to hold the answers to all life's deepest questions. I loved how any pothead on the block was an instant friend with an open door. In a way, we were all outcasts, none of us good enough to live up to the standards of the broader culture. I guess I liked that, too. Slowly, I became hooked, not just physiologically, but socially. Being a stoner was a way of life, a seemingly grand adventure that, in my own mind, had no parallel.

As I slowly numbed my mind with that sweet cloud of psychopathic impassivity and all of the ideologies of the hippie lifestyle, my heart gradually hardened. The few people who tried to pour into me during this lowly state of being found that it was paramount to pouring fertilizer on a rock. I would not budge; nothing could move me to change my mind, heart, or character. I had determined that drugs were ultimate, and nothing short of death was going to stop me from pursuing them.

Berry was one of the coolest kids in our school. He was the productive type of stoner, the kind that was able to work a job and maintain good grades, while getting high constantly. He taught me it was possible to be productive and party like crazy. He had a lifted Jeep with a giant smiley face bouncing on its antenna and the word "happy" plastered across the back window. We called him Parachute Sack because one time he'd gotten pulled over and successfully managed to hide a beer under his nutsack while getting searched by three different officers. Parachute Sack was a legend after that.

As the delightful high of smoking weed became more central to our lives, the idea of stopping became unfathomable. Why stop when we could function so well on it and it made us feel so good? Denny loved drinking and smoking cigarettes; they were her lifelines like weed was mine. We sat in her garage for hours with little smoke clouds fading around us. I skipped class as often as possible to spend time with her, wasting the days away. She slowly became acquainted with Graham, Aloe, Cat, Parachute Sack, and my other friends. I slowly opened up to her and learned to trust her. It was the first serious relationship I'd had. The more I got to know her, the more I fell in love, and eventually, I gave her my virginity.

I felt like drugs were the sole reason my life was suddenly blossoming. I accredited all the good changes in my life to drugs: my sudden popularity and ability to maintain friendships, my relationship, and the fact I finally had a social group. I credited drugs for all of it. Drugs not only brought us together, but they also filled our time together with laughter, chaos, and fun. If something brings us status, praise, and acknowledgement, we will keep doing it. At this moment in my life, drugs were bringing all of those things and helping me push away the anxiety and lessen the blow of being a social anomaly.

The obsession, the way I placed weed above all else, bordered on idolatry. When I started smoking weed, everyone told me it was a gateway drug. I told them to screw off. All that mattered to me was having fun, living in the moment, and weed provided that. Before I knew it, weed became more important than anything. We began wagering our most valuable possessions for just one more quick trip to the land of laziness. Whenever there was a dry season, the potheads would rally on a unified journey. We would scour our bedrooms, our phones, our contacts, willing to do anything for just one more hit. We stole things, we created lies, we hung around pawn shops, willing to do anything to please the shady dealers, just for one more fix.

During these years I learned that most people have secret obsessions. Some with melt-in-your-mouth chocolate, or the bittersweet sensation of hot coffee warming their belly. Some work tirelessly to sculpt and chisel a perfect body, while others live for the next savory bite of something delicious. Some live to seduce, while others search endlessly for acknowledgement and acceptance. The alcoholic finds the fuel to push through each day by imagining the sparking "ptch," as he tips his drink of choice briskly down his parched throat. Some are workaholics, fixated entirely on their bank statement, possessions, luxury experiences, and their next sweet buy. Yet as tempting and delightful as each of these things were, none of them seized my soul the way drugs did.

Most of us greet each day by scouring our phones as their beeps, alerts, alarms and notifications raise us into wakefulness. The pervasive world of entertainment marauds us day and night; texts, emails, social media alerts, television, binging, billboards, apps, movies, music, radio, and nightclubs all volley for our attention with inhuman persistency. We erect social media shrines in memory of ourselves, hoping to garner the attention and affirmation we need to fuel our souls. Yet with the passing of each hot new trend, each season of our favorite show, each social media post, we find ourselves anxiously scouring, scavenging for more. What is it that we're looking for? Why is it that no number of messages, movies, or outings with friends can bring us what we need? Instead, the more our phones explode, demarcating our popularity, the more our brains explode with the stress of trying to keep up with it all.

As satisfying as all these things were, I always needed more. I used them eagerly, to oil and grease the recalcitrant machinery of my life, hoping that *en masse* they could fill the holes and fix what was missing. When I used drugs in conjunction with these other things, it was like injecting them with steroids. I felt like I could do anything. Yet, the longer I went at it, the more I stalled out and malfunctioned. Basing my wellbeing on these quick fixes and drugs was like mixing water with my fuel. Sure, it was all readily available, quick, and cheap, but it did not get me very far. I thought I'd found my cheat sheet, but I didn't realize that by cheating I wouldn't figure out any real answers to the questions or problems of life.

This dreamy feeling of floating in the clouds was just that —a dream— one that, by definition, could not last. This feeling of ecstasy was merely a chemical process in which my brain wrang itself out like a sponge, thus eliminating all the neurotransmitters it needed for its long term wellbeing in a few unforgettable experiences. Drugs were a chemical cocktail that ignited my senses for a moment, only to leave me scrambling, trying, but forever unable to attain the same feeling and high. Thus, I lived in a constant state of nostalgia, scrambling to recreate what had been lost forever, striving to retrieve the irrevocable.

Whatever drugs gave me at this point in my life, they would cost me later. The fleeting pleasures I was pursuing would burden me for decades, creating life-consuming addictions, impairing mental stability, damaging emotional and social wellbeing, and causing broken relationships within my family and with most of my friends.

Chapter Five

Tangled in Barbed Wire

One day, when I came home from school, my mom was in an uproar, tears were streaming down her cheeks and she was pacing around the house too frantic to speak. I tried calming her and getting her to talk to me. Finally, after what seemed like an hour of incoherent bawling, she mumbled my sister's name...

"She's dying, Mike."

My mom couldn't even slur words from her mouth without going ballistic. She was still wearing her scrubs from work with small name tag reading Registered Dental Hygienist. As she wept, she flailed her arms in hopeless pain and frustration. As the gravity of the situation sank in, my stomach sank also, my eyes started to tear up. "What's wrong with her?" I shouted, angrily, trying to rouse any response other than hysteria. "What's happening? Where is she?"

Mom could not respond. In terror, I reached for the landline and called my dad. He'd recently gotten our family's first cell phone. Before that the only way to reach him had been via pager. Dad was always traveling for work, that pager of his beeping 24/7. He was out of the state close to 75% of the time. He most likely wouldn't be able to get the time off to come home, but in an emergency like this he would definitely be in the loop about what was going on. He always did his best to be there for us despite the demanding job.

"She's in the hospital," he said. "We thought we were so close to losing her Mike. They're saying it's a miracle. They life-flighted her and called in the most skilled surgeon in the state. They say she should've bled out already, but someone showed up out of nowhere and slowed the bleeding. They're saying without his help she wouldn't have made it until the ambulance arrived. She's in critical condition. For most of the day, they weren't sure she was going to make it."

Dad told me to tune into KSL for more details; her story was one of the main features on the news channels that day. As I watched, there were shots of the rugged mountains, a steep trail, and a Jeep that had tumbled down them and crumbled into pieces at their feet. I tried to control my weeping as I feared for my sister's life. *Why had we always fought so much? Why had I always taken her for granted? When was the last time I sat down and talked with her? Did people always feel like this when they were in danger of abruptly losing someone they loved?*

She had skipped class to go digging with her friends. When the Jeep started spinning out, the driver threw it in reverse, hoping to navigate backwards down the steep slope. Instead, he drove it straight off the cliff. As the vehicle teetered there, he shouted for everyone to bail. Since the driver's side door was on the downhill side, gravity assisted him in flinging open his door and bailing from the vehicle before it started tumbling down. My sister, on the passenger side of the vehicle, did not have such luck.

As gravity pushed down on the door, she grappled with the it. She got it to unlatch but couldn't manage to lift it open against the weight of the tilting vehicle. As she pressed against the door with all her weight the jeep started toppling down with her inside. As the vehicle cascaded downwards, the unhinged door flew open, and the thick steel snapped easily beneath the nearly three-ton vehicle. Since she'd been told to evacuate, her seatbelt was detached. As the vehicle flipped and rolled, she was tossed mercilessly around the metal cage. At some point, she flew towards the door that had been ripped off. As her leg stuck through where the door had been, the Jeep rolled over it, nearly snapping it off.

A smattered piece of mangled flesh is the only thing that held her lower leg to the rest of her body. According to the news, as the vehicle rolled to a stop, it flung her out through the hole and into a barbed wire fence. At this point, she went unconscious and was unable to remember anything that happened. The broadcaster told how, with an extremity virtually detached, she would've bled out in less than five minutes. The driver was in shock as he stared at my sister's body. Finally, after a couple minutes of total panic and confusion, he started running down the mountains to find the nearest home where he could call 9-1-1.

At that point, the camera focus changed slightly as it zoomed in on a scraggly-looking man in a biker's suit. He started talking about how each morning at 7 a.m. he went for a routine bike ride through the foothills.

He said, "This morning, my alarm simply failed to go off."

He distinctly recalled setting his alarm the night before, yet inexplicably, in the morning the alarm failed to sound. As a result, he woke up two hours later than normal, another abnormality. When he woke up, he had the strangest feeling that today, on his bike ride, he needed to bring his first-aid kit with him. As he scoured through his home, it took him nearly forty-five minutes to find the thing. By this point, he was so frustrated he said the only reason he didn't call it quits and give up riding altogether that day was because he'd recently retired. He didn't need to go to work, and he didn't have much else going on.

As he pedaled into the mountains, it became clear why he'd been delayed. He was so close to the accident that he could hear it, the screams, the crunching of metal. He said that as he rode up, he saw my sister there tangled in barbed wire. He said it was the strangest feeling; he just felt like he needed to have that medical kit. He couldn't for the life of him explain why, but when he saw the accident, he instantly knew. Because of the medical kit that he carried, he was able to slow the bleeding just enough so that she was able to survive until the ambulance got there.

The man claimed that God had sent him exactly where he needed to be so that he could help save my sisters life. He was so excited and grateful that he had been able to help her. He said something like, "I never could've imagined so much good coming out of me being late," and, "It's amazing how God uses us even when we're clueless as to what's going on."

She was on crutches for well over two years. They had to perform seven surgeries to ensure she could not only keep her leg but also maintain some semblance of a normal lifestyle. It was thanks to a new technology called an external fixator and her amazing orthopedic surgeon (one of the most revered in the country) that she was able to heal. The metal contraption had skewered metal rods which jutted in and out of her leg, shooting straight through the bone and poking out the other side. The device could be ratcheted to pull the bone in different directions to facilitate proper regrowth. To this day, it looks like a shark bit off her leg and that it somehow grew back on. My sister is a living, walking miracle.

I remember her getting pumped with oxycontin and oxycodone, like a baby is fed breast milk. I remember her getting hooked on opiates. I remember her coming off them: the screaming, the shaking, the vomiting. I remember her struggling and suffering, not for months, but for years, as she healed. I remember thinking that I lost my sister, and then got her back again. For some reason, I wasn't capable of seeing the good in it. I wasn't capable of seeing how God saved her life, how He had intervened. Instead, my mind was blind to it, to Him. The miraculous facts surrounding her rescue didn't awe me, woo me, or wow me; they meant nothing to me. I was as oblivious to God's kindness as the driver who almost killed my sister was about how to drive in the mountains.

I am not sure whether this event contributed to my addiction or not. Aside from my heart breaking each time I saw my sister's pain, the accident didn't change my life in any practical ways. I watched her fight, I watched her run for student council while in a wheelchair, I watched her win. I watched her, as a severely injured young woman, do the things I was scared to do as myself. As she was fed copious amounts of painkillers year after year, I also watched as the company she surrounded herself with started to change. Shadier characters started showing up, older guys drinking beer, other guys smoking white crystals out of unidentifiable objects. I didn't know what to think. I got angry at first, but when I told my best friend about it, he told me that his big sister did the same thing and that it was normal.

I wasn't capable of helping her and I was afraid to ask how she was really doing. Instead, I just watched from a distance. Whenever the pain woke her in the middle of the night and she screamed loud enough to wake the house, I watched, wide-eyed from a corner, as my parents administered her drugs. I am not sure if the screams from the pain of her leg, or the screams from the withdrawals were worse. Mostly, I just kept to myself. I could never have imagined that I would one day choose to make myself dependent on the same drugs I watched wreck her. Though my sister did not choose to become dependent on opiates, I later would. Despite having seen their negative side.

My friends who did drugs always focused on the positive components of drugs, sex, and partying. They told me all the positive ways that substances and relationships would benefit me, but they never shared how much these things would cost, how much they would take from me. I don't think they intentionally withheld the negative, they simply couldn't see the whole picture. We were all too entrenched in the present moment. We hadn't yet driven off a cliff, but we were already beginning to wrap ourselves in barbed wire. There was no warning label with my drugs that told me I would spend decades paying every cost for this brief season of delight.

"Therefore... stripping off every unnecessary weight and the sin which so easily and cleverly entangles us, let us run with endurance and active persistence the race that is set before us.

—*Hebrews 12:1* (AMP)

***

When I think of the staggering number of people who have died from overdoses, I imagine their families when they found the body. I imagine the hurt, the desperation, and the wailing and tears. I think of the abundance of emptiness that must've haunted their families for months and years afterwards. I think how easily it could've been me; when my friends overdosed, I felt like it should've been me. According to the 2020 World Drug Report, drug use is increasing in everyone ages 15-65 across the globe. Collectively, smoking, alcohol, and illicit drug use kill 11.8 million people each year. This is more than the number of deaths from all cancers combined [12].

When I think of my battle with addiction, I am often reminded of the pain I caused, and even more real to me, the pain I felt, albeit self-induced. It is in this setting that my story takes place. I was the fool who didn't even know what opiates were when I got hooked on them. I was the kid who cared about one thing and one thing only – having a good time. Statistics meant nothing to me; I didn't think they applied to me. I believed I was the exception to all the rules. I was willing to risk a premature death as long as I went out living it up and having a grand old time.

Chapter Six

Blowing Zeros

"*Whenever we make something ultimate, we begin to hate anything that stops us from getting it.*"*(MH)*

"For the time will come when men will not tolerate sound doctrine, but with itching ears they will gather around themselves teachers to suit their own desires. So they will turn their ears away from the truth and turn aside to myths." *—2 Timothy 4:3-4*

One day, Graham told me he'd started stealing clothes from the mall. I'd never seen him look so excited about anything except pot. He told me how he'd worn a baggy outfit so when he tried the new clothes on in the fitting room, he could rip out the sensors and layer them underneath. Of course, I took part. We didn't need to do this; we had parents who took care of us, but it was exhilarating. Each time we did it, we felt like we were living on the edge. Evading all the rules felt like evading gravity itself; we felt exceptional. The first time we took some of our younger friends to join us was also the first time we got arrested.

They were not particularly gifted in this area. They triggered the alarm and security quickly surrounded them. Graham and I got away but felt bad for our friends and decided to return. Before turning ourselves in, we took the clothes we had stolen and hid them in the trash can in the bathroom, carefully covering them with paper towels. We turned ourselves in and told security that it was our idea, we were to blame, and we had peer pressured our friends. We begged them to please let our friends go. They did not. Instead, they wrote all of us tickets, after which we thoroughly regretted having turned ourselves in.

The mall cop graciously explained the three-strike system to us. The first arrest cost fifty dollars plus a dozen or so hours of community service. With each arrest, the fines increased, as did the hours of service and other associated penalties. Once you passed three, you were deemed a threat to society and could be sent away to detention (DT). We didn't plan on making a lifestyle out of corruption, but we were triggered by the fact we'd gotten arrested and penalized for doing the right thing and going back to protect our younger friends. We were angry being arrested when we were not found in possession of any stolen objects. We felt robbed. After writing each of our citations, the officer commanded us to vacate the premises with our tails between our legs. After a quick bathroom break on the way out, however, we were feeling vindicated once again. The $200 worth of stolen merch still left us $100 ahead after we'd both paid our fines.

After a while, pulling off these feats and outsmarting the system became a high of its own. Our reasoning was modeled after Robin Hood: steal from the rich and give to the poor. It's just that the rich were the huge retailers like the mall, the big box store, and the authorities; and we were the poor. We had no ill intentions, we were just teenagers, tunnel-visioned, living in the moment, living for the thrill. My second strike came when I was stealing a shirt; I hadn't been smart or careful and I deserved it. At first the authorities had been so lenient that I was able to finagle each situation so I came out ahead. After my first three strikes, however, they started slapping thousands of dollars of fines on me and locking me up in detention. Over time the consequences became so crushing, overbearing, and suffocating that I did not know what to do with my life.

At first, our theft was just an experiment, but over time, we felt like the system was stealing from us by arresting us and giving us hefty fines, so we retaliated by trying to outsmart the system. Once we'd figured out how to locate gaps in the surveillance and remove the security sensors from objects, we felt like we'd finally found a way to get ahead. Most of us tried to hold down jobs as well, but it took us years of working part-time gigs at fast food joints to pay off all the fines. It was much quicker to steal goods, sell them in the secondhand market, buy drugs with our proceeds, and resell those for profits.

My third strike came when I was at my girlfriend Denny's house. She smoked like a chimney, had dropped out of high school, and was already becoming an alcoholic, but I thought she was the coolest girl in the world. One night, the cops showed up out of nowhere and insisted on giving us breathalyzer tests. We found out later that her mom's boyfriend had called the cops because they were having an argument. They were both sloshed drunk when they called the cops on each other, which I guess is why the cops wanted to test us. By the time the cop came banging on the door, both the mom and her boyfriend were long gone, but he kept pounding and shouting and we stood there terrified. He kept shouting that he knew we were in there and we better open up. When we finally opened the door, he insisted on immediately giving us breathalyzer tests.

I blew zero's twice, and he still wrote me a ticket for consumption of alcohol by a minor. In my understanding, it was illegal for him to write that ticket. I tried taking up the dispute with him, but there was no way to defend myself. Denny's older sister had dug four empty beer bottles out of some forsaken trash bin and brought them to him like a dog with a bone. At that moment, the cop cuffed me, sat me on the front porch, called my mom to come get me, and forbade me from speaking with Denny. I wasn't resisting him; I had complied with each of his requests. I also wasn't guilty of anything, so the fact he cuffed me left me despondent and unheard.

I was infuriated with his refusal to listen to me. He insisted I had been drinking. I insisted he could not give me a ticket for consuming alcohol when his own technology had proved I had not. Still, he did not listen. He did not budge. The matter worsened when my mom showed up in a car with my grandma in the passenger seat. If she hadn't thought I was a juvenile delinquent before this, she certainly would start now. The cop grabbed me by the cuffs and pulled me to the back seat of my mother's car. After he took off the cuffs, he shoved me in and ordered my mom to get me out of there.

Now that I finally had use of my hands I rolled down the window and shouted at him.

"You're an A-hole! You're supposed to uphold justice, not frame teenagers." And as we sped off, the words burst from my mouth and echoed through the air, "Yoouuu suuucccckk!" It was petty, but I felt so framed, manipulated, and angry.

To the best of my recollection, Denny did not get a ticket that day, nor did her raging mother whose backbiting boyfriend called the cops in the first place. That day the blame fell on me, and the blame would keep falling on me again and again. In this way, my frustration, fury, and despondency continued to grow until they ran as hot and fiery as my addictions. This event was the tipping point. It convinced me that the justice system was not just. From my point of view, I was innocent; his own technology had affirmed it, but he persecuted me, nonetheless. After this happened, I decided it didn't matter what I did, I would be indicted, regardless, so I might has well just DGAF everything. Each encounter after this seemed just as brutal and jarring, and each encounter solidified my defiance.

We were always looking for an excuse to sneak out and a place to crash at and do drugs. One time, our neighbor moved and while their house was on the market, we found a way to sneak in. We had a full month of non-stop partying in the deserted dynasty before we got caught by the real estate agent. We were halfway through smoking a bowl when it happened. I scrambled out of there so quick I left my favorite shirt and never got it back. Houses without adults to supervise were prime real estate for the likes of us, but also hard to come by. In the summer we could use any of our various smoke spots littered throughout the valley, but in the cold mountain winters getting high without getting caught was an art in itself.

One winter night Graham invited me to go robo-tripping with him and Cat. I neglected to ask where they'd managed to find a place to spend the night, a very pertinent question this time of year. I told him I couldn't make it. I'd been grounded ever since cussing out that cop in front of Grandma. It was not my parents' proudest moment. I couldn't risk sneaking out this time, and my parents refused to let me have sleepovers anymore. The next day was Saturday, and Denny called me. She sounded hesitant.

"Mike, Graham came here last night with Cat... they uh... they slept here, and they stayed with me... Graham tried to kiss me."

My heart sank into my stomach, skipped a beat, and a sickening feeling enveloped me. "Well, did you let him kiss you?"

A pause. "I was drunk, I couldn't help it, I couldn't stop him. It was his fault, not mine."

Red hot anger flushed my cheeks. "Did you kiss him back?"

Another pause. "Yes, I did, okay."

I was afraid to ask the next question. "Did you sleep with him?" The pause was too long and uncomfortable this time. I felt sick, but I needed an answer. "Well, did you?"

Finally, she responded, "He stayed the night with me, but it's not like you think. I swear I wouldn't have done it if I weren't drunk. He made the moves on me. I don't like him like that. You're my boyfriend."

A tear streamed down my face; a swell of impassioned fury boiled inside me.

I spoke firmly, "If you liked me, you wouldn't treat me like this. I'm sorry, I can't deal with this again. I've already had one girlfriend cheat on me with my best friend, I can't handle it happening again."

Despite having zero self-confidence, after managing to tell her that I deserved better than this I found the strength to hang up the phone. I stormed out of the house and ran into the mountains. A storm broke out, and the thick dark thunderclouds released a roar comparable to what I felt inside. Apparently, God was having a bad day too, or at least having pity on me because soon the waterworks bursting forth from the sky far outdid my own. Tears dripped down my cheeks, melding with raindrops and falling to the ground. That was the day I realized, *the amount of despair we experience when something goes wrong is directly proportional to the amount of hope we have placed in that thing.*

I ran, and I ran, and I ran. I eventually found a half-burnt cigarette under a rock protected from the rain. It reminded me of Denny. I stopped to pick it up and light it, relishing its stale taste as its decrepit filter bent in my clenched fist. That was the day I became addicted to nicotine, too. Until then, I'd always veered away from the substance. That day, I figured it didn't matter if it made me smell like hell itself, caused cancer, or killed me more quickly. It gave me a buzz, and that was what I needed.

Denny called me over a dozen times during the five hours I was away. Since she kept ringing the houseline my mother said the poor girl was distraught and required me to at least listen to what she had to say. When we finally talked, she apologized and promised not to do it again. She asked me to take her back, and my poor heart crumbled. I forgave her and took her back. Although she acted as if the event had never happened, I was not so quick to forget. The ache in my heart screamed for vindication. Graham was like a brother to me, but he hadn't hesitated to stab me in the back, just like my girlfriend hadn't hesitated to cheat on me. Even after settling things with her, I knew I still needed to confront Graham.

I thought about it all weekend, and at school the following Monday, I looked everywhere for him. The tension grated at my stomach. That morning, as I watched him pass by, I did everything I could to muster up the courage to approach him. He looked cocky and proud; he gave me a nonchalant wave as he passed by, smiling menacingly. I couldn't tell if the smile was engineered to mask his betrayal or to mock me for letting him get away with it. As he passed, I tried to speak up, but the words froze in my mouth like icicles; by the time I'd cleared my throat and caught my breath, he was gone.

Later that day, one of the Laurel brothers approached me. The Laurel brothers lived in my neighborhood and we had grown up going to Boy Scouts together. Both brothers were tough as concrete and always ready to either party or brawl. They were the toughest guys I knew.

"You look off today, Mike, what's up?"

I thought for a moment and then told him everything. I hadn't talked to anyone but my mom about it yet, and I spared her most of the details. With my emotions still fuming like a volcano inside me, I figured it was good to get it off my chest at least. When I'd finished talking, he looked at me incredulously.

"You can't just let him get away with that. He broke the bro-code. If we throw that code out the window, then there are no boundaries, no parameters, no rules, no reason to respect each other. Think about it: at some level, we all know it's wrong to sleep with our best friend's girlfriend, or any guy's girlfriend for that matter, but we can't help it. Maybe it's just in our nature to want something that we can't have, but the bro code calls us to a greater standard. If we all ignored the bro code, not only our relationships would go to hell, but our friendships would crumble along with them. If we ignore the bro code, everything is fair game. Even punks have standards, or at least we should. Graham didn't just betray you, he betrayed what it means to be a man, a brother, a friend. Lay it on him, man, don't be a sissy."

He stated it as if it were a mandate, as if there wasn't any other option in the world but to fight Graham. Laurel was the sort of guy that used his fists to do most of his talking, but I realized during this exchange that he had a lot more going on in his head than he let on. He was the sort of guy who could rally the whole school for a fight if he wanted to, the sort of guy who breathed courage, never shrinking back from a fight; he was always ready to stand up for what he believed in.

He grabbed my binder out of my hands and jostled my shoulder encouragingly.

"Go do this man! I'll get your back if anyone else jumps in."

We found Graham as he was just about to exit the school hall. Bolstered by my newfound courage, I shouted at him. He turned around quickly, and I closed the distance.

"Did you sleep with my girlfriend?" I asked.

His eyes shimmered with pride, and there was not the slightest trace of remorse.

"What does it matter to you?" he murmured defiantly.

Before I even knew what was happening, *wham*, my right fist rocketed into the side of his jaw. He tried to lift his hands into a defensive position, but he was stunned and was moving slowly. *Wham*. I connected again, and this time my full weight was behind the blow. The explosive boom that was my fist connecting with his face, silenced the crowds. The hall filled with an eerie tranquility. Then, crowds of people slowly began to circle around us like moths mystified by a glowing lamp.

As my fist flung through the air a third time, I started speaking again.

"What kind of (vulgarity), (obscenity), (expletive) friend are you?" I asked. "Why would you do that to me?"

He smirked condescendingly, as if some part of him were enjoying this. Blood was now pooling in his mouth and sticking awkwardly to his toothy grin. Drilled by countless hours of wrestling practice, he shook it off quickly. Now it was his turn to strike. Swing, swing, *wham*. Swing, swing, dodge. His arms were flailing mercilessly.

The second time around, both of his blows landed, but only partially. As they ricocheted off my forearms, one sunk into my ribcage, and the other skimmed the side of my face. I swung again, and he did likewise. He reached for my hoodie and pulled it over my face; he yanked forward, trying to pull me to the ground and blind me simultaneously. He was successful at pulling the hood over my head, but I wouldn't let him knock me off balance. I propelled myself forward, ducking under his arm and yanking in the opposite direction with just enough force to shake him loose.

We were dancing now, jumping back and forth, feigning strikes but no longer swinging, both of us assuming defensive positions. By this point, most of the damage had already been done. My first few blows were catching up to him now, and his adrenaline was wearing off.

A big Tongan stepped between us and separated us. He looked down at me amusingly. "Thanks for the entertainment, kid. Winner rides home with me."

He glanced over to Graham.

"Go on, get out of here."

Graham rushed off with Cat by his side and blood dripping down his cheek.

When he left that day, he went to get stitches in his face. When I left, I felt more confident than I had ever felt in my life. With adrenaline pumping and chest held high, I felt like a kid who had officially passed through his rites into manhood.

In the movies, the protagonist always gets their way. They always come out on top. In real life, it doesn't always work like that. In real life, sometimes we lose even while we're winning, sometimes we win at the wrong things. I won the fight, but I lost my best friend. I won the girl, but she cheated on me. Maybe "happily ever after" is just for fairytales? Maybe they never show us any scenes of what it looks like because "happily ever after" is messy and difficult, just like real life is. Maybe they never define it for us in the movies because there is no such thing, or if there is, it looks just like real life.

The movies teach us that we won't be happy until we find our Prince Charming or Princess Whatever. It's not just the jocks and cheerleaders who get wrapped up in this theme, it's all of us. All the TV shows and books (especially the young adult ones) feature teenagers who are finding their places in the world through the establishment of relationships and the acquisition of popularity. Whoever lands the cutest girl or guy is always esteemed above the rest, looked up to, and envied. Whoever gets good at sports is more likely to get laid. Whoever's cool is sleeping around. Whoever's sleeping around is desirable. To a large degree, our social status is defined by who we are able to seduce, intrigue, entice, and beguile.

In the same way, my friendship with Graham was there one day and gone the next. My relationship with Denny cost me my friendship with Graham, and then, after about a year, it ended abruptly as well. I was in juvie after going to court for a flock of fines and allegations. All of my various arrests were catching up to me and my world seemed to be falling apart. When I needed her most, when it seemed like she was the only thing I had left, she moved away and cheated on me a second time. I valued her above everything else in my life at that point, but these events made me realize not all people are worthy of our trust; not all things we value are able to reciprocate. To numb the pain of my messed up relationships, I started using more drugs, not knowing they would cheat on me too.

***

It is not only in the halls of the local high school that people are taught to evaluate their self-worth based on who their friends are or who they've hooked up with. Ideologies tying self-worth with seduction permeate the web. Social media and dating sites teach us that the more we market ourselves, and the more "likes" we get, the more desirable we are. These interactions and sites are teaching us to be dependent on what other people think of us, and to derive our sense of self-worth from them, regardless that these other people are unstable and insecure in their own right. All these avenues are drilling one lesson into our vulnerable minds: approval from others and is a primary source of pleasure, enjoyment and meaning for our lives.

We don't learn about the dangers of codependency, or how dangerous it is to base our wellbeing on another person. We don't learn that sleeping around, hooking up, and breaking up damage our ability to produce oxytocin at optimal levels [14], or how oxytocin is significantly related to our social bonding, social salience, stress and pain regulation, and that low levels of it have been related to mood disorders, substance abuse, and our ability to create healthy bonds [15].

We don't learn that sleeping around affects our self-worth. We don't learn about the longitudinal studies that have found that the odds of developing substance dependence increases linearly with the number of sex partners one has [13]. We don't learn how the damage of broken relationships, the real pain of a broken heart, can fuel drug use, how drug use can make us turn to sex and relationships, and how neither is entirely capable of meeting our innermost needs. Instead, we just learn to yearn, long for, crave, and idolize sex and intimacy.

So we keep chasing fairy tales, feeling discouraged, disappointed, or even despondent when our lives don't look the way Hollywood or social media say they should, and hooking up causes more problems than it solves. Most of our books and movies are modeled on the "happily ever after" theme for a reason: Somewhere deep down, we long for true love and acceptance. The movies teach us that the perfect someone will complete us while our culture tells us our own opinions and self-acceptance will complete us.

We really need both, and more. We need a type of love and acceptance that isn't fake or fabricated but is unwavering and unconditional. We can bestow love on ourselves in a limited fashion, but if we esteem ourselves while everyone else thinks we're a monster, then we are delusional, and our self-love is not rooted in reality. We need to be esteemed by those whom we esteem, but the esteem of others can be fickle, wavering, and paltry. Both sources for love and acceptance are inconsistent and unreliable; here one day, gone the next.

Chapter Seven

You Do You: Moral Relativism

"The acts of the flesh are obvious: sexual immorality, impurity and debauchery; idolatry and witchcraft; hatred, discord, jealousy, fits of rage, selfish ambition, dissensions, factions and envy; drunkenness, orgies, and the like. I warn you, as I did before, that those who live like this will not inherit the kingdom of God." —*Galatians 5:1-21*

So then, how do we define happily ever after? For me and my pubescent brain, the answer was simplistic: If sex and drugs feel this dang good, more must feel fantastic. I was a boy who had always been playful and imaginative, innovative and adventurous. A boy who believed that life could be greater than a storybook, more glorious than a fairy tale, more explosive than a firework. A boy who could not simply float through life living a menial existence. At some point, I was merely misdirected. Someone lit the fuse and pointed me in the wrong direction. When I was a kid my personality had been sheer optimism and curiosity. Before I realized that I did not, and could not fit in because of my lack of religious affiliation, I had always been the class clown; always carrying an abundance of laughter with me wherever I went, easygoing and eager to incite a moment worth remembering.

At some point, I became convinced that the best way to create a moment worth remembering was with drugs and a cute girl, but girls were good at breaking hearts and drugs were good at getting me arrested. Both of the things I turned to for joy and pleasure, acceptance and meaning, also created a lot of conflict and negative consequences. Because I didn't fit in with the rest of my society, I became isolated. Because I didn't know how to process those feelings, I became vulnerable, easy prey for the devil to chew on.

Despite my ever-increasing consumption of weed and other substances, I remained a generally sweet, quiet, and mild-mannered kid. With each successive arrest, however, my mind became full of criticism towards myself and the world around me. This unavoidable increase in conflict with the authorities waged war on my optimism and replaced it with hatred and despondency. Each instance of conflict led me to resent the authorities, the police, the education system, and anyone else who imposed their will on my life. Over time, I came to accumulate more than just stealing tickets. After I got arrested for blowing zeros, everything began to fall apart. I got arrested five times in a span of five months and faced over a dozen allegations.

The sheer number of officers who would show up at any given crime scene was unreasonable at best, but it ascribed sheer terror to us. It seemed they were intentionally trying to traumatize us. It seemed as if the tiniest infraction would beckon them. I don't know if it was just the fact that the people around us were a bunch of tattletales who called the cops over every minor disturbance, or whether the cops just didn't have real crime to worry about in "Goodie-goodieville." In reality, I think there were just too many of them employed for our city, which had extremely low crime rates and an extremely pronounced affinity for religion. The majority of these officers simply had nothing to do, so any time they saw a kid like me, with long hair, a skateboard, and pants hanging off his butt, they swung into action, showing up in hordes. A child such as this was an anomaly in the neighborhood in those days.

The more the police impinged in my life and arrested me for doing the things that I thought brought me joy, the more firmly I dedicated myself to those things. It was my life; I was free to do with it whatever I willed and whatever I wanted. Anyone who opposed me was violating my freedoms. My motto was, "I will do what I want. No one gets to determine what is right or wrong for me." Yet the things I kept choosing were self-destructive. Was it possible that they were inherently consequential, or intrinsically negative, or did I just have bad luck?

Although I didn't know what postmodernism or relativism were at the time, my life was ruled by their teachings. According to postmodernism, I was the acclaimed founder of my own reality. I got to choose what was right and wrong, not them. Everything in my life, including my self-worth, was based on my own ideas and constructs. I boasted in my ability to defy authority and responsibility, yet I could not defy the fact that every decision had consequences, some of them good and some of them bad.

The constructs of my reality were framed entirely upon the picture of pleasure. I had no concept of long-term wellbeing, delayed gratification, or working long and hard before receiving a reward. I was like an animal, rampaging against my caretakers, even as they tried to feed and nurture me. Even my parents, who put a roof over my head, food in my belly, paid for all my clothes, my phone, my computer, and all my other things —even they had no right to tell me what to do. At first it was normal teenage rebellion, I would bite the hand that fed me, as long as it gave me my food faster. After drugs had taken control however, I'd become infected, a rabid animal, unable to fixate on anything other than my next meal.

One of my favorite sayings was relativistic and I would say it every time someone made a funny face at me after I cursed. "People could have decided that 'microwave' was the f-word and everyone would get royally offended each time the word 'microwave' slipped from someone's mouth. It's absurd," I would tell them. So, I determined that all words were made equal in my mind, and that I would take offense to none of them. Still, my decision did not change the paradigms of others' realities. People continued to be offended, and I continued to "not give a microwave" about it. I not only constructed my opinion about which words were good or bad around relativism and postmodernism, but my entire reality.

Our postmodern culture teaches us that through our ideologies and belief systems we can construct our own reality. It teaches us that we get to decide what is good and bad for us, and that there *is* no absolute good or bad. I loved this! It excused me from all the moral obligations and accomplishments to which everyone around me strived and was accountable. This idea made me happy because it always allowed me to justify myself and my actions. Through this belief system, I was never in the wrong; I couldn't be.

But the minutia of these beliefs didn't add up. If there is no absolute bad, what do people call rape, molestation, or murder? Someone would have to be royally "microwaved up" to call those things good. I never thought about how many of the things I called good were just as abhorrent in the eyes of others as the above list is in my eyes. Relativizing good and evil not only enabled me to do whatever I wanted, but also to justify whatever I chose to do.

As I slowly grew accustomed to testing boundaries and bending rules, I became desensitized to what is right and what is wrong. My mind became warped, and I came to believe I was always in the right, even when I was doing something that society labeled "wrong." I would lie to my parents' faces and never feel conviction. I would steal and feel vindicated for doing so. If anyone called me to any "higher standard" I would get offended and find some way to accuse them of something. I would call them narrowminded or something else virtually irrelevant and feel like I had justified myself in doing so. It didn't matter to me whether their point was valid, whether their advice was logical, or whether following their advice would have genuinely made my life better. I would not take it from anyone. I had already made up my mind. I didn't want anyone holding me accountable to do or be better; I didn't want to "be better." In my mind, there was no better. You do you, and I'll do me.

✳✳✳

I felt like there was a battle raging between the police and me. My real battle, though, was not against the police, but against the law itself, against the ideology of right and wrong. If there was a lawgiver, my battle was also against Him. For years I believed all the tension hinged on my adoration of and their abhorrence towards a certain green fluffy plant, but it was more than that. My battle was cosmic. It hinged on the fact that I wanted to control my reality. I refused to obey or cooperate with anyone else's instructions or guidelines, even if they would lead to a safer society and an overall higher state of wellbeing. I would call the shots; It was my life.

I didn't realize that there would always be something influencing my decisions and weighing in on my life. At this moment weed was calling the shots and the desire to win approval from others controlled most of what I did. These were my idols, the things I functionally relied on to carry me through the hardships of life. I loved my weed, its dark, robust smell, the resounding buzz I got after smoking it that made my heart flutter and my mind fuzz. I didn't give a flip that it was ruling me. I didn't give a flip about anything. YOLO… DGAF…

One day, the Laurel brothers called me to smoke. They wanted me to drive them to meet their dealer and pick up a sack. Up until I'd kicked the crap out of Graham, they'd hardly acknowledged my existence. After that event, they finally started paying attention to me. I had a feeling that the only reason they were really calling me was because they needed a vehicle and none of their real friends were available. Still, I wasn't going to pass up an opportunity like this. After we picked up their weed, we headed toward the foothills. The snow was thick, almost two feet of fresh powder had fallen in the past 48 hours. My infamous Chevy S-10, with its two-wheel drive and automatic transmission, was struggling in the snow to climb the mountain that led to our usual smoking spot. After spinning out again and again on the steep slope, we finally skidded to a halt.

Two members of the group jumped out into the thick, tumbling flakes and disappeared into the white night sky. They came back, shouting for me to follow them. They led us into someone's driveway; the house looked empty and secluded, so we decided it would have to suffice.

We started hitting the bong, and after a while, someone exclaimed, "Oh my bleepity-bleeping microwave! There's a cop behind us!"

Sure enough, we all turned around to see a cop car just sitting there. They handed the bong to me to get rid of, and I did something so dreadful that I would retain the mockery of it for years to come. I did something that only a pothead who was stoned out of his mind would do.

I grabbed the bong, and I threw it straight out the window. For a brief moment, we thought the problem was solved until it slowly dawned on us that if the officer were to approach our vehicle, it would be the first thing that he would see. It was a Wile E. Coyote moment; by throwing our bong outside the window, I had ensured our impending doom. It was like throwing a bit of TNT out the window, only to realize, when it blew, the three-foot distance between it and the vehicle wasn't going to make much of a difference. This was when I made my second stupendously stupid decision. I opened up the door to grab the bong, and the second I did, the light in my car turned on. The light triggered the officer, who had actually not even known we were in the vehicle until then, and he immediately headed towards us to investigate.

Before slamming my door shut to turn off the light, I quickly grabbed the bong which was unharmed after landing in well over a foot of soft, fresh powder. Seizing the moment, I dumped its contents as quickly as I could. With one eye on the rearview mirror, I reached for a blanket, wrapped the bong in it, hid it under the passenger seat with lightning reflexes, and repositioned myself just as the officer approached the door. He signaled for me to roll down my window, and as I did, the thick fresh fragrance of weed rolled out of the vehicle in storm clouds. To our surprise, his first comment wasn't about the smell, although it was the first thing he wrote about in his police report.

Instead, the first words from his mouth were, "What's going on here? Are you a bunch of faggots?"

I don't know if he was more shocked or we were. Some of my friends were so macho that they had pummeled people for saying less to them. Nonetheless, this officer was obviously not acquainted with the pothead ritual of removing one's shirt before smoking so as to make the odor of weed less pungent when returning home to your parents. It was obvious that this dude was not a pothead in his teens.

We had taken off our shirts and set them on top of the vehicle so they didn't reek of smoke, but for him, all he saw when he looked into the truck was a bunch of half-naked men. He called for backup, commanded us to get out of the vehicle, and told us to put some clothes on. It must have looked like a clown car when five bulked up teens clambered out of the tiny four-seater extended cab. The cop handcuffed us immediately and plopped us in the snow. As he waited for backup, his flashlight methodically scanned each of us, starting with me and working its way down the line, only to come back again and again. He looked like a lighthouse as he surveyed the surroundings for any form of movement or any inconsistencies.

The light was not big enough to cover all of us, so every few seconds, each of us would get a moment without the blinding light beaming in our eyes. Those who hadn't done so before used this opportunity to take their weed and paraphernalia and shove it down their pants. This is an art that we had become fearfully good at, and the handcuffs only made this act slightly more difficult. The goal was not simply to put the weed inside your pants or boxers, since even then they would be able to discover it while searching you. If you didn't position it correctly, the crinkly sound the plastic bag made could be easily manipulated to disclose your secret. No, you had to put the weed under your nut-sack and move with careful precision so as not to trigger the sound yourself or dislodge the treasure within.

Soon there were four cop cars and two cops in personal vehicles with so many lights busting and blaring that it looked like the real circus had shown up. In some twisted way, this seemed to be like hitting the jackpot for them, finally catching us, the town hoodlums, at our worst, with no escape. When the backup arrived, the cops surrounded my friends and me in a semi-circle. One officer after another searched us and each of them turned up empty-handed. Round and round it went, yet regardless of who searched us, my friends and I were so experienced that after hours they could still find no evidence of our crimes.

The once raunchy odor of weed that had previously loomed in my vehicle was now beginning to fade as well. Three of the officers had searched my vehicle, and by some miracle, they were unable to locate the bong. Although the blanket was tossed to and fro throughout the vehicle as it was stripped apart, the tiny bong somehow managed to remain concealed within it. During the first hour of our arrest, we thought their inability to locate our drugs or paraphernalia would play in our favor. Yet as the time passed, our shivering frames froze in the arctic stillness of the evening. Our toes became numb, our fingers rigid, our bodies shook in the sub-freezing temperatures. The cops identified our agony and used this to their advantage. While we were skilled at concealing our crimes, they were skilled at softening their culprits, and they were dead set on arresting us despite their inability to locate evidence.

As they took turns digging through my vehicle and searching each of us, they also took turns mocking us. We were shivering and improperly clothed.

One of the police officers started to make fun of me, saying, "You look like you're wearing your four-year-old sister's pants. Oh, do they not keep you warm?"

I wasn't brave enough to say it, but I felt confident he was just jealous because he probably weighed well over 300 pounds and looked like a baby whale. At first, the officers didn't even allow us to grab our jackets from the top of my vehicle, although they wouldn't have been easy to put on with handcuffs clenching our wrists. They were smart enough to know that if they made us too comfortable, we would have played this game all night. They knew that the more we suffered, the more likely we would be to accommodate them.

They threatened to call the K-9 units, and the cold continued to take its toll. We were freezing. All sense of touch and feeling in my extremities was growing numb, and the nearly knee-deep snow had soaked through my skater pants (they were not girl pants). They told us they were not going to let us go until we confessed, and their threats of sending the K-9 unit disheveled me a bit. I decided I would take the blame. In one smooth movement, I turned towards the officers searching my truck and told them to grab the blanket and bring it to me. As my back was turned from the officer with the flashlight, I reached inside my pants, ripped off a tiny nug from my bag of weed and shoved it in a separate bag (which I kept on my person in case someone wanted to buy from me).

I placed the majority of the weed back in its safe harbor and pulled out the newly enclosed nugget in its baggie. In the same smooth manner, I turned to face the main group of officers and began to make my wager: "I will take the blame and give you the evidence you seek if you agree to only fine and arrest me." This was my chance to redeem myself in front of my friends. If I could get the blame placed on me, maybe they'd still like me. Some squabbling developed among the officers, and there seemed to be no general consensus. I went towards the vehicle, grabbed the blanket, and shook it. The bong flopped out, and the officer quickly leapt to recover it. Now they were getting excited.

All of these maneuvers were difficult with the cold jagged handcuffs grinding on my wrists, but luckily, they had cuffed us in front instead of behind the back. I turned to the original arresting officer and opened up my hand to him, saying, "Here, this is what you're looking for, now let my friends go." He grimaced; this was exactly what he'd been waiting for. He did not let them go, but rather he declared, "I knew it, continue the search." With their evidence substantiated, the officers grabbed us and dragged each of us toward separate cop cars. From this moment forward, I was unable to see what would unfold for the rest of my friends.

The officer in the front seat of my vehicle had the piece of weed squeezed between a pair of tweezers and was investigating it closely. The mischievous glower in his eye approximated that of a small child burning an ant through a magnifying glass for the first time. While never taking his eyes off the weed, he told me that he wasn't even on shift tonight but had been out with his wife looking for deer. He said they loved watching deer in the foothills during the winter months, and they just so happened to find us idiots, half naked in my truck. He said that he wrote me a fine for possession and paraphernalia, but that he could also give me a DUI and impound my vehicle if he wanted to.

As my world seemed to crush in around me, he looked back and told me, "I have been gracious to you this day."

It didn't feel gracious. My resentment boiled. First, the cops mocked me, making fun of my style and clothes, as if I weren't insecure enough already. They forcefully subjected us to excruciatingly cold temperatures, laughed as we shivered, and then blew my one chance at redeeming myself with my friends. Instead of letting me take the blame, they wrote citations for all of us. My friends never did let that go; to them, I would always be the imbecile who caused that arrest because of my failure to think things through. It didn't matter that they had put me on the spot by handing me the bong and asking me to get rid of it. In their minds, it was entirely my fault we'd been arrested.

We were kids, we had broken the law, but we still deserved —no, we needed— to be treated with basic human dignity. We needed to be treated like kids who were lost and in need of help, not like worthless criminals who were a mar on society and a burden for the planet. After my first few times getting arrested, I started to give up hope that I would have much of a future. I wanted to prove to them that I wasn't just a drug addict, I wasn't just a criminal, I was a boy, a boy who wasn't willing to be satisfied with simply existing.

After I got arrested for smoking weed in the mountains, it seemed like every decision I made led to getting handcuffed, thrown down on a hard, cold sidewalk curb, and talked down to for an inexplicable amount of time. This would last until they decided to either release me with an exorbitant fine or throw me in the clinker until my parents could come to pick me up. Yet, despite my bravado and my incessant efforts to shake off adolescence, I was still a fledgling teenager, which meant when push came to shove, Ma and Pop were always stuck with the job of picking up the pieces of mass destruction that their inebriated child always left in his wake.

Up to this point, my struggle with substance use hadn't affected or endangered anyone except myself, yet the police kept knocking down my door. After a while, it started to feel like the police were getting paid to ruin my life, like they were seeking me out, hunting me down, and finding pleasure in the process. After my first few arrests, I gave up hope that it would ever be any different. Instead of using my energy to try to change, I used it to try to outsmart the police at their own game. Of course, they had countless other tasks and duties to attend to besides me, but I really did feel like I was getting picked on. Since they were so big and powerful, the only way I could get a sense of justice was by outwitting them.

***

My mom and dad had both grown weary and disappointed after many unscheduled trips to the police station to pick up their rebellious kid. Neither my parents nor I could understand how I'd managed to draw so much attention from the local police force. Then one day my dad saw three police cars lined up to arrest and investigate one small teenage girl sitting on the sidewalk with tears streaming down her face. From his best judgement, it appeared that she had jay-walked. One officer had originally pulled her over and, as per the norm, numerous backups had soon become involved. After my dad watched this event unfold, seeing all of those officers hovering over that pitiful looking girl, he had a lot more compassion on me; he realized that despite my drug use, I did not always deserve the treatment I received. He saw that quite often in Valley Grove; there was an exaggerated response to teenage delinquency.

One time, after this nightmarish succession of arrests, when my license was suspended, my sister borrowed my infamous Chevy S-10. She was pulled over by an unruly police officer who demanded to know which of her companions was Mike Heil. She insisted that none of her companions went by that name, and the officer rather rudely disbelieved her saying, "This is Mike Heil's truck, where is he?"

She told him again, "Mike is not here, I'm borrowing his truck."

At this point he started shouting at her, "Fine, so it's going to be that way, is it? Give me your IDs, now!"

After thoroughly examining them, he realized they were telling the truth. He begrudgingly handed back their ID's and said in a stern voice, "Where is he?"

My sister politely told him that I was at home under our parents' supervision. He then stomped back to his vehicle, pulled away, and drove off without even writing them a ticket for speeding.

Most people told me I was being dramatic when I told them how it seemed like the police were always looking for me and pulling me over, how even when I wasn't doing anything wrong, they would appear behind me with their lights flashing. I felt like they must have had a picture of me posted in their break room. A Valley Grove's "most wanted" poster or something like that. I felt that they were out to get me, and this event gave me a lot of evidence to substantiate that belief. I later sold that truck to a friend of mine. Afterwards, he began getting pulled over at an abnormally accelerated pace. This always happened at the border of, or in, Valley Grove City.

I can't say the cops were foolish for putting this sort of target on my back. The numbers were certainly in their favor. The odds were, if they did pull me over on any given day, for any given reason, I would be up to something they could fine me for and collect money from it. In addition, my truck was blaring red, full of character, and hard to miss, just like me. As a teenager, however, I felt robbed of freedom, robbed of dignity, robbed of innocence. It took me years to realize that they weren't the ones who were actually robbing me.

One time, when I was nineteen and actually sober and doing well, I picked up mountain biking as a way to replace my bad habits. Driving home, I hung my CamelBak on the hook fixed above the rear seat door. I got pulled over for going 33mph in a 30mph speed zone. The cop was waiting right before the junction where the 30mph speed zone turned into a 25mph zone. Even though I'd only been going 3 mph over the speed limit, he marked me at eight. When the cop saw my CamelBak, he immediately called for backup.

"What's that IV bag hanging behind you?" he demanded. "You got alcohol in that thing?" he probed.

I tried to explain to him that athletes commonly used such devices to keep themselves hydrated and that it was most certainly filled with water and nothing more, but he insisted on calling for backup. Before long, aK-9 unit and two additional cop cars were at his side, totaling six officers plus the dog.

I sat on the sidewalk trying not to cry while they searched my vehicle for an hour-and-a-half.

After so many negative experiences with the police, every time I saw their lights flashing, my body went stiff and a chill would go down my neck. Whenever they pulled me over, my adrenaline would pump so hard that my body began to tremble with fear. Even when I wasn't doing anything wrong, my body responded in this way. As the search through my vehicle continued, I grew convinced that somehow, even though I was clean, I was going to go to jail that night; somehow I deserved it. I thought perhaps they would find some hidden remnant of a drug that had been lost and buried in years past, or if they couldn't, they would claim they did and frame me for it.

They were rather surprised when my story was validated; there were no drugs, my CamelBak was filled with water, and I was clean and innocent. It was one of the biggest reliefs in my life when after this encounter I realized everything was fine. They didn't impound my vehicle, take my license, and lock me up. Instead, they sent me on my way virtually unscathed with nothing but a speeding ticket.

Since I didn't like the law or the consequences for breaking it, I lived in denial of it. But pretending as if it weren't there did not make it disappear. So, I retaliated against those who represented it. If I couldn't divert the consequences, I diverted the blame. I blamed the Valley Grove police force for my consequences. I blamed them for "ruining my life." I blamed them for my arrests. I refused to accept that it was my fault for breaking the law in the first place. Blaming others allowed me to keep believing whatever I wanted and acting however I wanted. Blaming others only fueled my rebellion and made me look at what was wrong with everyone and everything else, while entirely ignoring what was wrong with me.

I was sad, angry, and full of self-pity. I hated being here, but I wasn't willing to accept that it was my decisions that got me here. There were and are predetermined fines and penalties that go with every crime; when we choose to do those crimes, we are risking the penalty associated with each violation. I grieved my situation; I grieved the fact that the fines existed and I was to be held to some higher standard. I grieved my arrests and fines and penalties with ferocity, but I did not grieve the actions that got me into these circumstances. I grieved my pain but I did not grieve my sin. In fact, I did not believe in sin, so I let it continue to destroy my life as I hopelessly, cluelessly, and despondently wondered what on earth was wrong. I repeated the same mistakes, feeling bad for myself, hating the consequences, but never changing a thing.

I found my identity in refuting the standards that society tried to impose on me. I refused to concede to anyone else's standard of good and evil, even if their constructs were rational and mine were not. Relativizing good and evil allowed me to dismiss any concept of a moral code. Dismissing the moral code did not get rid of my inward compass that told me when one thing was wrong and another was right, but it did allow me to mock others' concepts of right and wrong in preference to my own.

What I didn't realize was that destroying morality and replacing it with my own ideals was the definition of postmodernism. I didn't realize that both morality and relativism are societal standards. It didn't matter if I rejected the former in preference of the latter; I was still the lap puppy of my society's teachings. I wasn't defying my society and its teachings at all, I was embodying them.

My adherence to postmodernism made me hate absolutes. The police embodied absolutes; they enforced the idea of absolute good and evil. Their purpose was to curb murder, rape, theft, drug pedaling, and abuse. They wanted humankind to do and be better, and they were willing to give their time and risk their safety to ensure we would be. They weren't selfish, they weren't savage beasts, they were simply trying to keep society from unraveling itself. I wasn't proving society wrong by ousting moral absolutes, I was sucking from the bosom of its most seductive teachings.

When I broke the rules, I felt empowered, like I was redefining things for myself and reconstructing them in a way that better suited me and affirmed my values. As I got away with one thing after another, I slowly came to believe that the rules were made so Mike Heil could break them. Mine was a world where anything was permissible and all penalties were an object of mockery. I was the king of my own pitiful existence, an existence that was crumbling, largely due to my rejection of moral obligations and authorities. My rejection of them did not erase them but enabled me to do whatever I wanted. At least I was king in this self-obsessed reality.

Drugs felt good, partying was fun; I did both, regardless of whether others wanted me to or not. I was determined to make the most of my days. All hell would have to break loose before I would be willing to change any portion of my lifestyle. I was determined to prove that I knew better than they did about what my life needed to look like. So, I set myself the goal of outsmarting the authorities and all their bureaucratic processes. While the goal of their system was to change my direction, all they actually accomplished was cementing and solidifying it. Sure, they had me arrested, they fined me, they confined me, but I refused to let them define me. I would define myself, even if that meant the definition of Mike Heil was "a stubborn criminal, hopelessly addicted and unable to abstain from drugs."

Is what we were doing really wrong? If the point of life is to find meaning and purpose, and my purpose in life was to enjoy myself, was it really wrong to live like that? Was our country not founded on the belief that every human has the right to "life, liberty, and the pursuit of happiness"? Did it violate some greater universal law if my actions to please myself harmed and caused pain to others, or should they just mind their own dang business? I was convinced that if it weren't for one small societal structure called the police, the decision I had made to take this specific direction in life would have been infallible.

Yet, despite the fierce determination of my obstinance, I was ignoring the law of causes and effects. The effects of drugs were addiction, broken relationships, incarceration, shattered integrity, marred character, deceit, homelessness, laziness, depression, mental health disorders, instability, dependency, etc. Even if the police weren't there to enforce the law and hold me to a higher standard, the inherent consequences of drugs would degrade my quality of life. For years, as I attempted to prove myself right, my blood boiled with vindication. Yet the harder I fought against the law and its representatives, the more messed up my life became. At some point I had to ask myself, *why did I keep choosing drugs and rebellion when they only ended in chaos and despair? Was it really worth the fleeting blip of euphoria when it cost so much?*

Perhaps the police could have shown me more mercy, but their brash confrontation of my rebellion taught me something just as important: the world did not revolve around me. No matter how badly I wanted everything to benefit *me* and work out in *my* favor the world did not revolve around, nor conform to, my every fleeting fancy. There are such things as objective, concrete standards and ideals which dwell outside of and beyond myself. Whether I ignored or embraced them did not change the fact that they existed. I could build my life on them or I could continue doing endless mental gymnastics trying to excuse evil for good, all the while pretending neither existed.

Can you start to get the sense now why I rebelled so thoroughly against authority and authority figures? In my mind, I was on a simple journey to find meaning and enjoyment in life, but I didn't seem to be allowed to do so. In my limited understanding, this was the only lifestyle that promised laughter, joy, and at least temporary alleviation of pain and insecurity. I refused to believe it was intrinsically bad. In fact, I was convinced that the only negative thing about it was the stigma and the penalties imposed by the law. My heart hardened against them for trying to take this life away from me, for trying to remove my life's greatest joy. So, I rebelled. I did what I wanted when I wanted. All hope was lost for me anyway, wasn't it? That's what the cops had said. That seemed to be the general consensus.

"The authorities that exist have been established by God. Consequently, he who rebels against the authority is rebelling against what God has instituted, and those who do so will bring judgment on themselves. For rulers hold no terror for those who do right, but for those who do wrong." —*Romans 13:1b-3a* (NIV)

***

Aldous Huxley once said, "I had motive for not wanting the world to have a meaning…the philosophy of meaninglessness was essentially an instrument of liberation, sexual and political" [47]. By evicting God from our worldview, we free ourselves to commit every form of wicked atrocity our sinful heart's desire. In doing so, however, we are admitting simultaneously that our entire existence is void of any form of purpose or meaning.

Does ignoring God or pretending He does not exist change the fact of His existence, or does it only change the extent to which our minds are rooted in reality? If He does exist, He exists and we will face Him one day. If He does not exist, we will still face the immediate consequences of our actions. Whether God exists or not, any person who pursues these worldly pleasures for long will find that they enslave more than they liberate and never satisfy for long. While it is relatively easy to ignore God, it is much more difficult to ignore the conscience He has installed at the core of every human being that throbs even as we sedate it with seduction and substances.

Chapter Eight

The First DUI

"For me, drugs were ultimate, and the police were stopping me from getting them. We cannot help but hate that which stops us from getting more of that which we love most." (MH)

"Everyone who makes a practice of sinning also practices lawlessness; sin is lawlessness. You know that he appeared in order to take away sins, and in him there is no sin. No one who abides in him keeps on sinning; no one who keeps on sinning has either seen him or known him."—1 John 3:4-6 (ESV)

When our valley had its first dry spell, no one could get any pot for a solid month. It was the longest I'd gone without weed since I first started smoking. During this time, I had to revert to cough medicine and a small stash of odds and ends prescription drugs. When I went to my alcohol guy and asked him to buy me liquor, I was surprised when he told me no. He said a recent experience with mushrooms turned him away from drugs for good. I laughed, having heard that one before dozens of times, but in this case, it was true. He'd left his home when he was a teenager, choosing to exchange his family (who reached out to him regularly), for hard drugs and the homeless population. He'd been on the streets shooting up and getting spracked out for more than a decade. He was the last person on earth I'd expected to get sober.

He told me about the worst, most terrifying trip of his life. A dark cloud of fear, anxiety, and hopelessness began to enclose him. This dark and heavy weight grew more substantial as he shriveled up in chaos and fear. The weight was so heavy he couldn't manage to cry out and he groveled on the ground for hours in the fetal position. The intense feelings of meaninglessness and insignificance were nearly paralyzing. A bad 'shroom trip can make you more afraid of life than you are of death.

His feeling of fear grew for hours until, finally, he remembered what he'd been taught as a kid: that Jesus could deliver him from the darkness. He cried out for Jesus to rescue him and told Jesus he'd do his best to follow Him. At that moment, as if in response to his prayer, a song popped up on his laptop. It was Amazing Grace my Chains are Gone by Chris Tomlin. From a library of over 10,000 songs, it was the only Christian song on his computer.

As it played, a bright light broke through the darkness, pushing it away and scattering it in every direction. As he listened to the lyrics, he felt as if God were speaking directly to him, telling him, "I will break your chains away. If you let me, I will set you free." As he lay there weeping tears of glorious joy, he felt God break the chains off his back.

At this point, I stopped him mid-story to laugh at him. "Wait, you're really going to talk about Jesus, dude?"

Despite my unbelief, his life was changed forever. This was a great disappointment because he was the only person, I knew who was over twenty-one and willing to evade the law by buying me alcohol. But he was free. He had encountered something beyond the veil, and it totally transformed him. Yet, I wanted nothing to do with this God of his. I was determined to carve my own path.

Graham and I had not spoken since our fight a few months earlier, but our mutual obsession with drugs was much stronger than our hatred for one another. Graham was the only person I knew who had another hook-up willing to buy and distribute alcohol to minors. Alcohol was one of the rarest commodities of all among the high school-aged teenagers looking to have a good time. While we were skilled in the art of hiding our drug use, alcohol was a beast entirely of its own, with its potent odor sticking in my throat, its effectiveness at slurring my speech, the inability to hide it in my pants, and the undeniability of drunkenness when put to the breathalyzer test.

As soon as we got our grubby hands on some bottles, we drank with vigor until we were sloshed. Graham and I had become such bad influences on each other that our parents had banned us from visiting each other's homes, so we decided to get drunk in my truck. Yes, this is that very same truck that police officers in the "ghetto" unanimously associated with trouble. I had the man buy me an Iced 151 Mint Rum. I was on a vegan craze and got the ingenious idea to mix it with chocolate soy milk. This was the most extravagant drink I had yet created for myself. The minty, chocolatey combination was intended to taste like a peppermint patty, but the alcohol separated the imitation milk and its texture was more like that of milk gone bad. It was not chunky, but it was not pleasant until I had made my way through the first half of the bottle.

After this, I became too buzzed to taste much of anything. Graham and I, at the peak of our drunken stupor, had a sporadic burst of intellect and decided to go to the movie theater. I somehow managed to drive us there safely, and when we arrived, Graham said we needed to finish both bottles so they could not fine us for open bottle containment. I thought this idea to be wise at the time and followed his recommendation. Before we made it to the bottom of the barrel, both of us were seeing double. At this point, we realized that we had spent all our money on booze and the only way we would be able to enter the theater was by sneaking in.

With each of our independent roles assigned, we made our way into the bathroom to relieve the liter of liquor and however much soy milk and other chasers we had each consumed. While I was relieving myself in one of the bathroom stalls, Graham was stumbling around the bathroom like a drunken idiot, ranting and raving, and spewing utter nonsense as he fumbled about. Without warning, he fell straight into the locked bathroom stall that I was in with such momentum that two of the walls caved in on themselves. As they fell on me, I lost my balance, and my stream of pee flitted across the collapsed cavern, splattering on the wall.

As soon as I'd managed to set the stall upright and scramble my way out of it, an older gentleman appeared in the room. I moved aside, hoping that it wouldn't crumble again, but it was in vain. The stall crumbled once again and the old man started shouting something about damn kids these days. Despite our efforts to calm him, we knew we would be in trouble if we didn't get out of there. So we hightailed it back to my truck as fast as we could and hid there a while. We laid low until the coast was clear and then moved out for action.

Graham's job was to sneak into the movie while I made sure to distract all of the workers. I did my job quite well by hitting on the girl at the front counter and "accidentally" spilling something. When the person at the ticket booth came to help clean up the mess, Graham disappeared. I figured he was working on his part of the plan, so I went outside to the back of the theater per our plan. He was waiting there with one of the emergency exit doors cracked open with a pack of gum, ready for entrance. Once inside, we took our seats. After about five minutes, however, I was out cold. I'm guessing a couple of hours passed before I was awakened so rudely by my supposed friend Graham knocking me upside the head, trying to get me up out of my seat as the rest of the audience was beginning to leave the theater. He was trying everything he knew to wake me up.

I blinked. Everything was blurry, words scrolled across the big black screen, the credits were playing, the movie was over. I couldn't move, and I wanted to sleep. I laid my head down again and collapsed into my own lap like a rag doll. Another smack triggered my anger. As I lay there with my face in my lap, I swung my arm backhanded in the direction where Graham was seated. I got him square in the face. He hit me harder across the back of the head. Now I was awake; we stood up and started at each other, stumbling into one another with clenched fists.

Neither of us was landing blows very well, and our anger quickly subsided. Once we had both calmed down a bit and settled back into reality, we noticed a small crowd of people gawking at us and shouting indistinguishable accusations. We ran to the emergency exit and through the parking lot until we found ourselves outside my truck. I fumbled with the key, excitedly trying to insert it into the keyhole but failing again and again. A few moments later, I was in the driver's seat. I looked and saw my phone where I had left it with nine missed calls.

Graham shouted, "Come on, hurry up before they get to us."

Feeling like we were being chased by a lynch mob, I excitedly reached for the ignition and ignored my phone. I began pressing the gas pedal; the engine revved fiercely, but nothing happened. I checked again. The truck was definitely in gear. What was happening? I pressed harder as the pedal slowly made its way all the way down to the floor, but the truck still didn't move an inch. Black smoke started to rise behind us; the tires were skidding out ceaselessly on a patch of thick ice. My truck had been parked on a huge snowbank, and my endless whirring only wedged my vehicle deeper into the hole that was fastening it down. Reverse, drive, reverse, drive, and finally the truck caught grip and propelled itself backward onto the curb.

As it flung across the curb, a tree crushed the side of the truck, damaging the driver's side doors while also knocking the mirror clean off. I had so much fun in those three seconds of exhilaration that I drove on and off that snowbank two more times before I had the common sense to leave from there. After we made it out of that vicious, snow-ridden parking lot, I cautiously made my way up Center Street. Despite its conspicuousness, it was the main route home and was largely unavoidable. I'm sure I was driving perfectly, going the speed limit and everything, when Graham started mumbling something about the cops. I looked in my rearview mirror, only to be blinded by blue and red beams of light that seemed to be shooting in every direction. I turned around to get a better look.

There were four police cars driving behind me in v-formation. Lights blinded me and sirens blared as I hurriedly pulled over. As I swerved to the side of the road, my mind flooded with panic and fear.

Thick tufts of snow blanketed the streets, leaving three-to-six-foot tall snowbanks on either side. With sirens screaming I quickly navigated onto one of the thick mounds. As the cop began pounding on my door, I tried earnestly to roll my window down but it wouldn't budge. The damage from the previous snowbank had so thoroughly mangled the door that the window couldn't roll up and down any longer. The officer glared impatiently. As he continued pounding I pulled even harder on the knob that was supposed to roll it down. Suddenly it busted clean off. I held it up for the officer to see, looking apologetic about the inconvenience. His clenched fist slammed even harder against the window; he obviously did not find this inconvenience to be a laughing matter. He was flaring with anger at this point.

My only other option was to open the door. I did so, trying not to slop out of the vehicle like soup. As my feet hit the snowy slope, the policeman jumped out of the way as if he were under attack and commanded me to stick my arms out for him to see.

"Do exactly as I tell you. Say the alphabet. Alright now, walk forward."

Without hesitation, he handcuffed me and threw me into the back seat of his car. Other officers had already confined Graham. We drove a short distance to the police station where the officer ripped me from the back seat and took me to the station's alcohol breath-testing machine.

I was required to blow through a tube, and a magical number was to show up on the screen, telling the officer precisely how much alcohol I had consumed. These magical numbers appeared showing a .129, with the legal limit being a .08. I knew that I was entirely doomed. The fact that I was a minor and was not even allowed to drive at the legal limit only increased the likelihood of a more severe punishment. They gave me five tickets: DUI; open bottle containment; consumption of alcohol by a minor; hit and run, and reckless driving.

I was placed in a small concrete confinement with large glass windows on one side so they could look in at me. Its most prominent feature was a nasty yellow toilet that had years of residue and slime built up on it. I wouldn't have let anybody pay me to actually pee in that thing. It was disgusting, but I had so much built-up pressure from all we had drunk that night that I was nearly ready to burst at the seams. I ventured that they couldn't hold me here for long and decided to hold it.

I'm not sure if it was one hour or three, but I dozed off while sitting on the elevated cement platform they called a bed. I awoke to the officer who had locked me up, pounding on the glass and shouting at me.

"Hey kid! Hey kid, get up! Your parents are here."

When they released me from the cell, two cops escorted me out. As we entered the next room, I saw my parents looking utterly distraught. My mom looked like she had been sobbing and my dad was barely keeping it together. Seeing them like this filled my heart with remorse. I had let them down again. I felt utterly incompetent, like the most portentous failure that ever lived. *How could I do this to them, again?*

I was seated in a chair next to my parents, and one of the cops began to summarize what had happened. Only he wasn't summarizing; from my point of view, he was telling my parents a lie, a fabricated exaggeration of what happened. He said I was too drunk to know how to roll my window down, and that I'd done a hit and run. He didn't clarify any details, like the fact that I'd hit a tree and that had caused my window to break. From his point of view, the law was black and white. There was no area for debate, and to make matters even worse, this was the same officer who had caught me in the mountains.

He glared at me as he spoke, as if I were the scourge of the earth. *I already feel like a failure. Did he have to emphasize in detail how I'd added five more citations to the three pending ones that he'd given me last month in the mountains? I drank alcohol and drove, I skimmed a tree, I did wrong, but the way he made it seem was that I'd killed someone. Did he have to ignore the details?* I wanted to fling myself on the ground and weep and tell my parents I was sorry and that I knew I'd made a mistake. But as he spoke, I became disgusted, even with myself.

"Please," I said to him. "Don't I already look bad enough as it is? Do you have to make me look even worse? Please stop lying to my parents."

He responded harshly, "Kid, you need to learn your place. If we hear one more word out of your mouth, we're going to throw you back in that jail cell."

Every ounce of me was triggered with frustration, and my body flooded with anger. I couldn't take it anymore.

I erupted, "I don't know where you came up with this (vulgarity), but you are lying to my parents, and it's not fair…"

He was about to respond, but I flooded him out. "And officer, you can't shut me up. I can say whatever the hell I want —I have freedom of speech."

At that instant, three cops grabbed me by the arms and neck and picked me up — still in front of my parents — lifted me off the ground and threw me back into the jail cell.

When I landed on that hard rock bed, my anger fumed into vindication. I stood up with vengeance in my eyes. Looking at the dank, slimy toilet, I took aim and pissed all over the wall around, behind, and above it. If I'd had my wits about me, I'd have also aimed at the window where they were glaring at me. As I looked over, an officer started yelling at me and pounding the glass. I glumly flipped him off and continued peeing with vengeance.

I was generally quiet, generally shy, maybe even a bit awkward. I didn't know where all of this was coming from. I was generally hesitant to even talk back to my peers, but my world was imploding, exploding, self-destructing. It was ending. I felt like it was all their fault and I didn't know what else to do. The pressure had been building with each successive conflict, but at least the other arrests had been manageable. Now my truck was impounded, my license taken away. I was sixteen, and I had a DUI. I was one of those horrid statistics, I was a drunk driver, I was the thing everybody hated. Now I was in a jail cell and I was nothing. Whatever had once been my life was gone.

After an additional thirty minutes of waiting, they could not hold me from my parents any longer. I was finally told that I could leave my cell, and I left as quickly as possible. Once free, I was placed in the car to face the wrath of my parents. Upon arrival at the house, my parents followed me into my room, lecturing me the entire way. Only it wasn't a lecture, it was a plea.

"Michael, we love you, we're here for you. This track you're on is destroying you. We want to help; we want to be here for you, but you keep blocking us out. Didn't you see all of the missed calls from us? We called you nine times. Denny told us you were out drinking. All we wanted to do was help. We would rather have you call us and tell us you are drunk and need a ride than try to drive and endanger yourself and others. Don't feel ashamed to call us, we love you even if you're drunk or on drugs. We will come and get you ourselves. We would do anything to keep you safe. Please, just be open with us. Please, just let us help you."

But I couldn't.

I felt so isolated, so broken, so lonely. I felt like no one on earth could understand me. I didn't even give them the chance. I just assumed they would never understand and used that assumption to block them out all the more. I had the most loving, gracious, and understanding parents on earth, but instead of opening up and working with them, I pushed them away. It was as if I couldn't control it, as if the darkness ruled my life, as if I were void of any hope. Was it my mind and beliefs that kept me so isolated, always assuming others won't understand, always pushing them away? Was it my own insecurities, my sin, my decisions?

Their love was sincere, but I almost couldn't tolerate it. I felt awful, agonizingly awful, for so thoroughly rejecting them. Despite their boundless love, I pushed them away; I didn't want their help. I kept telling myself they don't understand, they'll never understand… But they might have if I would've let them. Instead, I yelled at them, angry about their love, angry that I was unable to reciprocate, but angrier with myself than with anyone else.

Realizing that nothing could break through the dark cloud that enshrouded me, they gave up and left me to sleep. Only, I couldn't sleep. My mind was filled with gloom. My guilt increased. I felt so ashamed to have such loving parents and to have let them down like this again. I did not deserve them. They did not deserve this. They deserved better. The pain and weightiness of what I'd done soaked into my bones, chilling me to the core, hardening my splintered heart. I brewed in this anguish for an hour, steadily feeling worse. Unaware of what I was doing or why I was doing it, I started scavenging around my room. I picked up a pair of scissors, and before I knew it, I was using them to create incisions on my wrists. I pressed as hard as I could and pulled again and again; small cuts appeared all across my wrists, but it wasn't enough.

I had more anguish than I could bear; I had more anger than this action could alleviate. I needed to be punished, and instead all I got was love. I went out to the garage, to my dad's workbench. I found a razor. I went back into my room and, using the same amount of pressure I had applied with the scissors, I pressed and then watched as the razor slit my wrist so deep that I gasped, terrified by what I had done. The cut didn't extend down into the bone, but the crevice was deep enough that the flesh on both sides had canyon-like ridges as the blood spewed like a fountain from between them. I hadn't meant to cut this deep. I didn't realize how sharp the blade was. I ran to the bathroom, my tears now flowing as steadily as the blood from my wrist.

I grabbed a full roll of toilet paper and pressed it on my wrist. After a few minutes of brooding in my own blood I heard a knock, followed by my dad's voice breaking through the sound of my sobs.

"What's wrong, Mike, what did you do? There's a trail of blood all over the tile out here. What happened? Are you alright?"

I sobbed even harder, "Dad, I'm sorry. I'm so sorry. I couldn't help it. I'm sorry, Dad, I don't know what I did. I don't know what I'm doing. I need your help. I need help, Dad."

"Open the door, son, it's going to be alright."

Still sitting there, I stretched up my good hand to unlock the door. By now, the toilet paper roll had soaked through completely with blood. He took hold of it and applied pressure. After the roll sopped with blood, he changed it for a new one and kept pressing. He spoke softly to me as he did this. Slowly, the flow began to lessen and so did my sobs. He removed the roll to get a good look at the cut. He told me we had two options: either we go to the hospital immediately for stitches, or we get superglue and doctor it up the old-fashioned way.

Through slimy tears and sobered eyes, I told him after having already spent the entire night at the police station I couldn't bear the thought of spending several more hours in the emergency room. So, after an hour of applying firm pressure, he found all the proper supplies, cleaned the wound, and glued it shut.

I didn't want to take my life, I just didn't know how to process everything that was happening to me. It happened so quickly.

I felt like I deserved punishment for all the pain I had caused my family. I felt like I needed some sort of rebuke, but instead, all they showed me was love. I deserved pain, I had merited pain, the only just reward was some form of retribution, some form of punishment. I didn't want to die, but I was in over my head. I didn't know how to live, how to handle all these consequences. I didn't know what else the arrests would bring and I was afraid to find out. I was drowning and the lifestyle I thought would bring me freedom had carried me, unprotected, into the unknown depths. It was limitless and boundless, exactly as I wanted, but as the waves hammered down on me, I grew increasingly aware that there was nothing of value out here.

"Floating on the remnants of a life that once was, a vessel, now broken, betrayed by its love. Clinging to wreckage while drifting astray. Increasing isolation keeping others at bay. There are not many old addicts, for before we arrive at the shores of old age, the waves crash in and sweep us away."

"'I was angry, so I punished these greedy people. I withdrew from them, but they kept going on their own stubborn way. I have seen what they do, but I will heal them anyway! I will lead them. I will comfort those who mourn, bringing words of praise to their lips. May they have abundant peace, both near and far,' says the Lord, who heals them. 'But those who still reject me are like the restless sea, which is never still but continually churns up mud and dirt. There is no peace for the wicked,' says my God." —*Isaiah 57:17-21* (NLT)

***

In America, roughly 300,000 people drive under the influence of alcohol every day. The average drunk driver has driven drunk 80 times before being arrested. I got arrested my first time, although I suppose most of them don't run into trees [16]. The laws about drunk driving are based on statistics. They exist to protect lives and reinforce responsibility in humans who have otherwise lost control, or who have started caring more about their addiction or having a good time, than they care about the safety of others. When people drive drunk, they endanger society. Sadly, there is a huge number of people across our nation who, like me, fail to heed these warnings. Thirty percent of vehicle related fatalities are caused by people under the influence of alcohol [17].

Chapter Nine

Judgement Day & The Law

"Do not be deceived: God is not mocked, for whatever one sows, that will he also reap. For the one who sows to his own flesh will from the flesh reap corruption, but the one who sows to the Spirit will from the Spirit reap eternal life." —*Galatians 6:7-8* (ESV)

When I showed up for school on Monday, Graham was there. We filled in the holes in one another's memories until he noticed the thick layer of gauze and sports tape wrapped around my wrist and asked what happened. I made the mistake of telling him, and rumors began to spread. Graham told our friends that I tried to kill myself after the arrest, that I couldn't take the pressure of it. It wasn't true. I hadn't really tried to kill myself, I just didn't know how to live with my mistakes. I'd just felt so hopeless, I didn't know how to press on with the pain. Without really knowing what I was doing, I found myself inflicting damage. I didn't know it would end up so bad.

Those who heard about my injury called me emo. They didn't care about the story behind the wrap, they just thought I was a freak and that I had the scars to prove it. At this point, it wasn't just the social pressure that was bearing down on me, but even more so the looming and impending reality of judgement day. Every time I got arrested, they pushed back my court date because they wanted to include all fines in one hearing. With my two most recent stealing tickets, the arrest at Denny's house while blowing zero's, the mountain arrest, and the DUI, I'd been arrested five times in as many months, accruing over a dozen allegations. The DUI alone left me with five additional tickets to account for. Thanksgiving was coming up, and after that, Christmas. I didn't feel like I had a thing in the world to celebrate.

I had already been dreading my court date, but now, with these added charges, what was going to happen? How much money would they fine me? When would I be able to drive again? My truck was gone; they'd towed it. How much would it cost to get it back from the impound lot? Would I get locked up or put in a program? Would I be able to keep going to school like a normal kid? It was my second year on the wrestling team and I was a sophomore now.

I just kept going to school, pretending like everything was alright, but I was crumbling inside. I was grieved that my life had come to this point; it had all happened so quickly. I just found myself running from one thing to the next and the things I was using to cope started more problems in and of themselves. The cycle spiraled out of control when one coping mechanism created consequences that led to the next coping mechanism, which created consequences, and on and on, without ever addressing the hurt and confusion inside.

I started smoking even more pot as consolation. It was hard to focus on anything but judgement day during the months I awaited my court date. I decided it would be to my benefit if I were to make a positive impression on the judge, so I homed in on my schoolwork, got a job, and strived to maintain a good work ethic. I set money aside for fines, preparing for my court date with studious intensity. Everything was a formula to me. This was my newest discovery: the more positive things I did, the more positively I would be perceived. This was definitely something I could use to lessen or even reverse the consequences of my negative actions.

I wore my best clothes. I prepared a hand-written letter for the judge. I worked to create a report card that many parents of exemplary children would have envied. But I allowed none of these good decisions to refine me; I was as insidiously rebellious as ever. I was determined nothing could change me. I was set in my ways. My heart was hardened, my beliefs were set, nothing could sway them. My positive actions were nothing but a way to preserve myself and mitigate my punishments. On the outside, people thought I was doing better, but every good decision that I made was superficial. I did what I needed to do so my love affair with drugs might continue lustfully. By this time, it was growing to be more than mere infatuation. It was dependency.

The judge stared down at me antagonistically. I looked up, quivering inside, yet still able to maintain the shroud of unwavering confidence that haughtily defined me. She began spouting off a list of nearly a dozen allegations.

"Mr. Heil, you've quite a serious record here. I've not seen a person rack up this many tickets in such a short time."

Standing in my nicest button-up shirt, I looked up at her and spoke firmly. "Ma'am, before we address any of this, I've written you a letter… It would be an honor if you would read it."

Upon that parchment was my neatest handwriting, organized with an orderly account of sob stories, pleas, and references to my suddenly surging grades. After unfolding the letter, she sat for several minutes, carefully perusing its contents. When she began to tire of reading it, I spoke up again.

"I mean it… I mean every word of it. I'm sorry. Look at my grades, my report card, the letter from my manager at work. I made a mistake, but I'm fixing…"

She stopped me dead in my tracks, speaking even more firmly than I had, "Son, you made *a lot* of mistakes. Don't come in here downplaying stuff, saying, 'I made *a* mistake.' You are here to account for *everything* you've done… And yet, I can see that you are trying."

She contemplated a moment, then went on, "Your crimes allot no less than thirty days in the juvenile detention center, and yet, such a charge would pull you out of school entirely. School may be the one thing you've got going for you still. We don't want to pull you out just yet."

Again, she sat in silence, until finally she declared, "You will pay $2,500 in fines over the next two years. You'll be required to do twelve individual counseling sessions and twelve group counseling sessions, after which your counselors will determine what further treatment will be required of you. You must get signed off for twenty-four AA meetings and attend the Prime for Life class. You will be under the surveillance of a probation officer for the next ninety days. Your license is suspended for eighteen months. You will serve eight days in DT over the next four weekends. The rest of the days that you were supposed to be in DT will be put in the bank, meaning if you are arrested again, you will serve all of the time we abated, plus whatever your next crime incurs. Based on the leniency of this verdict, I anticipate that I will not be seeing you again, Mr. Heil. Case closed."

I was flushed with relief; it was nearly palpable. My parents and I were almost certain I would be locked up that day, but I got to return home with them. We ran and hugged each other, struggling hard to hold back the tears.

We didn't entirely understand what was happening, but my public defender had asked the judge to hold my plea in abeyance. By pleading guilty and pleading in abeyance, I made it easier on the court so they didn't need to find evidence that proved me guilty. Essentially, I told them I was guilty and surrendered all rights to defend myself. In exchange for placing myself in their hands, at their disposal, they assigned me a probation officer whose job it was to ensure that I followed all the terms the judge had outlined. They agreed to lessen my sentence and fines as long as I followed their protocol. If I failed to uphold any part of the agreement, I would be brought back before the judge. If I couldn't provide a good reason for my failure to uphold the agreement, I would enter judgement, conviction, and sentencing for all of the crimes and penalties that had been previously withheld.

In the wake of this pardoning, I worked hard to convince my counselor and probation officer that everything was fine, flawlessly performing each of the tasks they set before me. But if I were honest, my only reason for complying was self-gain. Sometimes we look like we are compliant on the outside, but on the inside, we are callous and cold. I worked hard because I believed the faster and better that I could perform these tasks, the quicker they would get out of my life. I was not willing to succumb to the monochrome monotony of the goodie-goodie life. I was determined that the rebel life was the good life. As long as I held this belief I would manipulate every situation to enable me to continue pursuing drugs, sex, and partying, despite the consequences.

I suppose this anger and manipulation was my pseudo-conscious method of giving the system, and all it entailed, the big fat birdie finger. What I failed to realize was that my inward disposition of fuming vindictiveness and self-justification only caused me to rob myself. I was giving myself the middle finger, not them.

All activities, things, actions, and ideals have consequences; it's the law of cause and effect. What makes us so angry is not the consequences themselves, but when something we believe in brings about negative consequences. By nature, we want the things we believe in to yield positive results. Usually, drugs yield a positive experience short term, and negative consequences long term. The irony is that even when we can see that something we believe in yields negative results that harm us, instead of changing our beliefs, we try to change the consequences associated with them. In my case, I continued believing that drugs were life's ultimate joy and pleasure, instead of accepting that they were harming me. I refused to change my life, continued using drugs, and expected there to be different consequences.

The destructive cycle of my life ran like this: Instead of stopping drugs, which often cause stinky breath, shortened breath, sore throat, cottonmouth, slothfulness, rotten teeth, and myriad other things, people use cologne, makeup, inhalers, and oxygen machines to cover up the problems that result from drug use. Instead of addressing the causes, we address the symptoms. Instead of stopping drugs when I was getting drug tested, I started using different ones that were easier to hide.

By arresting me and putting me in courses and mandatory programmed counseling sessions, the authorities had shoved me onto an assembly line, believing it would fix me without ever accurately assessing what was broken. I was a broken person in need of wisdom, love, patience, and hope, not an object in need of fixing.

After my sentencing from the judge, I started getting drug tested regularly. As a result, I had to stop smoking weed. In place of weed, I started doing other drugs that stayed in my system for shorter amounts of time and were harder to detect. It started with nontraceable substances like mushrooms, acid, and 2-CB (a derivative of mescaline), but it quickly turned into hard drugs. While weed was detectable on tests for up to a month, hard drugs were only traceable for a few days or a week at most. Ironically, the drug tests which were meant to discourage me from drug use, turned me on to hard drugs.

The more I "outsmarted" my drug tests and the system, the more messed up I became. The more things I got away with, the worse my problems became. The fact I could manipulate any situation to get what I wanted, when what I wanted, was killing me.

As bad as my drug use was, it was a symptom of something much deeper. And their assembly line method of dealing with addicts did very little to help me pinpoint the real issues, let alone address them. So long as I believed that this lifestyle was best, I would find a way to keep doing it, regardless of the penalties. So long as I kept throwing out God, my life would be void of any purpose or meaning greater than making myself feel good before I died.

I was so stuck in my ways, my beliefs, my biases that I was determined to let no one persuade me out of them. Though I couldn't be persuaded out of them, I couldn't avoid the consequences of them, either. Drugs, sex, and partying had first been something I stumbled across, something I used to alleviate the dullness in life and the pain of loneliness. Now they were my god, my ultimate objective, my end goal. They were all that I lived for and they were the fuel that got me there. I was willing to risk my future for them.

"Claiming to be wise, they instead became utter fools. And instead of worshiping the glorious, ever-living God, they worshiped idols." —*Romans 1:22-23* (NLT)

***

Being served justice made me angry. I didn't realize if the judge simply let me off the hook for my crimes, she would have to let *everyone* off the hook. If there was no penalty for breaking the law, people could do whatever they wanted without consequences. Crime would increase until society crumbled. When people aren't being held accountable for their crimes, there is no justice. Sin and lawlessness multiply without anything to stand in their way. In the same way that a human judge is only just if they hold the perpetrator accountable for their actions, so also, if God is just, He must hold each individual and the human race accountable for their actions. If He does not do that, there will be no ultimate reckoning or righting of wrongs. Our sin, selfishness, and destructiveness will echo into eternity, with no one to stop it.

My judge was trying to help me change my trajectory, the path I was on, the place I was going. She wanted me to be okay, to be normal, to be a regular, teenage citizen, having fun in healthy ways instead of destroying my life. Her strategy for getting me there was basically court-ordered repentance: 1) acknowledge that you messed up, that you "sinned"; 2) ask the judge for forgiveness, and 3) change your trajectory; stop repeating the mistakes. The only problem was that you can't force someone to repent. You can't force someone to change their heart and mind about something. You *can* force them to change their actions and even their behavior, but if their beliefs remain the same, they will only get angry with you for it.

Even though my judge had pardoned the majority of my penalties, I was still angry with her for holding me accountable to any of my actions. The only reason I confessed that I was guilty was to lessen my penalty. It was out of self-interest. The reality is that I was guilty. Until I owned that fact, however, I would never heal. As long as I told myself that I didn't have a problem, nothing could help me. My denial didn't only make me delusional but it prevented me from getting the help I needed.

The process of acknowledging our faults forces us to pull our heads out of our butts and consider how our actions affect others, for once. The process showed me that all actions have consequences; it also showed me if I continued in my actions, I would throw away my future.

Chapter Ten

Dragon Counselor

"Your kindness to the wicked does not make them do good. Although others do right, the wicked keep doing wrong and take no notice of the Lord's majesty." —*Isaiah 26:10* (NLT)

As a freshly adjudicated youth, it was my responsibility to attend every group and individual counseling session, every AA meeting, and every correctional class that the judge assigned me. It was also my duty to pay my fines on time, check in with my probation officer weekly, take randomized drug tests, and provide evidence of regular school attendance. Any failure to do so could result in a warrant for my arrest and subsequent incarceration. During my first counseling session, I was required to complete a survey to assess how bad my addiction really was. I cheated.

I answered all the questions in such a way that I looked as if I were a child dropped straight out of heaven, placed in counseling by mistake. This maneuver minimized the amount of counseling I had to go through. The only downside was that I didn't get the help that I needed because I made them think I didn't need help. I led the counselor, probation officer, my teachers, my parents, and everyone else to believe that I was a good kid who'd just slipped up and made a few blunders. I made them think I was putting my all into recovery when, in reality, the only thing I was putting my best effort towards was deceiving each of them. My intellect allowed me to maintain the style of life I wanted, right underneath their noses.

It had only been two years since I'd first smoked weed. I was now a sixteen-year-old who had not only incurred the highest tier of probationary punishment, but also managed to become a target demographic for the local police force. Hunted down by the authorities, and now firmly enmeshed within their correctional procedures. I felt like a rat in a serpent's quarters, and I was about to face one of my strangest challenges yet. I had been under the scrutiny of the local police force for over a year by this point. The bottom line was, if I could outsmart the judicial/legal system, then I could keep my addiction. But was that really what I wanted? Here I am, talking about my addiction as if it were some small and innocent pet, something that merited my unconditional affection. Wasn't it tearing my life apart? But to feel so carefree…To feel, even just for a moment, like nothing mattered in life. That feeling of all of the dopamine in my brain being forcefully dumped out was like a cargo truck of ice cream being unloaded on a carousel of small children. That ecstatic euphoria lasted… for a moment, but then left me scavenging, stealing, and wandering the streets until I could find my next fix. At least drugs bought me acceptance with the cool kids. That had to count for something, didn't it?

I kept telling myself that everything had been fine until I drank that bottle of 151 rum, tipped over the bathroom stall in the movie theater, and got chased by that v-squad of four cop cars right down Center Street. That incident left me truck-less, license-less, and job-less, while also leaving the Valley Grove police force thoroughly pissed off, if you'll pardon the pun. But I hadn't been fine. I'd been digging my own grave, and that was my fifth arrest in as many months. You can't do that much stupid stuff in such quick succession without it catching up to you. In the immediate aftermath of all that crap happening, I was forced to be sober, at least until I figured out how to work the system. The process of regaining my mind made me feel as if I were losing it. Drugs were my coping mechanism, my source of confidence, my sanity.

As I sat in class, my mind settled on an image of a packet of morning glory seeds. A series of golden eyes stared at me from the hollow depths of an overgrown shrub. In my mind, the spherical blue star-like flowers bobbed wistfully in the wind. From under each bonnet a glowing golden eye peaked out glaringly. It had a treasure buried inside of it, and it would soon be mine. My brain was more than ready to get back in touch with its more "creative" side. I hadn't gotten high in almost two weeks and this golden blue flower happened to be one thing that would not show up on a drug test. I had stolen a few packets of these seeds from the local grocery store and had been saving them up for a moment like this.

This flower also was one that just so happened to come naturally laced with a hallucinogenic substance called 2-CB, a substance strong enough to take Bigfoot himself for a joy ride worth bragging about. It didn't matter to me that I had school that day. It didn't matter that I could get locked up for breaking the terms of my probation, or that I was on court-ordered probation with mandatory counseling and randomized checkups with drug tests. In my world, there was little time to think about the consequences of my actions. I kept busy by living life, not worrying about it.

It was not that I had ill intentions, nor that I didn't care about my life. I simply couldn't understand why some things were labeled "bad" and others were labeled "socially acceptable." I didn't get why some things would merit praise and other things judgement. All I knew was what made me feel good. I knew I could only live each day once, and I believed each day ought to be lived to its fullest. It didn't matter that I couldn't define what that meant. What mattered was that I try to live it out. If I could carve out an adventure into any given day, it didn't matter how much it cost to do so; I considered it a day well-spent. Lately, that happened to entail an excess of illegal activity, but was it my fault that the most entertaining things to do also happened to be illegal?

I mean, how does one even live their life to its fullest, anyway? More parties? More girls? More drugs? None of my solutions seemed to fit the bill. What about all of those super-industrious nerdy kids who kept talking about good grades, excellent schools, and dream jobs with exciting career potential? How did those kids even have time to think about success and prosperity, anyway? Weren't they a little too young to be trying to make a name for themselves? What happened to adolescence and carelessness? Was I merely behind in my development? I mean, hanging with the loony tunes wasn't a bad gig for a high school student dead set on self-satisfaction, but what kind of future would partying and drugs bring?

For some reason, at this point in my life, it didn't matter to me. The only aspirations that seemed to move me were getting high and getting laid. There was no motivation for anything else in life. Had it always been this way? Or had there been a time in my life when I'd had dreams as well, but somehow, I simply lost them along the way? When a girl I worked with hanged herself in her closet and another kid at school overdosed on heroin, I just knew it was coming for all of us. Life was too short. I didn't feel like I had time to think about tomorrow at the cost of wasting today. I was guaranteed the present moment, but I wasn't guaranteed tomorrow.

These were the types of thoughts that meandered through my hollow dome as I heartily ignored the teacher lecturing at the front end of the classroom. I wanted to get high. No, I *needed* to get high. My mind raced. I wasn't used to this racing. Usually, a fuzzy blur saturated my thoughts. Zoned out, careless, inconsequential —that was my norm. When the bell finally rang, I jumped out of my seat and scrambled for the door. If I could just find a ride home, that flower's cavernous gaze was penetrating its way deeper into my limbic system. I was practically aching for it now. The morning glory flower was about to make my day a lot more glorious!

After finding a friend to give me a ride home for lunch, I ground up the seeds and chomped them down. I began to experience a throbbing pain in my stomach. The shells of the seeds are poisonous for human consumption, and I had skipped several steps while removing the poison in order to expedite the process. Nonetheless, I removed most of it. I puked a few times (a motion which bothered me very little at this point in my life) and when I finally re-emerged from the bathroom, I stood up feeling dauntless.

I returned to school with a particular new hop to my step. In my next class, we had finals. That was a trip, to be sure, but somehow, I still managed to pass the test. I am very grateful that the person sitting next to me wasn't tripping balls and seemed to have a knack for the topic. My brain could not compute anything that was going on around me, which was ironic because the class we were in was computer science. I kept zoning out as the various shapes and symbols flashed across the computer's glowing screen. My most strenuous efforts to combine those symbols into words failed drastically, sentences eluded me, and time passed in a chirping swirl of incoherent madness. Was I even copying the right answers off the screen of the person next to me? It didn't matter if I failed, I could make it up some other time.

The bell rang. I tried to ignore the teacher who was looming over me, asking questions. I couldn't make sense of them.

"Later," I retorted, "can I finish this later? I need to go now. I am not feeling..."

My face must've turned green because the teacher looked puzzled and then realized I was about to puke. I turned quickly and clambered out of the classroom. That would be a battle for another day. After a quick trip to the bathroom, I walked down the hallway, scanning my surroundings. I saw the rosy cheeks of a brunette light up with laughter. My brain could compute that. I started straight for her and momentarily found myself sitting on her lap. I started speaking in a tone that seemed surprisingly confident —real sentences this time, too, and a smile lazily spread across her face.

My words appeared to make her laugh. I was funny. *Good job, Mike*, I thought to myself.

I sat there for about five minutes, and to my great surprise, she didn't even try to evade me. Before too long, a friend of mine came and pulled me off her lap.

"You're way out of your league, dude, don't push your luck."

Dragged along by my friend, I turned to give her a wistful smile and told her to call me if she needed anything. Never mind that I hadn't given her my number and could probably not have remembered it correctly, even if I'd wanted to. I knew I would never have the audacity to talk to her again (at least while in my right mind).

It was my norm to go to events high. I passed my driver's exam high on weed, and I had intentionally gone to detention shrooming, just to see if I could do it without getting caught. I was determined to convince the world that every form of drug use should be legalized, determined to overthrow the authorities by proving their fickle policies futile. I was an advocate of anarchy, dead set on self-satisfaction. As a result, I went through most of high school either high, drunk, or locked up, with some sort of crumbled prescription up my nose.

The extent of my depravity was ruthless: graduation, family events, weddings, funerals, Grandma's birthday, Christmas, Thanksgiving, and every other holiday. The one common denominator amongst these occasions was that the only thing I gave thanks for was an inebriated state of being. If I had to go a day without drugs, it was a bad day. If a day went as I preferred, I would get high in the morning, at lunch, and in the evening.

When I got home that day my mother nearly trampled me, as she ran down the stairs and out to the car. She shouted at me to get ready for my drug test and counseling session.

"What are you talking about?" I asked her. "I'm not going to counseling."

She gave me a look that said, *I'm sorry, son, have you forgotten who the adult is around here?* But her words were more direct, as she reminded me, "You are supposed to call the hotline every day for your random drug test. You have counseling every Thursday. How could you forget?"

I chose to get high on 2-CB because I knew I wouldn't have to worry about it showing up for a drug test. What I was not prepared for, however, was the counselor. I could hardly face her on a good day. How on earth was I going to convince the counselor that I was sober when I was tripping balls? I could hardly talk, my brain kept short-circuiting, and even my mom was on to me. How was I supposed to convince anyone that I was a decent and responsible teenage citizen?

Screw it, I thought as I uneasily resigned myself to whatever consequences lay ahead of me. There was no getting out of this one. Whatever was about to happen, I would face it with all the courage and determination I could muster.

The counselor's job was twofold: First, to ensure my sobriety by subjecting me to a series of sessions that I referred to as "brainwashing", and second, to make sure I understood the long-term consequences that drug use and rebellion would have on my life. The end-goal was to persuade me into willing conformity to the law. By successfully undergoing counseling treatments, completing questionnaires, and proving myself to be of sound mind and understanding, I would be able to earn my way to freedom.

Today's "slight" misconduct would surely lead to an interference in my path forward unless I could convince her there wasn't anything wrong with me. As we climbed into the car, I felt a sudden sense of impending doom, a moment of mental clarity. This counseling was court-ordered, and if she knew I was on drugs, I would be locked up on the spot, not to mention a whole array of other penalties.

The campaign ahead would inevitably erase and undermine all past successes from the previous months of counseling. As I sat and waited for my counselor to call me into her quarters, I found myself rocking back and forth like a child in the fetal position. I couldn't keep steady. The walls around me were caving in. If I were caught in my charade, I would be pulled out of school, deemed no longer suitable for development in the outside world, and placed with the rest of the outcasts in a long-term detention facility. As the floor spun like a Ferris wheel, up-right-down-left, up-right-down-left, launching itself in symmetric circles, I suddenly felt like puking again.

As the floor lifted up, the ceiling would close in on it, steadily grow shorter and stouter. Then the ceiling would lift up, and the floor would drop down, making that same door elongate and stretch tall enough for a giant to step through. In one moment, the ceiling and floor seemed to be fifty feet apart, with the door filling the gap in between. As the circular motion completed its sequence, that same door would shrink down to become three feet tall and five feet wide, just the right size for a fat hobbit to stumble through. Sadly, it would not be the warm, friendly face of a hobbit that crawled out of that hole to greet me, but a being who held the authority to crush my very life.

Finally, my counselor came sprawling out of the cataclysmic mess. She loomed in the door, standing tall, skinny, and elongated, before beckoning me to the basement. I looked down the stairs nervously, trying not to tip over after that lengthy Ferris wheel ride had made me so nauseous. By the time I made it to her office, I didn't just feel like I was in a dungeon, I felt like I was dungeon crawling, ready at any moment for some fowl creature to jump out and attack. I made a cautious crash landing into the nearest chair and stared awkwardly at my lap trying to avoid her gaze.

When I finally did glance upward, I choked for a moment when my eyes met with a long giraffe-like neck. My eyes followed the seam of the neck upward until they met with a surprisingly unfamiliar face. A face, rough, rugged, and scaly, peered fiercely back at me as a contorted grimace worked its way unevenly across its surface. Its sidelong glance nearly sent me scrambling out of my chair. Jagged teeth protruded from the abysmal glower, and I suddenly felt sick to my stomach again. Her head followed seamlessly along the giraffe-like neck as the two rotated in a perfectly perturbing sequence with one another. The steady gesture much resembled the motion of the door through which I had entered this dark realm.

I found myself rocking again. I knew I was tripping balls, but my counselor looked like a dragon. Who could have even imagined? The conflicting pressure almost burst from inside me. Half of me tried not to explode with laughter at my strange predicament, and the other half was terrified by how portentously accurate this new representation of her was.

"How have you been?" she asked.

Me? Wha? Um… *Respond*, I told myself. But no words came out. *Don't laugh; avoid the eyes; tell her you're sick.* These thoughts raced through my mind, but still, no words came out.

By now, the head hanging on the giraffe-like structure was no longer just spooling in circular alignment with the elongated neck but was now moving forward and backward as well, drawing closer to me with each passing second. I looked down at my twiddling thumbs awkwardly. Her face was so close by this point that I felt like I could reach out and touch it. Had she walked over to me or was her neck literally stretching across the room? Was I imagining the breath on my face?

A slithery voice hissed out from the dragon-like face, "Not feeling like talking today, are we? That'sss fine, I've prepared ssomething elsse for today's lesson anywaysss."

The body upon which the long neck and crooked face were situated looked surprisingly human. As it made its way towards the bookshelf, the neck straightened a bit and stopped doing that creepy swirl thing that reminded me so much of the cat from *Alice in Wonderland*. From behind me, a book was shoved into my lap, and the voice spoke up again.

"Consssult with me when you're finisshed reading; we'll have a lot to disscusss."

I quickly looked down and opened the book, and wishing I could retreat into it, I stared at it blankly. I tried reading, but my mind couldn't grasp the letters upon the page. To my advantage, it was a children's book, and there were only a few words on each page. Anyone with a second-grade reading level should have been capable of adequately digesting its content.

I sat staring until the inquisitive voice asked me if I was alright.

"Yes," I retorted. "I just want to make sure I understand it well."

No matter that I was still looking at the title page, which only had three words on it: *The Missing Piece*. The black title stood out in bold contrast to the white background. I intentionally spent about one to two minutes on each page of the book, hoping to pass the time, but when I was done perusing it, a hefty chunk of our session remained. I was able to absorb its contents fairly well, yet when I tried putting it into words, it was like triggering the "on" switch of a blender. Something was definitely jumbling around in there, but the process of transferring it into phonetics was beyond my best efforts. The idea of having to sustain a civilized conversation with Puff the Magic Dragon was growing more intimidating by the moment.

In a brief moment of clarity, I told her that I liked the book and asked if there was more to the story. She stood up to take the book from my hands, and I feared that I'd been discovered, but to my great surprise, she was only taking it to the bookshelf. After a moment she placed the sequel in my hands.

As I looked through the sequel, something magical began to happen. All my life's questions and quests were boiled down into stick figure format in front of my very eyes. Because of the drugs pulsating through my brain, the experience of identification was more than just a feeling. As I read, I felt like Max from *Where the Wild Things Are*. I climbed inside the book and departed on a grand adventure. Like Max, I knew precisely what my life needed: more mischief, more wild things. Yet, somehow like him, the sum of my adventures had only shown that none of the wild things could ever satisfy.

The sad sum of all of my actions burned like a signet into these meager pages. I had believed my quest for drugs would fulfill me and meet a need that I felt at the center of my being. I was wrong. Every human will experience emptiness and loss. Every human has a hole inside that they try to fill at different times in different ways. Most of the time, the solutions we find satisfy temporarily but create more problems in the end. We go to a thousand different things, trying to find what's missing in our lives. We find pleasure for a moment, and then we need more. None of the things we turn to are permanent or long-term solutions, and we begin to wonder if there is any solution at all.

The book my counselor had me read insisted that something was missing in my life, not a feeling of euphoria that lasted a moment and left me wanting, nor the approval of others, which always proved inconsistent; what was missing was a component at the soul of my being.

I had been looking to other things and other people to fix what was within me, and they couldn't. Something within me needed to change. It wasn't just my actions, but my belief systems. My beliefs were contributing to the actions I took. They were the why behind the what. At best, my counselor could help me moderate my actions, but until my beliefs changed, I would resent the change. I was at war within myself, my mind telling me one thing, my emotions telling me another. The missing piece in my life was not merely more knowledge, nor was it more experience, it was something much deeper than that.

I had a hole at the center of my being, and I had been trying to fill it in all the wrong ways.

The book never addressed how the hole got there or why the methods I was using could not meet my needs, or solve any of the problems in my life. The book never told me how I could fill the hole, it simply urged me to question the efficacy of the strategies I'd been using, thus generating a whirlwind of questions. If drugs, pleasure, and adventure were not capable of providing lasting fulfillment in life, then were relationships? If the right relationships with the right people could not meet my needs, then could wealth, status, or luxury? What if the solution isn't quick but lengthy, isn't easy but painful, isn't cheap but costly? What if there is no magical solution but a difficult process in which the cost we pay is determined by the choices we make? What if it doesn't always feel good or make me happy? What if hope and purpose are refined through the trials rather than by avoiding them?

My goal was to find something that would fill the hole, but everything I turned to seemed fleeting and temporary. The only things that proved enduring were my tenure in the justice system and the consequences of my actions. In my innocent pursuit of lasting pleasure, nothing was lasting except the fact that I became a pothead, an alcoholic, a womanizer, a heroin addict, a smoker, and a bulimic who was completely obsessed with what others thought of me.

"Man without faith can know neither true good nor justice. All men seek happiness. There are no exceptions… This is the motive of every act of every man… So, while the present never satisfies us, experience deceives us, and leads us on from one misfortune to another until death comes as the ultimate and eternal climax… What else does this craving, and this helplessness, proclaim but that there was once in man a true happiness, of which all that now remains is the empty print and trace? This he tries in vain to fill with everything around him… though none can help, since this infinite abyss can be filled only with an infinite and immutable object; in other words, by God himself [35]." —*Blaise Paschal*

Chapter Eleven

Pissing Zeros

"But mark this: There will be terrible times in the last days. People will be lovers of themselves, lovers of money, boastful, proud, abusive, disobedient to their parents, ungrateful, unholy, without love, unforgiving, slanderous, without self-control, brutal, not lovers of the good, treacherous, rash, conceited, lovers of pleasure rather than lovers of God—having a form of godliness but denying its power. Have nothing to do with such people."
—*2 Timothy 3:1-5*

While the assembly line of counseling and probation addressed my symptoms, it never did address the root, so my symptoms sprang back without delay. After my first couple months of being "sober," over-the-counter cough medicine, morning glory seeds, and other nontraceable substances like psychedelics couldn't cut it anymore. Because of my experience with the dragon counselor, I knew that drugs weren't a long-term fix. I knew they were destroying me inside and out; I knew they weren't the way to live life to its fullest, but by this point I was so addicted that logic couldn't reach me. The harder it was for me to get high, the more I wanted it. I needed weed. I needed real drugs.

So, I calculated how many drug tests they would do in a given period of time, peed in a few baggies, and saved them for those moments of truth. After one month of being able to successfully utilize my pee bags to pass the drug tests, I stored a stash of bagged piss in my closet. There were a few close calls when I ran out of pee and had to gather it in bags from my sober friends, but after a while I had to adjust my strategy because I really didn't have a lot of sober friends and I didn't feel comfortable asking strangers.

I did some research on the most effective methods for cleaning my own system of drugs. Each month I would take a concoction of over-the-counter drugs, alongside a few gallons of water. I would sit in the steam room and sauna for several hours, for several days in a row. I did this every time I had an upcoming meeting with my probation officer, when they would almost always test me. I had friends who would steal drug tests and self-administer them to make sure they were clean, but I trusted my regimen. After performing my regimen, when my test showed up clean, I would store my own pee in a few baggies again and hide them around the house.

Many people were not sleuth enough to pull off the pee bag trick. They always managed to make their baggies crinkle too loud or made some other blunder that unveiled their deceit to the constable monitoring their case. I, however, nailed it every time. And by doing this, I enabled myself to continue spending time with the few and only people whom I called my friends. The only reason they hung out with me, of course, was just to smoke weed, but they were all I had, and sacrificing them would have messed me up good.

One day, when these friends and I were smoking, they playfully began spreading rumors about the latest and greatest in the world of probation. I wasn't sure if they were trying to joke with me or if they were being serious, but after some long, hard contemplation, I figured the latter to be true. They said that the courts were now requiring that drug testers start recording the temperature of the pee to make sure that people like myself who were cheating the system could not get away with it. I laughed it off; the concept seemed ridiculous. I could picture some government worker dipping their hand into my cup of pee with a thermometer dangling between their fingers in an attempt to measure the precise temperature and ensure I hadn't faked it. It seemed improbable, laughable even.

The next time I had a drug test, I arrived home from school to find my mom rushing down the stairs. She nearly pushed me out the door as she slammed it behind her.

The first thing out of her mouth was, "We're late, get in the car. You have a drug test today, and they're closing soon!"

She was already whooshing toward the car and frantically urging me to do the same. If I missed or failed the test, it meant jail time, and her fuming frustration showed me that she knew it. I told her I needed to go to the bathroom and pleaded with her to please let me in the house. She caved and threw me a key.

I quickly sprinted downstairs to pick up one of my plastic bags, and then a little light bulb went off inside my head, reminding me that pee now needed to be warmed up to pass the new tests. I looked around frantically, but seeing no other alternative, I decided to throw it in the microwave. I gave it one minute and thought it should be fine, then I pulled it out and tucked it inside my pants (the only place they weren't allowed to reach into and check to make sure I wasn't cheating the system). At that exact moment, I knew I'd made a bad decision. Almost instantly, I started cringing. The pee was scalding my skin; it was scorching hot. At the same time, though, my mom was honking from the car. I ran outside as quickly as I could, and boy, was that car ride awkward! I couldn't stop shifting around, just trying to spread out the burn.

Despite the red-hot blistery marks melted into my skin by the bag of molten piss, I passed the drug test. I would prefer the consequences of a small burn over getting locked up and put on house arrest any day. I am not exactly proud to say, however, that in my battle to outsmart the justice system, this instance was not an isolated one. While my other engagements with bagged urine fortunately did not give me blistering welts, they did throw me through the wringer once or twice. But now I'm getting ahead of myself again.

***

One day, one of the Laurel brothers called me. He had just gotten off probation from the time we got arrested together in the mountains for smoking in my truck. He had never robo-tripped before and he asked me to teach him how. I showed him which types of cough medicine and pills he could use. By this point, I'd robo-tripped so many times I was beginning to despise it, especially after my heavy reliance on the substance during the first couple of months of probation, before I learned how to fake the tests. Each time would leave my brain feeling like freeze-dried mush for a couple days, and each journey into La La Land was getting less and less enjoyable.

Despite the negative consequences of drug use — the grogginess, the lack of energy, the delirium, the impaired physical health — I had trained myself to desire that exact state of being. Despite the impracticalities and discomforts of being high, it had now become my preferred mode of operation, but all highs were not equal. I preferred real drugs to this over-the-counter crap. Yet this was a chance to win some favor back with the Laurel brothers, who were much higher on the social ladder than I was, and who had mostly cut conversation with me after blaming me for our arrest in the mountains.

During probation, my parents had me on strict lockdown; the only time I was free was while they were at work. This was the first evening I'd been out of the house in a long while. I had been in the system for about six months by this point. I had successfully navigated my parole and was feeling celebratory. My parents allowed me to go as a sort of test to see if they could start giving me some of my freedoms back.

We parked in a desolate neighborhood behind one of the big box stores and we each popped twenty-five pills. The driver was one of the Laurel brothers' friends. He pulled out a big sack of weed, and we smoked to our hearts' content. I thought about asking them to wait a minute before smoking so I could run into the store and get few baggies to pee in, but I decided the one bag of pee I still had under my mattress would have to suffice. After about an hour, the driver dropped my friend and me back at my house. We crept downstairs, only to be confronted by my mother who was looming in the hallway.

Without hesitation, she said, "I'm taking your friend home right now. You have school tomorrow. You've spent enough time with him for one day."

I was incredibly disappointed. The only thing worse than tripping out on your own was tripping out in DT or a hospital or the loony bin. I didn't want to trip on my own.

So, I told her, "No, it's not even late."

She took him home anyway. When she got back, she came directly to my room to confront me. I was lying on my bed, strewn out like a scarecrow. I looked at up her clumsily and started speaking my friend's name.

"Laurel, dude, where have you been? What class are you going to, bro?"

My hallucinogenic folly was only just beginning to blossom. After staring at her for another moment, I proceeded to ask, "Hey man, do you wanna go smoke a bowl?"

She backed up to the doorway, looking distraught, and then she flipped out.

"Damn it, Mike, what are you on? I'm not Laurel; you're not acting right!"

She disappeared and returned with my father. They dragged me to the car. I clung first to the bed, then to the frame of the door, and then to the tile as they pulled me across it. I refused to go with them. I tried my very best to explain that I was fine. I only wished that I could've spoken more intelligibly because it would've been a lot more convincing. In my mind, I was telling them that I knew what I was doing and that I was going to be fine. I had taken these drugs before, and they were harmless. But words failed me. I was not capable of telling them that I had researched the stuff and knew it was impossible to overdose on. So as my mom looked at me, she feared the worst and presumed I was overdosing.

I pulled away, refusing to go. Everything went black. When I came to, I was sitting in the car. For some reason, my brain told me I was on my way to get ice cream. I relaxed momentarily. Everything went black again. Suddenly, we were in a parking lot, my mother clutching me. Puzzled, I looked around. I could make out a fuzzy red sign that read EMERGENCY. I ripped my hand loose of her grip and tried to run. Again, all went black.

I was sitting in a room with numerous schematized chairs. Everything went black again, and then I was sprawled on my back on a white table. I was screaming; someone was shoving something up my… I looked up to see a man in white with a mask over his face. I saw a machine hooked to me, and I could barely make out the number 220. It was my heart rate. The pain was excruciating. I couldn't understand why they were doing this to me.

Eventually, they pulled the catheter out, and along with it came every ounce of liquid that had entered my body throughout the past millennium. It hurt so bad; with every drop of urine that left my body, it felt like someone was cutting me from the inside with a razor blade.

Eventually, the doctor told my parents that they weren't able to detect anything in my system except weed. He said that a spinal tap would show if I'd taken mushrooms or acid, but they decided against it. I guess stabbing a tube through my private area was enough for one night's work. He said the only thing they could do to be of any real assistance would be to pump my stomach, but it didn't seem necessary in this instance, so they decided to send me home.

I felt like a rat in a laboratory subjected to haphazard prompts and punishments with little or no explanation as to what was happening. The doctors, despite their torturous methods, were able to do nothing except subject me to pain and then send me off; they stated they had no idea what was wrong with me but it'd most likely sort itself out if I went home and slept, which is what I'd intended to do in the first place. Somehow, that was enough to put my parents at peace.

The next morning, I found my dad on the couch outside my room. He was sleeping there because he wanted to make sure I was safe, but I was angry with him for taking me to the hospital. I would've likely forgotten the whole ordeal, except that morning when I first woke up, I found myself nearly screaming with pain when I tried to go to the bathroom. It felt like I was pissing out needles and it jolted all my memories of the previous night back into place.

I told my dad he should listen to me next time and that, even when I was high, I had more common sense than those doctors did.

"They didn't do squat to help me out," I said. "If anything, all they did was scar me for life by sticking that hardware up my dick."

Dad wasn't having it though. He shut me down real quick.

"Mike you were not fine, you were so messed up you pissed in the trash can while we were waiting in the public waiting room. That's why you couldn't pee for the pee test they were administering."

"Well," I probed, "why couldn't they have just scooped the pee up out of the trash can and used that for the stupid drug test? It would've been easier on all of us. Plus, there was nothing in my system but weed and Benadryl, two drugs nearly impossible to overdose on. I did my research, Dad; I know what I'm doing."

He looked at me dumbfounded and then he said something about the two of us having very different definitions of what it means to "be just fine" and "have nothing wrong with us" and to "know what we're doing." Then he grounded me indefinitely. All that meant to me, though, was that I'd need to wait until two or three in the morning before climbing out of the window instead of risking it at midnight or one.

I hadn't even taken into consideration how my parents felt. I didn't know my dad had slept on the couch outside my room to make sure I'd be alright. I was letting drugs divide me against the people who cared about me and worked hard every day to keep me alive and provide for my needs. I put drugs in a higher place than I put my own family. My family cared, the others didn't.

Maybe a normal person would've been ashamed of an experience like this, but I thought it was just grand. Who pisses in a public waiting room? Who pisses to their own demise? How high must I have been to be so incredibly stupid?

My friends also seemed to think my stories were hilarious. That day at school, I told some of my friends what had happened the night before. By the time lunch arrived, I had a whole crowd of people gathered around me, pressing me for the juicy details. I stood on the lunch table as if speaking from a podium on stage. I held their rapt attention as I told them the story with enthusiastic suspense. It was like this every time I did something stupid or got arrested. Everyone wanted to hear what Mike Heil had been up to this time. How had I evaded the police or outsmarted the system? What kind of stupid thing would I do next? I wasn't doing the stupid things for acknowledgement, I did them because my life was spiraling out of control, but I did love the attention. I needed it. In a way, it was a lifeline.

Each time I held an audience, it confirmed to me that despite all the horrendous trials and consequences I was facing, my life was more interesting than theirs and, therefore, that drugs were more interesting than abstinence. Each time I grew more determined that my lifestyle was ultimate, drugs were ultimate, partying was ultimate. Over time, I convinced myself that my life was grander than the fairytales they watched on television.

I'd talk about the adrenaline rush I got when fleeing from the police, the phantasmal delight that I experienced when evading the law. The pride I felt when able to outwit the great and omniscient Uncle Sam. I was not only beginning to like my reputation, but also to glory in it. I didn't have time to stop and think how bad I was screwing up my life, or that the more I succeeded, the more messed up my life became. I had awesome stories, and that made it worth it to me. Stories of excitement, thrill, and grandeur—isn't that a sign of a life well-lived?

What mattered most to me was what I said and thought about myself. I'd learned earlier that other people were not a stable foundation to build an identity on, so I changed my strategy and began building my identity on what I said and thought about myself. I tried my best to ignore all the negative things that other people said about me and only focused on the positive, but their opinion inevitably had some impact. It's hard to pretend like you're the greatest, most desirable, and coolest person on earth when other people call you a loser, a pothead, or a weirdo.

Nonetheless, I decided, from here on out, I would be responsible for making myself feel valuable and important. Since drugs and sex always fell short, I was in charge of bestowing significance on myself. I believed that through primarily loving myself, I could bestow happiness on my life.

I kept telling myself that I was great, that I was enviable, that I was attractive, and wonderful, but this source of self-worth seemed trivial, because whenever my circumstances changed, so did the narrative that I told myself. It's hard to think you're the bomb when your life looks like a bomb hit it. It seemed disingenuous to tell myself that I was awesome when the people around me thought otherwise. In a way, it felt like I was lying to myself. The deep, inward insecurity probed at me, exposing that one opinion —mine or theirs —was not rooted in reality.

During this time of my life, I started latching onto hedonism and existentialism, because that gave me even more power over my own life. I started to believe that no one created me, I was here by chance, it was all an accident, there was no greater purpose to humanity, and no one would ever come and fix humanity, because there was nothing outside humanity. Therefore, it was up to each human to determine their own worth and significance. I not only needed to fabricate the path I followed in life, but also the purpose for my life. I was responsible for making my own life meaningful. The difficulty in this belief system was the fact that if anything went wrong in my life, or if my life lacked meaning, I couldn't rightfully blame it on God anymore. If you don't believe in God, it doesn't make sense to blame Him when you lose a loved one or are having a hard time.

I latched on to all sorts of weird ideas that empowered me to do whatever I wanted and blocked the thought of God from my head. After doing this long enough, I lived an existence that was void of Him. I was tunnel-visioned. I couldn't see past myself —my needs, my wants, or my next high— and I would believe any worldview that would allow me to justify my decisions, even if it meant making God irrelevant, the human race a cosmic mishap, and my own existence virtually meaningless. All I could believe in was what I saw in front of me. There was no God, no heaven, no long-term accountability, only this life and the pleasure I derived from it. I believed every teaching that could help me oust moral authority from my life.

Over time, existentialism gave way to hedonism as I made pleasure into my God. Using pleasure to fill the gap that my empty worldview created. Even though I said I was my own authority and I acted like the world revolved around me, my actions revolved around whatever gave me pleasure. My feelings were the real authority of my life. Feelings dictated what I did and why. I sought what felt good, almost to the exclusion of all else. The only purpose of my existence and my identity was to make myself feel good. I guess I simply wanted to feel good while I still could, before I passed from this life and couldn't feel anything ever again. I didn't have the presence of mind to ask why base everything on feelings when they're so misleading, deceptive, and unreliable. For some people, probably the best they ever felt was when they overdosed and were killing themselves.

I believed everything my culture and the education system trained me to believe. My existence was an accident, I would die and turn to dirt, I was nothing but a sophisticated animal, and I needed to make the most out of my life while I still could. I sat on the throne of my life, I chose what I would do with it. No one created me and there was no purpose for my existence. Ultimately, when I died, there would be no penalties and no one to hold me accountable because there would be nothing period. Believing these ideas meant my life had no ultimate purpose, no end goal, and no ultimate hope. Secularism, hedonism, existentialism, Darwinism taught me to scrutinize and criticize any prospect of a creator. All I had was this short life, but I got to rule it and do whatever I wanted with it.

I was trying to live a meaningful life, but the pendulum upon which I was swinging tick-tocked back and forth between rebellion and pride, enjoyment and arrest, insecurity and proving myself. Like a grandfather clock's pendulum my life was ticking away. Time was a limited commodity and I wanted to spend mine well, but everything seemed to backfire, shooting me from one end of the spectrum to the other.

I laid low for a couple of months after getting taken to the hospital, but before long, I started sneaking out at night. I just needed more: more adventures, more girls, more of all of it. It was never enough. I'd climb out the window near my room and go meet friends or meet up with various girlfriends. On several occasions, I came home to find the window that I had climbed out of locked from the inside. Whenever that happened, I would sneak in through the garage or some other window and usually find my parents sitting there like wraiths waiting in the shadows. After a while, they took the hinges off the door to my room. They knew that I was doing drugs and sleeping with girls behind closed doors. They thought that removing the door would solve the problem. It didn't. The inability to lock them out did make things a bit trickier, but it was addressing the symptoms, not the cause.

One morning, I woke up to my dad rifling through my closet searching for drugs. I had provoked him by being reckless and smoking weed out of the bathroom window while running a shower to dampen the fumes. I suppose he had planned his attack for early morning since he knew that potheads were slow to rise. I went back to sleep figuring there was no way he'd be able to locate my stash. An hour later, when my groggy eyes flittered to wakefulness, I saw him holding my teddy bear by the throat as he put it up to his ear and squeezed. It crinkled in just the wrong way, and he perked up like a hunting hound locked onto its prey.

After squeezing it again, he turned it around in his giant hands and glared at it. My precious teddy bear had gotten me so far in life. Up to this point, it had never let me down. I had carefully cut a hole where its butt crack would've been, where the seams met together at its back. The hole was big enough to stick a bag of weed in, but small enough to make it difficult to get out. When Dad's giant hand went into it, he nearly tore the poor thing in half. To my dismay, he found exactly what he suspected, my last and only bag of weed. My sweet and savory refuge, a small sack that I had been calculatedly consuming for the past three months, in-between drug tests and counseling sessions, to mitigate my anxiety and sustain my addictive propensities.

He was enraged. "You're still doing this stuff? I don't know how your counseling facility isn't detecting this, but this is finished now. I will start drug testing you myself if I need to."

***

Billions of people base the foundation of their existence on the secular/humanist worldview, claiming there is nothing but humanity, nothing but biology. They claim, as I once did, that we humans are the beginning, center, and end of our own existence. It is our responsibility to give purpose to our own lives. There is no one who made us, cares about us, or has a purpose for us or our world. There is no greater good. The only thing we can do is enjoy this life before we die. It's no wonder that so many of those who ascribe to this ideology turn to drugs, partying, and wealth to find their meaning. Many of them, like me, follow these paths to their end, only to find themselves consumed by the emptiness of it all. Only to realize, when they die, they cannot take any of it with them, and the sum of all their successes amounts to nothing.

Chapter Twelve

Heroin: Understanding Addiction

"I felt awful, full of grief, terrible for all the hurt and pain that I had put my parents through." (MH)

I could not function without drugs anymore. I needed to find some way to get lit each day, through any means. I absent-mindedly scurried through my daily activities, remembering almost nothing of what I did or what I learned in school. Even though I was making bank selling drugs, it was still hard for me to come up with enough money to keep them flowing as regularly as I was using them. I thought, *if I could get prescribed Xanax then my parent's insurance would pay for my drug addiction, which would be nice.* After convincing my parents I suffered from anxiety, they scheduled a doctor's appointment for me. After several tests and surveys, the doctor prescribed an antidepressant instead. It was depressing. Who on earth wants to be prescribed Zoloft?

While Xanax was a good buzz, all the SSRI did was contribute to my blurry and apathetic state of being. Only a few events stuck out during this time. The night before my grandma's birthday, I took so many over-the-counter pills that I was high for three days straight. I showed up at the party looking like a cloud, pale as snow and flimsily trudging about. I could not speak coherently, so I avoided all conversation until I eventually fell asleep in a corner. Later on, I was able to convince the doctor that I had ADHD, which may or may not have been true. Getting prescribed amphetamines helped me stay on top of my schoolwork, while also keeping me from getting too dependent on their big brother methamphetamines. The researchers didn't know it yet, but the Vyvanse my doctor prescribed me would later be shown to help with binge-eating disorder as well.

The trouble was, after such extended and demonstrable drug use, it's impossible to be happy just being yourself; instead you *need* something else to feel okay. The whole cycle is a trap that not only creates potholes in your brain, but also takes away control of your most valuable possession: yourself. It takes away your independent ability to obtain happiness, your ability to produce internal peace and comfort. It places inside of you a parasite, like a tapeworm that must be fed more and more; if it is not, your body starts to decay.

Within the drug addict, a battle rages. We become highly attuned to our own needs and numb to both others and the world around us. We crave above all else that we might acquire our next high, and somehow, we become oblivious to the fact that we are not okay without it. We used to be okay without drugs, but no longer. Now we need them. And yet, even when we are in this position, we will deny it. Denial reigns truer than our obvious dependency, but we don't seem to notice either; maybe it's because when we are subject to the drugs, they reign over our lives, they are in control, not us. Others can see it in us, but we cannot see it in ourselves.

In a nationwide survey The Center for Behavioral Health found that 95.4% of those classified as needing treatment for their substance use problems did not think they needed treatment [18]. Despite being classified as having a substance use disorder that needed treatment, they thought they were fine. They denied the problem, or like me they were impervious to the idea that it even existed. Denial, they say, is the first sign of addiction, but denial, by nature, hates to be found out. It manifests in anger, blame, and avoidance. It manifests in excuses, lying, and rationalization. Our world crumbles around us and it is always everyone else's fault but our own.

In the same way that my truck had been impounded by the police, my life had been impounded by drugs. Something else had seized control of what should've belonged to me. The worst part was that I'd bought into the lies by believing that drugs were ultimate. My deluded beliefs not only convinced me to accept the fact that drugs were robbing me of my life, but also to believe that was a good thing. So, I stood there with a smile on my stoned face, defending them vigorously as they pillaged me.

The more I had to fight to smoke weed, the more obsessed I became with it. Over time, it became more of a necessity than a luxury. But weed wasn't the only thing stealing my life.

One day when I was with Cat, I asked if he had any weed to share and he said he didn't. The valley had been dry; I hadn't gotten high in weeks, and I was jonesing out of my mind. He kept going into the bathroom and igniting his lighter. Then he would come out looking blitzed.

"What were you just smoking?" I asked.

"It wasn't weed."

"What was it?"

"It's black."

"What's that?"

"It's really addicting. You don't want to try it."

"I don't have a problem with addiction, I've got super strong resistance," I said. Then I followed up with burning curiosity, "Does black feel good? How long have you been doing it?"

He responded, "It feels better than anything I've ever done in my life. It feels a hundred times better than weed. It doesn't stay in your system very long either. It's a lot easier to pass drug tests on black than it is on weed."

I didn't know that "black" meant heroin; in fact, I didn't even know what heroin was at the time. But if it felt as good as he said, I needed to try it. I needed to get high. It was the only thing available. I'd take my chances. Cat got out the tinfoil and showed me how to do it. I breathed in, and time seemed to collapse in on itself. If weed made me feel like I was soaring, this stuff made me feel transcendent. From the first breath, I felt like I'd finally found my answer.

At first, I just started doing black every once in a while, as a side dish to my weed. But when they placed me in the system and weed became the most dangerous substance to take because of how long it stayed in my system, my dependency on black really started to kick in. This addiction would have me scavenging the streets for the vilest characters, seeking anyone who looked like they could have connections with the Mexican mafia and spending every moment of spare time traveling by bus to the most populous and drug-riddled areas in our state.

After trying heroin and experiencing how good it felt, I tried cocaine, meth, ecstasy, acid, and just about any other drug I could get my hands on, figuring if they felt half as good that they'd be worth it. Our monthly runs turned into weekly runs, and soon we were heading up to Midvale, West Valley, and Downtown SLC two to three times a week to hit our connections, get our fix, bring it back to the valley, take a portion for ourselves, and resell the rest for profit. Despite the income we got from selling, our personal drug use increased as well; there was no such thing as equilibrium in this life. We increased our Robin Hood runs to the big box store to offset the imbalance, but being an addict is an expensive pastime.

The more drugs we sold, the more danger we were in if we got caught, so we kept our inventory limited. We weren't trying to stock the valley with drugs, we were simply trying to maintain our own addictions. Before long, people started crawling out of the woodwork; strangers would ring my number and ask if I could hook them up with whatever drug they were looking for. My outgoing personality allowed me to develop a vast and broad network of connections, not only with other addicts, but also with other dealers and the Mexican mafia who had access to black even when everything else went dry.

After putting these anonymous buyers through a series of tests to evaluate their sincerity and make sure they weren't undercover police officers, I would arrange to meet them in scenarios I'd learned from the Mexican dealers. When I met with the Mexicans, they would tell me which gas station to meet at and what kind of vehicle to look for. A few minutes later, they would pull through at lightning speed and expect me to follow them as they twisted and turned into a back-alley neighborhood. When the coast was clear, they would pull aside, and I'd pull up next to them. I'd toss them the money, they'd count it, and toss me my fix.

My life was at a teetering point, and I was about to fall off the edge of a cliff. I was spiraling down a black pit, and there was nothing that was going to stop me. Once you're falling through the air, it's impossible to turn yourself around. The gravity of my actions was pulling me down, down, down. I used black until sanity began to creep from the confines of my mind, leaving little more than a skeleton-like remnant of who I once was. Not inanimate but inactive, still alive but very much aloof, I passively floated through the steps of life, numb.

The more we tango with various things, the more our hearts get entrenched with them. The more we repeat something, the more that thing becomes intertwined in our identity. We slowly become the things we love most, just as our wellbeing grows dependent on the activities we do most. Not everyone turns to drugs to cope with their problems, but everyone turns to something. Whatever we turn to, we will justify.

I did not call the things I turned to an addiction. They were a habit, a tendency, a craving, a weakness, a preference, a compulsion, a fixation. I was so affectionate about drugs and the lifestyle I had chosen, and so enamored that even if it enslaved me, I would still find positive affirmations with which to adorn my captor. I would never admit it was out of my control. Even if the whole world said I was unnaturally dependent on substances, I would fight them. I would deny it.

I don't know at which point I crossed the line. Maybe it was the first hit that first night, or maybe it was after the first year of regular use. In one sense, it didn't matter; once I stepped over the line, the rest was history. They were in control from that point on, not me. I may have initially done drugs to feel good, to fit in, to escape the pressures of daily life, to party hard, to feel cool, and to make scandalous memories, but now I was doing them because I had become dependent on them. At first, they had temporarily alleviated some of life's pressures and ailments, but they had only left me wanting more, and they had never really been a solution.

I thought of drugs and sex and partying as essential tenets of a well-enjoyed life. I had no idea it was possible to expect or rely too much on them. It was beyond my understanding that drugs or relationships could meet a need one day and leave me in want the next. Yet the more I had each of these things, the more I realized it wasn't that they over-promised and under-delivered, it was that they were completely incapable of delivering or doing what I desired them to do. Their inability to satisfy long-term led to dependency and overindulgence; as my tolerance grew, I needed more in order to feel okay. Not only could they not meet my needs, but they left me dysfunctional so that I was unable to face life without them.

My problem was internal, something inside of me, but I didn't know how to address it. So, I just kept running, round and round, like a hamster on a wheel. I blamed my problems on the education system because it kept me busy and required me to maintain some semblance of sobriety. I blamed my problems on the authorities because they drug tested me. I blamed my problems on the police because they kept me in check and held me accountable for my actions. The real irony was that it was probably these things that kept me alive. Drugs were my solution to the problem I felt inside, and yet they had become a problem of their own. The solution I chose created innumerable other difficulties in my life.

Knowing that this lifestyle would lead me nowhere didn't help me to stop. Knowing that in most cases addiction leads to a ratty, nasty, unclean, and unhealthy life of lies and deceit, to rehab, or to a premature death didn't help me stop. The fleeting high and temporary buzz became so captivating that it was irresistible. Somehow addictions, once ignited, can overrule even common sense. Just like the 1954 Milner and Olds Rewards/Pleasure rat experiment [36]. Once the rats experienced what it felt like to press the lever and activate the pleasure region of their brain, they sat around doing it, virtually to the exclusion of all else—food, water, mating, social interaction, playing, grooming—and everything stopped. If they'd never experienced this quick fix, they would've had happy, healthy, normal rat lives and been able to raise happy, healthy, normal rat families. But they couldn't. Instead, they starved themselves to death pressing the pleasure lever in place of and in exchange for every other form of positive interaction or relationship.

The good feeling gives us the false impression that we are meeting a need and that we've finally found a solution to our problems. Yet, we're really creating additional problems. At the core, every person has legitimate important needs that must be met and there is nothing wrong in having them. We can feel our needs deep down, but we don't always know the best way to meet them. The more we try to meet these needs in illegitimate or negative ways, the more difficult it becomes to meet our needs in positive or constructive ways. So, we choose the wrong things, and the wrong things feel right, for a minute. Yet they leave us even more empty, sometimes even numb and hopeless. Illegitimate methods usually create more needs than they address. The longer we use them, the more hopeless things seem.

This cyclical pattern drove me round and round, hitting rock bottom again and again, each time breaking through to new all-time lows. I knew the cycle was running me dry and eating me alive, but I couldn't resist the temptation. I was like a fish on a hook. An inanimate object had more power over my life than I did. The desire for that tiny, fleeting buzz replaced my will for anything else. The emotional stronghold (my perceived need for that specific feeling) had become greater than my rational thought. Common sense told me that I didn't want to lie to my family constantly, steal all the time, and drug myself into a coma. Common sense also told me that if I didn't want to keep making these same stupid mistakes, I would need to change and stop performing the same stupid actions. But I didn't have the power or discipline to change. So, I kept doing the same things over and over, each time feeling more hopeless than before.

I got so caught up thinking about how drugs felt, I didn't realize what they were doing to my health and the rest of my life. I'd seen drugs, drinking, and pornography addictions destroy marriages, families, homes, parents, and children, but I still kept believing I needed these things for my life to be pleasurable and good. I was almost as shortsighted as the rats.

As my life started to derail, my parents prevailed on me more to go to their little church. Some weekends I would simply go AWOL, but on those weekends I returned home, I would always show up on Sunday morning, looking like hell after having partied all through the weekend without sleep. When I arrived, they would prime my inebriated carcass for church and drag me with them. And I'd prime myself by taking some sort of upper. Sometimes I'd still fall asleep on the pew, but luckily, I was not the only one. After church, I would smile and strut my charm with the doting church mothers. I was so cunning about my addiction that most of them didn't have a clue, other than the occasional rumor of an arrest, but those could easily be blamed on bad company. When I got home, I would sleep through the rest of the day and night until I finally awoke for school on Monday.

I didn't mind being dragged to church because, as I said, it was a social club. I got to hang out with other teens there. And it was nice to spend time with other kids my age who could relate to the isolated weirdness of growing up and going to public school as a non-Mormon in Utah County. Because of my insecurities, I tried to fit in with whatever crowd I was with. If they asked me if I believed in Jesus, I might have said yes, but then I'd show up at church on ecstasy or acid. I didn't have any faith. I didn't know what a relationship with Jesus looked like. Going to church was just something my parents made me do because they thought it was good for me. I didn't know what I believed. I just latched onto whatever I could, or more fundamentally, whatever would benefit me.

I recall telling people I was a Presbyterian when they asked. Being able to respond this way to the Mormons gave me credibility; it showed I was a part of some tribe too, albeit a tiny and hard-to-define one. I would get puzzled looks in response and then they would ask me what on earth a Presbyterian was. I probably would've had better luck telling them I was a Rastafarian, and at times, in fact, I did. When they asked, I would say, "Oh we believe in God too, only we're allowed to drink wine and coffee and stuff... It's not as strict." I guess I just took that approval and ran with it. But at some point in this journey, my mother started to rise up in her faith. Maybe it was from those countless nights of worrying where her son was and if he'd be alright, wondering if I'd make it home safely or when I would come back on the radar. And there were the nights she sat up praying for her lost son to come home.

Whenever they grounded me, I would sneak out the windows. Whenever they took my keys, I would arrange a ride with friends. Whenever they took my phone, I would use the house phone. Whenever they restricted me, I would leave and not come home for days at a time. Whenever they tightened their grip, I would get a job and go to wrestling tournaments, finding every legitimate excuse to get out of the house, evade responsibility, and keep partying. I was completely uncooperative and manipulated everything in my favor.

As my parents tried more and more to help me, the darkness wrapped its grip tighter around my decrepit soul. One day, a man crawled out of the darkness and into my life. His name was Rogue. He was like most heroin addicts: scrawny, pale-skinned, and disproportionately cocky. He positioned himself as my new best friend, and I embraced him blindly. He would nonchalantly shoot up in my bathroom and was always talking about how much better it felt to shoot up than it did to smoke it. Week after week he would invite me to shoot up.

I was defiant and said, "I have never shot up, and I'm not going to."

But each time he shot up his drugs, he made sure I was watching. He was not my only friend who was shooting up at this point, but he was the only one who made sure to explain each and every step; he'd take me through it like a tutorial, explaining how normal, how easy, how enjoyable it was. He explained how he would simply go to the pharmacy and tell them he needed insulin syringes for his mother, who was very sick. He would ride home with bags of them. Each time he came over, he made sure to leave a few unused ones where I could find them. Rogue was like that little demon on your shoulder that knew your weaknesses perfectly and kept nudging you to indulge them.

"I've got some cheese," he said. "It's not enough to smoke, but if we both shoot a little, it'll get us feeling real good."

I told him to shoot half and that I would smoke the other half.

"Sorry, man, there's not enough for that. It won't do anything for you if you do that. I'll just take it all."

"But... but, that's not fair," I said.

His response was quick and aggressive. "Just try it, don't be a pussy. You'll be fine. I do this all the time."

Rogue placed the needle in my arm and sent me off.

"The soul who sins shall die." —*Ezekiel 18:20* (ESV)

***

I remember seeing signs and billboards pop up everywhere across my state, warning people of the "opi-demic" (the statewide epidemic of opioid consumption). These ads blazed and blared warnings, telling us it's not only heroin and hard drugs that kill, but also prescriptions, alcohol, weed, and pills. If we heeded these warnings long enough to break free from our boxes and peer into the world of these victims, we'd see that the people becoming addicted to opioids (and other things) and overdosing are a lot like us. They're not bums on the street, but grandmas, business professionals, and athletes. They are mothers and fathers, and children. They are people with faces and families, or at least they were. Sadly, this epidemic of opioid consumption is not isolated to my state. Approximately 80% of the global opioid supply is consumed in the US [10].

Four of five heroin users start with prescriptions [8]. That means 80% get hooked on opiates under their doctor's orders, either getting prescriptions after surgery or an accident, or they borrow them from a friend, or steal them from some relative's medicine cabinet. In 2012, there were 259 million prescriptions written for narcotics, which was more than enough to give every adult American his or her own bottle of opiates [4]. Since opiates are so addictive, it is recommended that doctors only prescribe a three-day dosage, yet less than 1% of doctors adhere to that protocol [9].

Along with the increase in prescriptions, heroin use has increased 40% each year since 2010. The first decade of the 21st Century saw a 400% increase in lethal overdoses. Perhaps the saddest part about this is that 91% of those who survived an overdose continued to refill their prescriptions [5]. When I think about those statistics, I wonder how many of us turned to drugs because we thought it would be the best option, because we couldn't see a better choice. Then, even after they nearly killed us, we keep returning. According to the American Addiction Center, in 2017, roughly 19.7 million American adults battled a substance use disorder with either alcohol, drugs, or a combination of the two [6]. In the US, more people die from drug overdoses than car accidents and gun deaths combined [3]. About 70% of overdose deaths are from narcotics, but the problem is clearly not limited to narcotics alone [7]. According to the National Institute on Drug Abuse the number of deaths from drug overdoses in our country has increased every year except one, since 1999 [2]. In 2021, the NCHS reported 100,306 deaths from drug overdose, a 28.5% increase from the year before [1].

"Since they thought it foolish to acknowledge God, he abandoned them to their foolish thinking and let them do things that should never be done. Their lives became full of every kind of wickedness, sin, greed, hate, envy, murder, quarreling, deception, malicious behavior, and gossip. They are backstabbers, haters of God, insolent, proud, and boastful. They invent new ways of sinning, and they disobey their parents. They refuse to understand, break their promises, are heartless, and have no mercy. They know God's justice requires that those who do these things deserve to die, yet they do them anyway. Worse yet, they encourage others to do them, too." —*Romans 1:28-32* (NLT)

Chapter Thirteen

Lost Boys

"If the dead are not raised, 'Let us eat and drink, for tomorrow we die.' Do not be misled: 'Bad company corrupts good character.' Come back to your senses as you ought, and stop sinning." —*1 Corinthians 15:32b-34a* (NIV)

Over the next few months, I injected everything I could get my hands on. The pulsating sensation of inserting the drugs straight into my veins was unparalleled. The first time I injected meth, I felt like an electronically powered device that had been struck with lightning. The amount of pleasure was so strong I couldn't do anything but close my eyes and enjoy it. At some point, the pleasure grew so immense that I found myself clambering around like one of those toy monkeys clanging cymbals with uncontrollable ferocity. I was not angry, I simply could not contain the massive influx of pleasure, so instead I exploded. Shooting up was like having sex without a condom for the first time, but better.

When some friends and I went to one of the many raves that Utah is famous for, we were required to go on a treasure hunt and compile various clues that had been left throughout Salt Lake valley. Eventually, these clues yielded GPS coordinates that led to the rave itself, which was in the middle of the desert. Since my license was still suspended I always had to hitch a ride with fellow partiers. The only real problem with the rave being in the desert was that I lost my ride home in the expansive space. It helped that I was extremely social because, in no time, I had found myself a new crew, a crew of misfits that would eventually come to label themselves as the Lost Boys. They were soon to become my closest friends.

As our friendship grew, the Lost Boys started selling ecstasy. We all found it to be a more and more highly utilized substance in our catalog of frequently used drugs. Over time, my friends came to sell boats of the drug, which means they were selling it by the hundreds. While most people had to pay ten dollars a pill, we ate them like candy. Ecstasy was the bartering chip of the rave life and having access to it was like being the owner at the casino. Everything was rigged in your favor, and all of the partying and gaming centered around what you had to offer.

The night I met them, we stayed at the rave until the early hours of the morning when the cops raided it. The desert landscape was so massive that floods of people simply disappeared into its crevices until they slowly reemerged at their scattered vehicles. The police were only able to catch so many people, and we got away scot-free despite the chaos. We headed to a gas station to get cheap coffee and drove over a bridge that seemed to climb its way straight into heaven. As our vehicle escalated towards the sky, driving for the rising sun, our jaws dropped in awe. The sunrise was so stunning that we weren't sure whether it was real or a figment of our imaginations.

Even though I typically avoided close friendships, I was steadily warming to the Lost Boys; they'd worked their way quickly past my guard, and I couldn't help but think that maybe things would be different this time. The Lost Boys had all either graduated from high school or dropped out. Their empty schedules and frequent availability led to a quick decline in my occupation as a student. Their full-time occupation was partying, doing drugs, and sleeping around—seven days a week; they had nothing else to do, no bills to pay, no jobs, just that. They would show up at my school, urging me to skip class, elaborating on all the epic adventures they were having without me.

They would plead with my parents to let me have sleepovers, to let me leave for the weekend and not come home. They would promise my parents that they would keep me out of trouble and away from drugs. They would promise them that they were clean and sober and doing just fine, but everything was lies.

As we did more and more drugs, however, I started to lose the exuberant part of my character. Instead of gathering the group together, I would hide away in the bathroom, snorting or smoking something. Or I'd just get so high I didn't know what was happening around me. Sometimes I would get high and look at myself in the mirror for hours. I called myself Meagral, kind of like Smeagol, but the Mike Heil version of the thing. I would mock myself as if I were an unwitting creature, saying, "You look like a sloth. No one's ever going to actually like you. They just like what they can get from you. You're nothing, you're wasting your life." But no one else saw that side of me, so I just kept pretending like I had it all together.

***

"But each one is tempted when he is carried away and enticed by his own lust. Then when lust has conceived, it gives birth to sin; and sin, when it has run its course, brings forth death." —*James 1:14-15 NASB*

On another one of those weekends partying in Salt Lake, I decided not to return home for church in the morning. I had casually done some heroin. Then we smoked weed and drank. I felt okay. I had done these drugs in combination many times before; it was nothing new. I drank some more and smoked some more; I was feeling good. Drex, one of the Lost Boys, showed up with ketamine. It was the first time I'd ever seen it. He offered me a line and had it ready for me on the bathroom counter. As he turned and started telling me what to do, a cute girl who we had a mutual crush on walked in looking like a strip model in pajama pants.

She looked both of us up and down with hot seduction in her eyes. As she did so, to my dismay, she sat on the counter and squished half of the line of ketamine onto her butt. My eyes shot back and forth between her and the drug. As Drex and I both shouted, she sprang up reactively, sending the dust, as expensive as powdered gold, poofing through the air. Drex looked at me and said, "Alright, Mikey, you get whatever is left of that line, and what's stuck on her pajama pants." I did my best to salvage the substance but ended up losing over half of it. Upon breathing in, I didn't even have time to lift my head up straight before it started to hit me.

While everyone else resumed their normal pace, I felt like I was walking on marshmallows, my life slowed to a pace I had never experienced before. It was as if my feet were stuck to Velcro, and I wasn't quite capable of lifting or using my legs. At some point I tripped. The prolonged fall seemed to take thirty minutes, while standing up took twice that time. I remember looking around while falling; I seemed to be moving an inch a minute while the scurrying bodies around me shot to-and-fro as if they were on a television screen with the fast forward button clicked to x16. By the time I had fallen down and managed to pick myself back up, the party was pretty much over.

After a while, I entered what must have been the second phase of the high; I felt like a scratchy record stuck on repeat. Now the people around me slowed to a sluggish scuttle, and their voices also seemed to lower three octaves. Somehow, I lost my phone, which disappeared into the framework of the couch like a coin in a vending machine.

For the next couple of hours, as I searched for it, I went in and out of consciousness. First, they set me on the couch until they realized I seemed to be having a seizure and had nearly flung myself onto the hard floor. The party around me was too raucous for anyone to take much notice. So, they leaned me against the wall and tried to set me upright. The convulsions happened a few more times, and a few hours later, when I finally came to consciousness, I didn't even know that I had been out of it. They had tried shaking me awake for at least an hour, but it was to no avail. When I finally woke up, I went outside to have a smoke. The girl who had sat on the line came up to me and asked me if I was alright.

"Of course I am," I replied snobbishly. "Why wouldn't I be?"

She explained what happened; embarrassed, I tried to pretend like it must've been someone else. At that point, Drex came up to me. Acting as if I'd risen from the dead, he asked me how I was. They told me I'd been seizing up for hours and that they both wanted to call an ambulance but didn't because they didn't want to get in trouble. They both stared at me with awe-painted faces as they shared how concerned they'd been.

When everything was said and done, I blocked the event from my memory. I didn't realize it at the time, but if that girl wouldn't have come in and sat on the ketamine, I would've ingested twice as much. If I were already overdosing, the full amount probably would've killed me. That one minor alteration in history, a moment which deprived me of my true desires and seemed tragically disappointing at the time, probably saved my life.

To overdose is almost like being betrayed by your lover, your greatest friend, your confidante. The substance is your idol, your ultimate satisfaction, the thing that fuels you in life and keeps you going. If it is given a place in your life, it will fight relentlessly until it becomes the supreme substance of your life. An innocent puff, a momentary euphoria, will eventually become more valuable than every other thing. It starts off as a fling, but the one-night stand gets you pregnant, and in a moment, the course of your entire life is altered.

Drex really worried about me after the overdose. He had lost one of his best friends to heroin. He saw the path I was on and pleaded with me to stop but I felt it was hypocritical because he did more drugs than me. Every month, we promised each other to stop but inevitably we'd start again, often causing each other to relapse. I would get sober for six months but when I went to see the Lost Boys, they would always say, "Wow Mike, you've been doing so well, you need to take a break and relax." Then they'd offer me free drugs and I'd have trouble resisting. I always lasted longer than they did, managing to increase my stints at sobriety a little more each time around, but it wasn't until I moved away for college that I was able to stay off their radar long enough to overcome that cycle.

Whenever the Lost Boys came to my house, lying to my parents about where we were going and what we were doing, my mom would sit and talk with us. She knew we were all doing drugs and lying to her face about it, but she also knew she couldn't stop me. At some point, she started responding to our lies in a way that made us think we'd tipped her over the edge of the cuckoo bin.

She would look us in the eyes and say, "Whenever you're tempted, you've got to shout." She then would scream the words so loud that we needed to cover our ears, "Get thee behind me, Satan."

Then she'd talk in a normal voice again and say, "The devil is ruling your lives. You need to learn how to say no. Stop throwing your pearls to the swine. Your lives have value, but you're throwing it away."

Her voice would get desperate again and she'd say, "You must not give yourself over to these things. They're damaging you. They'll destroy you. You must learn to stop."

Then she would turn to my friends and plead with them, "Please don't lead my boy astray. He's trying now, he's trying to be better. Please don't drag him down again."

I thought my mom had gone totally nuts, but she hadn't. She had finally, through her faith, found a way to voice herself and stand up to me; to share how she felt about what was going on; to voice her concern, fear, and worry; to state that her son had been taken from her and that she wanted him back, and to say she was not going to stand aside and let him be besieged any longer.

"You boast, 'We have struck a bargain to cheat death and have made a deal to dodge the grave. The coming destruction can never touch us, for we have built a strong refuge made of lies and deception.' Therefore, this is what the Sovereign Lord says: 'Look! I am placing a foundation stone in Jerusalem, a firm and tested stone. It is a precious cornerstone that is safe to build on. Whoever believes need never be shaken. I will test you with the measuring line of justice and the plumb line of righteousness. Since your refuge is made of lies, a hailstorm will knock it down. Since it is made of deception, a flood will sweep it away. I will cancel the bargain you made to cheat death, and I will overturn your deal to dodge the grave. When the terrible enemy sweeps through, you will be trampled into the ground.'" —*Isaiah 28:15-18* (NLT)

Chapter Fourteen

Self-Actualization...?

"You felt secure in your wickedness. 'No one sees me,' you said. But your 'wisdom' and 'knowledge' have led you astray.'"
—*Isaiah 47:10* (NLT)

"For me, sex was ultimate: Family, laws, discipline, respect, responsibility, growing up, I despised every good thing that prevented me from getting more of that which I loved most." (MH)

I remember when I learned about self-actualization in my psychology class. I learned every human has physiological, safety, social, and esteem needs, and we can only reach our highest potential after these needs have been met. When we are housed and fed, when we are sheltered and safe, when we have a good social life and feel esteemed, we will experience self-actualization. If we feel unloved, insecure, and unappreciated, we cannot accomplish our highest potential. According to Abraham Maslow (1908-1970), the normal development of a healthy human is to progress from one tier of needs to the next and, when those needs are met, to proceed further; the primary goal of human existence is to self-actualize or reach our highest potential.

In my life, reaching my fullest potential meant getting high, getting laid, and doing so in a fashion more impressive than anyone else. I focused so much on self-actualizing my physical self that I became a bulimic. Reaching the highest tier of my potential in each of the essential areas did not satisfy. One second I would be achieving all my greatest hopes and dreams, and the next I'd feel like a slug... or feel like I'd gotten slugged. The whole cycle was misleading. Life has ups and downs, it's not linear, it's cyclical. Sometimes our friends betray us and our social needs get reconfigured; sometimes we make the wrong investments and our sturdy foundation becomes insecure, and sometimes, the things we believe will enable us to self-actualize, are empty.

The more I reached my goals, the more money I made from drug dealing, the more girls I hooked up with, the more adventures I had, and the more accomplishments I reached, the more messed up I felt. For years, I strived to reach my fullest potential, until one day I had to ask myself: *What if the whole purpose of life isn't getting everything we want and living to make ourselves feel good all the time?*

If we base our well-being on temporary things, whatever self-actualization we accomplish will also be temporary. It may be grand for a fleeting second, just like a wave is, but it will come crashing down. In addition, we can only accomplish this feat so many times before our lifespan comes to a decisive conclusion. Isn't it futile to work so hard to reach what I thought was my potential, only to die and lose everything I've ever worked for?

There was a black hole inside me that no level of self-actualization could fill.

My problem wasn't my parents, it wasn't my friends, it wasn't my education, it wasn't even the weird environment I grew up in. I chose to do drugs, I weighed the reasons for and against them, and I chose them because I thought they would provide meaning and pleasure to my life. I chose them because I believed life was a cosmic mishap and all we could do was make ourselves feel good before we die and slip away into nothingness. I chose them because they helped numb the pain of my hopeless worldview. I chose them because I didn't know there was an alternative that could meet these needs in a better, more permanent, more fulfilling way.

At the time, I didn't realize that my core needs could not be met through this cycle and could only be truly met in God. Instead, I thought it all came down on me, every mistake, every correction; I believed I was responsible for adding meaning to my life, fixing my faults, and filling the emptiness. So, I enslaved myself to a cycle that could not satisfy. As a human being, I am social, psychological, biological, neurological, and spiritual. Without acknowledging and addressing all of these components, I am incomplete. Maslow's pyramid could not provide me with anything that lasted beyond this life or give me any hope beyond myself. It left out the deepest part of my being; it ignored my spiritual needs.

My obsession with attracting the opposite sex and training my body to reach its highest potential was killing me. It started after my first weigh-in when I joined the wrestling team. It continued through college and was harder to give up than heroin. The harder I tried to quit drugs, the more I reverted to puking. I would fast for three days or a week, then binge and puke it all up. Every time I consumed a piece of food, I headed straight to the bathroom; there were no exceptions. Even when I ate a salad or a tray of vegetables, there was no food I did not try to puke up later.

I could puke on demand without sticking anything down my throat, and I became so skilled at it that I could time the flinging of my vomit with the flush of the toilet. Even in a public restroom, crowded with people, no one would have heard me. Somewhere deep down, I clung to this belief that if I were skinnier, then I would be more attractive, cooler, and have more friends. Yet, even when other people did acknowledge me as attractive or cool, it still didn't satisfy. My counselor told me I was doing it to get a sense of control because I felt like my life was out of control. In truth, I think I was looking for approval and acceptance, but I was using control and bulimia to get it.

One study found that men comprise one-third of all cases with bulimia nervosa in the general population [37]. I had what experts describe as atypical multi-impulsive bulimia: "people who purge without having overeaten at all… people who overeat and purge for weight control, who also overuse drugs and alcohol, or who engage in other forms of addictive behaviors to help them to manage stress and life in general [38]." This was a problem in which people regard "weight and shape as central to one's self-worth [39]."

The longer I was a bulimic, the worse it got. I spent more and more of my day inside the bathroom wherever I happened to be. Whether it was at school, a restaurant, a fast-food joint, home, a friend's place, every time that I could not be located, there was no shadow of a doubt as to where I was. My need to puke consumed almost as much time and thought as all my other addictions combined, perhaps because it was so tightly entwined with my identity and security. At Thanksgiving, Christmas, birthdays, or any other type of family gathering, I would eat my fill and puke, and eat my fill and puke again. People would comment about how much time I spent in the bathroom, but I convinced them into thinking that I was just that vain.

I trained my body until it naturally knew that puking was what it was supposed to do. I became inseparable from this internal need to maintain my weight and appearance through absurd amounts of vomiting and exercise. I was not content just puking once, I had to get everything out. Sometimes I would puke twelve times, just to get up every drop. I could be in the bathroom for up to two hours after each meal. My parents grew sick with fear as this habit got worse and worse. Each time my family tried to talk with me about it, I flared up in anger because I felt like they were collaborating against me. After an extended absence or missing an entire night of activity, my parents or my sister would come to the bathroom door to check if I was alright. I would shout at them to mind their own business, telling them that I was fine. Sometimes they'd stand outside the door awkwardly, not knowing what to say or how to help me.

My mother pleaded with me constantly. She would tell me stories of people she knew who died from eating disorders. There was one story of an elementary teacher whose esophagus had been burned through with stomach acid, causing esophageal varices and resulting in her dropping dead in front of her class of students. She told me that in addition to swelling in my esophagus, extended vomiting could cause food and blood to leak out into my lungs and even lead to veins rupturing. Despite the intimidation factor of these reports, I did not stop. I could not stop. This is who I was.

The fact that I was skinnier than my girlfriends did not matter; the fact I was skinnier than most girls did not matter. I was so obsessed with my appearance that I grew blind to it. The way I thought I looked became distorted within my mind, and I saw myself to be larger and less appealing than I actually was. After a time, I began developing ulcers, and the doctor prescribed me a chalky substance that I had to drink every day. It was the one thing, other than my drugs, that I tried not to puke up.

"Do not let sin control the way you live; do not give in to sinful desires. Do not let any part of your body become an instrument of evil to serve sin." — *Romans 6:12-14*

***

When the momentous day finally arrived for my suspended license to be returned to me, I was ecstatic. In a surreal moment after I paid the state $600 in reinstatement fees, they handed it over to me. It had been eighteen months since I'd last sat behind a steering wheel. The price of my insurance had risen $200 a month for the next five years, an estimated $12,000. For me, the cost was worth it. It meant I didn't need to longboard everywhere and bum rides from people anymore. After the DUI, my parents had bought the truck back from the impound lot on my behalf. My dad told me as long as I was willing to help him fix it, he would pay for all the parts and teach me how. For him, it was worth it just to have the father-son bonding time. The idea of being able to drive again made me feel like a bird who just got its wings back.

Since I could drive again, I picked up a job at Universal's Best Care and Training Center, a facility where I got to help individuals with mental health disorders. This was one of those jobs that drew in mischievous characters like a magnet, so my coworkers were always smoking, drinking, and getting high. They were easygoing and fun to be around. For several months, I became much like them: mellow, balanced, just your average pothead going to school and working a job. I was genuinely trying to do better, and I kept adding more and more good habits on top of my poor ones, hoping that they'd balance one another out. But from the day I met Storrie, all that was history.

Storrie reaffirmed to me that the path of rebellion is the greatest delight a human can experience. He taught me that whatever we needed to expend to get pleasure in the moment was worth whatever we had to sacrifice, even if that meant our future. I watched him lie, steal, seduce, and cheat to get his fix; nothing was more important to him than getting and staying high.

He was a raging addict two years my senior, another cool kid I could look up to and hang out with. Every day when we clocked out, we embarked on journeys of epic proportion. Storrie was fascinated with my knowledge of drugs. He was like a lab rat and I was like a mad scientist. He loved drugs more than any other person I knew. When I taught him to create different types of highs by combining different over-the-counter medications, you'd have thought he'd died and gone to heaven. He would disappear for days at a time, tripping balls until someone discovered him sleeping on the ground outside a gas station. The various drug cocktails Storrie was consuming were the type that a drug user should only try a few times in his or her life, but he was trying them twice a week, sometimes even more.

Whenever I suggested to Storrie that things were getting a bit out of hand, he would mock me and say, "What, you can't keep up anymore?" I tried to reason with him that it wasn't a matter of keeping up, I just wasn't finding joy in it. At some point the high became overshadowed by the hangover, and the euphoria started to pale in comparison to the unending grogginess. We would pop hundreds of pills, and the more we did, the more my brain felt like a sponge; my intellect steadily degrading until finally I felt as dense as SpongeBob or, even worse, his friend Patrick. The first time I'd tried these chemicals with CD, they hit us so hard that we managed to light a forest on fire. I suppose Storrie was having just as much fun now as I'd been having back then.

After operating at this groggy level of consciousness for several years, these cheap drugs had lost their appeal and their luster. Part of it was that I now preferred the high of hard drugs to the imitation high that over-the-counter medicine provided. At the same time, I'd become so used to being high that I would choose cheap drugs that made me sick over no drugs. It didn't matter if it was cough medicine with alcohol, allergy medicine, an energy drink, six shots of espresso, or a cigarette. Even puking provided some sort of dopamine release.

I was not enjoying this any longer but I kept turning towards it, and I could not explain why. Was it just because my friends did drugs? Was it because of social pressure or loneliness? Was it because of dependency and habit? For some reason, any alternative seemed better than sobriety. I kept telling myself that I chose this path because it was more fun, more interesting, and more eventful. I told myself that the people who failed to choose it were just afraid to let go and live. Then I would go and have the craziest adventures, and each one would propel me deeper into this lifestyle. Somewhere deep down, I knew that I was lying to myself, and yet each escapade pulled me deeper into my own little biosphere of lies and delusions.

Storrie pulled at me constantly to go and party with him. The fact we worked together allowed us to collaborate by telling our families we were working graveyard shifts. We would meet up at work and then go to various parties or raves. It was at one such rave that I saw a guy with five girls hanging off him and decided that one day I'd be like him. As for now, I was tripping out too much to function, let alone pick up any girls. I managed to find my way to the outside stage, where there was an alien with eight arms throwing glow sticks at everyone. Somehow, all eight of its arms could move, even though it was only the size of a normal human being.

It was a bright glowing figure that looked like it had originated out of the stars themselves. Its natural, incandescent glow was only enhanced by the fact that it was carrying hundreds of glow sticks in its arms. I stood flabbergasted, with my jaw dropped, until one of the glow sticks slapped me across the face. I bent over to pick it up, and by the time I regained my balance and stood back up, I saw hundreds of people holding the glow sticks up to their ears like antennas and bowing down to the alien. I scrambled as fast as I could. They were worshipping the figure, and even high on ecstasy, I could not bring myself to do such a thing.

I went inside, where I found another alien running inside a giant hamster ball across the top of the crowd. He ran atop the crowd as seamlessly as a ball floating on water. I reached up in total fascination, imagining what it would feel like if I could float across the people myself. Before my fantasies could take me too far, I saw another alien made of laser beams projecting its light in every direction. Another one made out of mirrors soon appeared, looking like a giant mobile disco ball.

Soon a freakish-looking alien with a chainsaw appeared and began sawing at one of its friends, only to produce massive amounts of sparks that shot across the smoky stage.

Everywhere I turned, I saw people making out with one another. I saw the guy who had five ladies trailing off him again, and my mind was blown. I wanted to be like him. I wanted to be that cool and desirable, too. So, I tried my shot at a couple of ladies who seemed to be lonely, but after several rejections, I realized I was too unaccustomed to the high of ecstasy to muster up that sort of game while on it. Instead, I passively observed the scenes around me, inwardly determining to find a resolution. After stumbling around, watching scenes like this until three in the morning, we finally departed. My coworker dropped me off at work, where I fell asleep behind a shed until 8 a.m. Then I called my mom to come and get me. She wondered why I smelled so robustly of cigarette smoke and weed. I merely told her a lot of my coworkers smoked, and then I slept through the entire weekend.

That rave opened up another world to me, and not just because of the aliens. I realized if I wanted to be the guy getting all the girls — cool, smooth, and in control — I needed to take my wrestling more seriously. I needed to be an athlete worthy of envy, or at least have the body of one. The small room was padded from floor to ceiling with thick blue mats and after four hours of training, it was always foggy with sweat; sweat dripped from the ceiling, landing in puddles on the ground. My body was chiseled not only by the constant exercise but also by my bulimia. I had maintained a weight twenty pounds below my average for two years while exercising four hours a day. I turned my body to pure muscle and bone. I was sculpted and tough, I just needed to learn how to utilize it more to my advantage.

I made a game out of going to as many concerts and raves as I could with my shirt off. Women would flock to me and write their numbers all over my naked torso. Once the first girl wrote on me, others thought it was cute and followed suit. At the end of the day, my skin would be tie-dyed with technicolor webs of sharpie scribblings. I'd always try to remember which ones I thought were cute and have someone underline their name for me. Some would just run up to me, kiss me, and then run off, giggling. I know men are shallow, but half the dudes I know live for this. Our pride is completely and irrevocably intertwined with the women we associate with. The hotter they are, the more of them there are, and the more they like us, the more confident we feel about ourselves.

When Benny Benassi came to town, I'd been drilling hard at wrestling and looked better than I ever had. I still was not confident in myself, but I suppose that is why I lived like this. As soon as we arrived at the rave, I scoped out the terrain and found three beautiful girls I would have gladly spent the night trying to win over. When I finally got to kissing the first girl, the second, who was her friend, joined us excitedly. When I lost these two girls in the crowd, I found the third and danced with her for a while until she too couldn't help grasping me tight and pulling my face towards hers. As we danced, another girl, whom I'd met at a previous venue, came out of the crowd and whispered in my ear, trying to win me over herself. As soon as the opportunity arrived, I slipped away with her. It went on like this all night and all morning at the after-party, until finally, I'd made out with eleven girls. I wasn't sleeping with them. I was convinced they wanted me just as badly as I wanted them. I think all of us were seeking value and affirmation where it couldn't be found, in a place where no one was truly valuing anybody else and we were all just using each other.

I was totally caught up in the culture of my day, where every guy constantly talked about the girls he was flirting with and how he was trying to seduce them. And the ladies put just as much value and self-worth in how many guys they could lure. Just like in everything else, I determined not just to enter the endeavor but to give it my all and outpace the competition. Other than the fact that everyone I knew and considered cool was living like this, I think this whole rat race was just another way of trying to find value and security in something fleeting and temporary, as well as proving myself a man to the many supposed friends who had used and deceived me.

The first day of school following Benny Benassi, after finally feeling like I had proven myself, I remember one of the jocks cornering me and saying. "What's wrong with you?" "Why are you so weird" "You're gay, right? You must be. Why else would you be so obsessed with your appearance? I always thought you were a faggot." It felt like the anticlimax of a lifetime.

Some people made fun of me and called me metrosexual or gay because I was so meticulous about my grooming and appearance. I felt like these nights out justified my existence and proved them all wrong. These raves and concerts gave me a feeling of transcendence; I would not be held back by my problems, nor would I let them define me. I was living it up. I could make of myself whatever I wished.

To most teenagers, college kids, and addicts, the fact that I was getting paid to party was pretty badass. The fact that I always knew where the party was, and people were always calling me for their fix, made others want to be around me. I carried myself confidently and got a lot of girls (regardless of what I felt like on the inside). I was fun and funny and therefore got invited to a lot of things. I loved entertaining people and could do so for hours. Sometimes the group would ask for "story time" with Mike. We'd turn off the music and I'd stand on the table. People would always say, "Who needs a TV to entertain us when we've got Mike Heil?" And this was the attention that I lived for.

One of the guys would strum a guitar excitedly, and I would tell my story in rhythm with the beat. Whenever the music sped up, so would the intensity of the story. Sometimes I'd sing the story, and sometimes I'd whisper it, making sure to pause at certain intervals for suspense and emphasis. I would enrapture people in a story, laughing and inviting those who were there into the storytelling so we could volley off one another. I could make a group of strangers feel like a group of friends.

The more I excelled at this life, the more drugs I sold, the more girls I got, the more parties I went to, the more messed up I felt. I was running a race to see who could screw up their life the most, and I was winning. The higher up I climbed and the more successful I became in this lifestyle, the more messed up things were. I needed someone to look me in the face and tell me that the people who win, succeed, and excel at this lifestyle end up in jail, in rehab, homeless, or dead, and these are the only four options for those who follow this path to its end. I needed more than that, though. I needed someone to offer me a way out, a better path forward, a more meaningful life.

On the days I felt down, I would just knock myself out with drugs, then I would sleep like a corpse buried six feet under. When the drugs wore off, I would sometimes be fine, but other times the darkness would clench its tight, choking grip around me. On the nights I remember, there was an empty abyss so dark and consuming that it saturated every millimeter of space in my proximity. When I was in withdrawal, I could ignore the thick feeling of darkness because the pain of my neurons as they retracted and screamed out for more drugs was a considerable distraction. I didn't mind it so much when my body jerked back and forth like a rag doll that screamed as if cursed by some form of voodoo.

What I did mind were the nights when I was confronted with myself, the nights I had no girl to distract me, no drug to satisfy me, the nights when I actually had to think about life and face it. On the nights when I had to look straight at who I was, who I had become, inexplicably, I would punch myself in the face as hard as I could. I would pummel my face until I fell asleep, eyes bruised and full of tears.

I don't know which ingredients stirred up these feelings within me. Whatever the cause, those brief daunting moments were the few ephemeral instances when I clearly felt the agony of my addiction. At every other point in time, I was running too fast, too hard to notice whether anything was wrong. It may have been denial, or I may have just been too blazed to rationally explain things, but for the most part, the cost of my addiction went unnoticed, and I focused instead on its rewards. Externally, I had it all together. My friends would imitate me, copying my colloquialisms and my mannerisms in order to attract girls themselves.

One night, after partying until the wee hours of the morning, I remember one of the Lost Boys turning to me and saying, "Mike, how can I be more like you? You always get the girls. You're always having a good time. You've got all the hookups and connections. You're even making money to party, and you're not doing half bad in school. It seems like you're paving out a pretty good future for yourself."

"You…" I stuttered, and then I tried again. "You don't want to be like me," I said.

Superficially, I was fine. In fact, superficially, I was great. I looked good on the outside, almost enviable, but inside I was scouring for something more. I constantly scoured my phone, messages, emails, and social media platforms for any form of hookup, party, or connection, but eventually I realized they were all just distractions. For me, one of the most genuine marks on my handsome face was the black eye that I gave myself.

In the eyes of most, I was winning at the life of partying, so I could see what most didn't see: it was empty. I kept thinking if a little feels good, more will feel better, but I was wrong. It was a lie. It was only once I'd attained everything this life could offer that I could see clearly what a lie it really was. The best this life had to offer was a slew of broken relationships, mangled trust, a compromised future, destructive habits, friends who used you, people who only wanted you for what you had to offer, and an empty hole that no matter how much you threw down it, it hungered all the more.

So, on and on we went, raving, going to concerts, and partying, obsessed with women and hooking up. Even after I realized it was an endless pursuit, another form of neurochemical release that would nurse further dependency on something other than myself, even then, I could not stop. At times, it felt invigorating, and at other times, it felt empty and vain. In my roller coaster ride-of-a-life, one day, I could feel like king of the world, and the next, I would feel like a big steaming pile of turkey dung.

Sometimes, I could convince everyone I knew to be envious of me, and other times, I couldn't even convince myself. I was bouncing between drugs and women like a pinball, using both to give my life meaning, only to find that winning at this life was equivalent to getting the high score on a pinball machine. Acquiring the best that drugs, sex, and women had to offer was virtually meaningless, like placing three-letter initials on some old arcade machine. Although I felt like a lunatic for not being satisfied, my experience was not unique.

I tried to use relationships to cope with my drug problem and drugs to cope with my relationship problem, round and round again. The relationships I developed would make things better when things were going well, but as soon as they began to falter, my integrity and self-worth would crumble as well. Each broken relationship caused a sort of identity crisis because I didn't have an identity of my own. I was as much a living incarnation of inconsistency as the culture around me. Eventually, I realized that the fuel from relationships was about as substantial as that of a fart to a fireplace. It never lasted long, always blew up on itself, and more often than not, left an agonizing mark.

Sometimes the relationships would help me keep sober, but whenever a relationship failed, it always caused me to relapse harder and fall further than before. Sometimes a failed relationship would send me scrounging for drugs in an attempt to numb the pain. Other times, it would send me to clubs or raves, looking for rebound girls to put a band-aid over the blow to my ego and self-esteem. I didn't have any tools or methods to process my failures and disappointments so I could learn from them. Instead, I kept repeating the same mistakes and cycles over and over.

I just couldn't get it through my thick head that the fuel of acknowledgment and appreciation from others was merely supplementary, that it was no more substantial than the fuel from drugs and partying. It was enough for a thrilling night out and gripping story, but not enough to fill the leaking reservoir of the human heart. Hooking up, being the life of the party, having people hitting you up day and night, being loaded, none of these things were substantial foundations upon which to build an identity, nor could they ever be.

Our culture tells us to want sex, pleasure, and instant gratification. Every hit song raves about it. Consumerism tells us that we need it now. There are a thousand voices that will sell us on these things; they'll tell you everything you want to hear, being sure only to leave in the good parts and leave out the bad. They'll sell you 'til you're hooked, then you'll sell yourself. Heck, at that point, you'll sell your soul. At some point I would have to realize that my feelings, instincts, wants, and desires were highly unreliable and unpredictable things to base my wellbeing upon. I already knew they were not capable of satisfying, but I kept letting them call the shots. More than that, I let my feelings hijack my life like a teen thug committing grand theft auto. Only I gave them the keys.

"So God abandoned them to do whatever shameful things their hearts desired. As a result, they did vile and degrading things with each other's bodies. They traded the truth about God for a lie. So, they worshiped and served the things God created instead of the Creator himself, who is worthy of eternal praise! Amen. That is why God abandoned them to their shameful desires." —*Romans 1:24-26* (NLT)

Chapter Fifteen

Steam Rollers & Bunny Rabbits

"There is a way that seems right to a man, but its end is the way to death." —*Proverbs 14:12* (ESV)

Now that I had my license back, everyone was asking for rides and wanting to hang out. One of the Laurel brothers asked me to give him and one of our drug dealers a ride to Orem. I wasn't sure how much they were getting, but I told them I wouldn't allow any more than a half ounce in my vehicle. Any more than that and we would be held liable for a felony with possible distribution charges on top. Ever since my sentencing, I had concocted a list of guidelines and boundaries to keep me safe and prevent further arrest. The first rule, and by far the most important, was that I would not drive under the influence of anything, regardless of circumstance or substance. Another was that I would only transport people when they were willing to take responsibility for their own substances and when they were carrying a small enough quantity that they could shove it down their pants. My friends thought I was a nutcase, but they agreed to my rules.

As we were *en route* back home, a cop pulled directly behind me and started following me. I didn't change my path, I just kept driving straight, trying not to have a panic attack. When it came time to turn, I put my blinker on, and he put his on as well, indicating that he was going to follow me. My dealer shouted at me to change directions. So, I turned my blinker the other way, but as I approached the stop sign, I ended up going straight out of nervousness. It was hard to focus on what I was doing, with one person yelling left, the other yelling right, and my own brain telling me to stay on course.

We were relieved when the cop continued in his original direction, only to find out that the road I had gone straight on was a dead end. The only way out of the neighborhood was to turn around and go back, straight past the cop who was now parked on the edge of the road, waiting for us. There was nothing we could do. Our hearts were racing, so we quickly threw the opium and some of the weed in the bag of chips my friend was eating. By the time we had done that, the cop was behind us with his sirens blaring.

He abruptly approached the car and asked for our identification, which we quickly handed him. After he ran our information, he asked me to step out of the vehicle. I hesitantly agreed and opened the door. I was trembling; flashbacks were playing in my mind. I was confident he was going to handcuff me right there. I was shaking violently, and beads of sweat dripped down the side of my face. He stood me squarely in front of himself and straightened me out with a kind but firm gesture.

Then he proceeded to speak, "Kid, you have quite the record. The reason I pulled you out of your vehicle is because I didn't want to embarrass you by mentioning your record in front of your friends and telling them that you're an alcohol-restricted driver. I'm going to have to search your vehicle."

My jaw dropped, and, still shaking slightly, I gave consent. I figured that we had already acted suspicious enough by avoiding him earlier and that if I refused him, I would give him evidence beyond a reasonable doubt that we were indeed trying to hide something from him, so I obliged.

He didn't make my friends get out, he just started shining his light around.

The first thing he saw were the packs of cigarettes that we had intentionally left out in the open. He confiscated them but didn't give us a ticket for them, even though we were underage. This was extremely strange and unusually kind. He continued searching, and as he was looking in the driver's side door, he reached down and grabbed something. He pulled his hand up slowly, revealing his thumb and forefinger, which were reluctantly clutching a small plastic bag. He pulled it close to his face and started to smell it, most likely assuming it would have the scent of alcohol.

His face wrinkled grotesquely as he exclaimed, "What is this?!"

It took all of my might to refrain from bursting with laughter.

I thought for a moment and replied, "Well, officer, have you ever really, really had to pee before?"

Realization slowly crept across his face, and he flung the bag from his hands as if it were a live snake.

He didn't believe me at first, and he was flabbergasted at the idea that I would have a bag of old pee just sitting in my truck. He obviously didn't know that it was my bag of clean pee, and that it held quite a bit of value to me, as it was my last dose of so-called sobriety. It didn't help that the thing had been marinating in my sauna-like truck for several months. I wasn't being actively tested by my probation officer anymore, but I never knew when it might come in handy. Especially if my dad ever decided to test me as he had threatened.

He turned to me, looking a little bit confused, and said, "Alright, I'm going to let you go with just a warning, but," he said sternly, "my one condition is that you have to leave this bag of pee on the ground."

Laughing, I said, "So you're asking me to litter?"

"As long as it keeps that thing out of your car, then yes," he replied.

I was a bit discouraged that my source of clean pee was to be diminished and left out on the street as if it were nothing more than simple rubbish, but more than anything, I was astonished to hear the cop say he would let me go with nothing but a warning. I had never met a cop like this, someone kind, understanding, courteous, able to laugh, joke, and be respectful, even toward a snotty nose kid like me. The way he treated me gave me a lot of hope. Despite my track record, he seemed to believe that I could still change. He treated me like a human, like there was still good in me. For the first time in my life, I left an encounter with an officer of the law reprimanded and exhorted, but not beaten down. In his administration of the law, he showed me a clear path forward. In his kindness, he nudged me along that path.

***

The leaves had finished changing colors and were steadily dropping from the trees. The tangible cold brought a shift to the air, the type that made the hair on your arms stand up, the type that was refreshing at first until you spent too long in it. At least this year I wouldn't have to longboard through the snow. Storrie and I had gotten used to waiting out in the cold, shivering beneath shared flannels as we waited for others to come and pick us up. The drugs always helped numb the impact of the cold, so even when it took hours for us to find a ride, we didn't mind it too much. Now, with my license in hand, things like that weren't going to happen to us anymore. Now we could go anywhere we wanted without hindrance.

One night we sat with our phones to our faces looking for, I guess, what all teenage guys are looking for, a teenage girl. I suppose a party would have equally sufficed because parties also had girls, and that was what mattered. In the end, we found both. Two girls we knew invited us to a party at a quirky apartment that was situated underneath a Mexican grocery store. On our way, we stopped and pilfered some over-the-counter brain manipulators. As we descended into the dungeon-like abode, the drugs kicked in.

I tried to keep myself awake, but ever since that night my parents had taken me to the hospital, this particular combination of drugs always made me black out. My vision kept clouding to black and eventually, when I regained consciousness, I found myself in my truck with my friend at the steering wheel. It was pitch black outside; it must have still been the early hours of the morning.

I started to ask him how we had gotten there but was quickly distracted by the steamroller that was headed straight towards us. My body stiffened, and my gaze shot out the front windshield. Sure enough, in the middle of State Street, driving straight towards us, was a massive steam roller that took up most of the road. I rubbed my eyes, blinked twice, and looked again. This time I could see little bunny rabbits hopping in front of the massive iron wheel. I screamed and pointed shakily towards them. As I did so, one of the rabbits jumped in front of the giant steam roller's dome-crushing anterior.

I watched as the poor thing was squished right in front of my very eyes. I looked frantically to the left and to the right where there were a half-dozen more of them, a small family heading straight towards the steam roller. After a minute of worrying about the stupid rabbits, it suddenly dawned on me that we were going to be next in this sequence of chaos. We, too, were steadily progressing directly for the steamroller. We were close enough now that I could smell the hot tar burning beneath it. I leaned over and grabbed the steering wheel. I yanked it as sharp as I could.

"You're driving straight for the steamroller!" I shouted. "You have to turn! What are you doing?!"

As our vehicle swerved into the other lane, nearly bashing into another car, my friend smacked me and said, "What the hell are you talking about?!"

And one last time, everything faded.

I woke up alone. A little bit confused, I looked around, trying to figure out where I was, and then a glimpse of the previous night shot through my mind. There was a steamroller, and we were headed straight for it. Had I been squished to smithereens like one of those bunnies? Outside my vehicle, everything was luminescent and glowing. The gleaming rays of light broke through the windshield, transmitting a radiant warmth into the vehicle. The heavenly-looking lights made me feel slightly out of place, in contrast with my hangover from hell.

Eager to figure out where I was and what had happened the night before, my mind scrambled to piece together every bit of information it could gather. I was used to this type of scenario by now: Waking up and not remembering anything from the night before, not knowing where I was or how I'd gotten there. My go-to solution was typically to search my phone to fill in the gaps. I reached for my phone and found nothing. I tumbled frantically around my vehicle, searching every crevice. It was gone.

I spent the next hour searching outside the vehicle, beneath the vehicle, on top of the vehicle… Nothing. Maybe, if I could find my friend, he would know where my phone was. I knocked on the nearest door, but the man who answered said Storrie had left hours ago. Next, I drove to his house, but he wasn't there either, so I made my way back to the house from the night before.

My phone was my lifeline. Not only did it provide me with my drugs, but it also provided me with my income by enabling me to pedal those drugs. More than that, it was the fabric of my social existence. All of my contacts were stored on my SIM card, including the numbers of all of those lovely ladies who had written all over me. If it was gone, so was my entire social life, and my primary source of income. I pounded on the door for thirty minutes, and when I realized no one was going to answer, I contemplated kicking it in. I'd depleted my options; I'd looked everywhere and met with nothing but dead ends.

Begrudgingly, I made my way back home. When I got there, I found that my parents were almost as worried about me as I was about my phone. After a brief interrogation, my father explained that he had some work to do, and he wanted me to help him. He informed me that he was not planning to reinstate my driving privileges after I'd gone MIA the night before. I kept returning to my truck like a wounded animal drawing attention to its injury. I scoured my closet in the delusional hope that I'd somehow come home while I was blacked out and lost my phone nearby. I wailed and moaned, I droned on and on, willing it to appear, imagining the types of withdrawals I would be forced to endure without it.

Finally, I looked up to the heavens and shouted, "Give me my phone… I need my bleeping phone."

A realization struck me, a brief remembrance from another time, a memory from my former life, from the Mike of the past. A memory of flames dancing under a moonlit sky. A memory of CD and me bowing our heads in that dark corner room of my grandma's house. And then I remembered that our prayers had been answered.

"God," I said hesitantly, the word sticking in my throat, "*if* You are real, please show me. Please give me my phone back."

At that moment, my father entered the room, handed me my keys, and said, "Go find your phone. Try looking where you slept last night, maybe you'll find it there."

Instead of being grateful for the compassion he showed me, I looked up annoyed and said, "I already looked there. I spent a freaking hour in that spot looking everywhere for it."

Nonetheless, I figured I had better take advantage of this moment now that I had my keys back again. I hopped in my truck and set off to retrace my steps. I'd completely forgotten where I'd woken up this morning. I knew which city I'd been in, but I wasn't sure if I could find the neighborhood again. As the scenery passed by on either side of me, I realized the last time

I'd acknowledged God's existence and tried to connect with Him was three years earlier during the forest fire.

I whispered again, making my requests known to Him as if He were some sort of genie, "God, I need my phone. If You have any power at all, please help me find my phone."

I continued driving haplessly, turning at random through various neighborhoods and surveying my surroundings. At some point, my eyes registered a familiar background of trees. I looked again to make sure I wasn't imagining it and recognized the rugged-looking house that I'd woken up in front of that morning.

I climbed out of the truck and slammed the door. As I did so, I murmured to myself, "This is stupid. What good does it do?" I had spent an hour looking here, in this exact spot, earlier in the day. It was pointless to be here again.

I looked up and stammered at God, "Fine, I'm here. What do You want?"

And to my surprise, I nearly stepped on my ugly little phone.

Chapter Sixteen

The Storrie of Adventureland

I told myself it was just a coincidence. There was nothing more to it. All that really mattered to me was my phone. God was a just a means to an end. Once I got it, I jumped in my truck and sped off, treating the Being who had helped me much like I had treated my father before, brushing off His kindness as if it were due to me.

I saw on the screen of my little Nokia brick that I had a few missed phone calls from Storrie. My father had only given me the keys back for the purpose of finding my phone under the strict expectation that I would come straight home afterwards. I hesitated, debating if I should obey the terms I'd agreed to or call Storrie back. Before I knew what was happening, I was on my way to pick him up, and from there, we were headed to a party the two girls from the night before had invited us to.

Up to this point, I had been able to observe my strict no driving while drunk or high rule. The night before, Storrie had driven us home, and today, Doc was the DD. He called himself that because he had an uncanny ability to get his hands on drugs that only doctors should be able to prescribe. As he drove, we smoked ourselves into a near coma until we flitted in and out of cognitive assertion. We aimed to smoke all of our weed that night and were pleasantly surprised when the party we arrived at was not a party at all, but a smoking session.

We had two-eighths of weed, and the host matched us weed for weed, which meant in one night, we smoked a half-ounce. We spent the entire two-hour car ride up there smoking, and once we got there, we smoked from a bong for at least three more hours. I still felt groggy and hungover from the night before. I was so pale that I looked incandescent. After the two-hour drive back home, I asked Doc to drop me off at my car. I planned to stay the night there. I decided I would sleep and sober up before even thinking about operating my vehicle, and then I'd head home in the morning.

When I asked Storrie what he was planning on doing, he told me that he wanted to spend the night at the other girl's house. I tried to convince him it would be easier to stay with me than to try and sneak into her place, but he wouldn't have it. We said our goodbyes, and I quickly fell asleep.

As Storrie sat outside of the girl's home, he soon realized that she was not going to come back out. He waited until he couldn't bear the cold any longer. He pulled out his phone and began to call me. Once, twice, three times, no answer. He called again and again. For a half-hour straight, he let the phone ring. Nothing. No response. He began to worry. His worry was not for me but for the cold he so begrudgingly endured.

He called again and again until the shrill rings of my phone haunted me into wakefulness. Half asleep, I finally answered.

"Come get me, Mike. I'm freezing, I can't stand it. I need you to come and get me."

"What happened to your friend?" I asked groggily. "Weren't you supposed to stay with her? I can't come to get you, it's my most important rule. I'm not fit to drive, and I can't risk getting another DUI. I just can't bring myself to do it. I'm sorry, my friend."

He hung up the phone, and I dozed off again. When I awoke, my imprudent cellular device was vivaciously buzzing. I was beginning to regret ever having found the dang thing. If it were not for that phone, I would be sleeping peacefully through the night. But now, it harassed me incessantly. Twenty-one missed calls, it said. And then it continued bellowing in my flustered face.

Exasperated, I forced myself to wake up enough to answer it again. When I did, I heard the cold, trembling breath of my horny friend as he said, "Please, Mike, I need you to come get me. I don't want to have to walk there. Come get me. I'm only a few minutes' drive from you. If I walk, it'll take forever. I'm freezing. I need you to come get me."

I was too stupid to register the fact that if he'd started walking after his first phone call, he'd already have made it to my vehicle. The horny idiot was just sitting there waiting for the girl, hoping to get laid, and bugging me all the while about how cold he was.

I had set the first boundary in my life and made it clear that under no circumstance could it be broken. Storrie knew my rule, yet, without the slightest restraint, he was urging, pleading, and begging me to break it. My heart had always been bigger than my brain, and I could not stand the thought of him out in the cold. The more he whimpered and pried at me, the less I could resist.

"Where are you, Storrie? I don't want you to freeze. I want to help you. I was just afraid to risk another DUI. It's not smart for me to drive right now."

He dismissed my last remark and responded excitedly, "Yes! I knew you'd come through! I know where your truck is. Go straight from where we left it and turn right past the light. I'll be on that road."

As I drove slowly and cautiously to the aid of my shivering friend, I thought about all the times I'd gotten arrested while trying to help the people I cared about or trying to take the blame on their behalf. I thought about that night when the police were swarming us and how they had put all of us out in the dumping snow to freeze. I remembered stepping forward and making an agreement with them, if only they would let my friends go and place the blame on me. I realized, in that moment, that even heroic acts count for nothing when you're in the business of corruption.

A green traffic light shined brightly in the distance. *Okay*, I thought, *I need to go past this light and then turn right. Or was I supposed to turn right at this light?*

His directions weren't clear. I picked up my phone and tried calling him, but he didn't answer. I didn't want to stop in the middle of the road while there was a green light, so I proceeded hesitantly. My truck slowly crawled across the intersection, and as I drove, I saw a car parked on the opposite side of the road in front of me. As I passed it, my head turned to get a better look. There was a figure whose gaze seemed to be tracking with mine, our heads turning in symmetry as we observed one another's movements. When my brain finally registered what I was looking at my body went rigid and my heart stopped in its tracks. It was a cop, sitting there, waiting. I hastily turned my face forward, fixing my eyes on the road, hoping that my driving looked smooth.

The path I was on slowly started to narrow. I gripped the wheel as if it were my lifeline. I couldn't believe it; I'd driven for three minutes to help my friend who was freezing, and now I was going to have to go to jail for it. No matter what happened, I couldn't risk turning around and having to face that cop again. I didn't care if it meant a full-speed police chase, I was determined to avoid him. I would not get arrested again, not this time. As I drove, the road steadily got smaller and smaller until I was driving along a small winding path.

At this point, I felt like I was on some sort of jungle expedition. There were big bushes and trees that shot out in various directions, making it feel as if I were navigating an obstacle course. I had absolutely no idea where I was, but I was sure of this; there's no way that cop would be crazy enough to follow me down this trail. By this point, it wasn't even a road anymore. The trail had gotten so small that my truck could barely fit on it, but I pressed on, nonetheless. I couldn't get arrested again; I couldn't put my family through that. It had been over a year since my last arrest. For me, that was a record.

I'd been fighting to pay off my fines and climb out of this pit of hell. If I got another DUI, not only my progress, but my whole future could be ruined. Whatever happened, I could not stop moving forward. My only option was to evade the police at all costs. The small trail continued to swerve back and forth, and I continued strategically dodging plants and trees that had their arms outstretched as if they, too, were trying to grab me.

As I turned the bend, I mumbled to myself, "When the freak did I fall into, a forest? Where am I?!"

I felt like Alice falling through the looking glass. *Why did this place even exist, and how on earth did a normal road lead me here?* There was a branch in the way, a bush, and then a bridge. I stopped and gazed as hard as I could at that bridge, trying to measure its size and calculate its breadth. I jumped out of my vehicle to get a closer look. It was undoubtedly smaller than my truck. I needed to gain ground, I needed to find a way out. I almost collapsed with anxiety and despair.

It was happening again.

I jumped back in the truck and started slowly creeping forward. My only other choice was to back up straight into the hands of that hungry cop. I edged my vehicle forward until my wheels hit the bridge. I could feel the tension. My truck was squeezed onto that thing like a hippo in a doghouse. I literally thought it would either collapse or burst, but slowly and grudgingly, my truck grazed its way across it. When I made it across, I sighed with relief. It was the first and last bit of relief that I would experience that night. Excitedly, I trekked forward, thinking there was no way on earth any officer would be ballsy enough to risk taking their vehicle across that thing, even if their Dodge Charger happened to be a lot smaller than my truck.

After crossing the bridge, I was sure I had the worst of it behind me. I looked forward and proceeded down the newly-found path. Instead of experiencing relief, however, I became filled with increasing dread. The small path was disappearing, and as I gazed at the slope in front of me, I stopped my vehicle dead in its tracks. My reasoning was this: I would rather go to jail than drive my vehicle off a cliff. I desperately looked around, trying to peer through the darkness and into my surroundings. My headlights lit up enough of the terrain to see that the small path teetered off into a dark abyss. As I looked closer, I saw that the dark, motionless pit was actually a reservoir, a pond, maybe even a lake of some sort. I thought I must have been hallucinating again. With one last volley of hope, I gauged the fading trail in front of me and the lake to my right before obstinately inching forward.

When my vehicle began slipping, I stopped, knowing that if I drove any farther, my truck would slip off the ledge and into the pond. The trail just wasn't quite big enough. I picked up that dreaded phone and called my friend. No answer. I didn't know what else to do, so I kept calling. Finally, after the fourth attempt, he answered.

With a whiney voice, he said, "Where the heck are you, man? I've almost walked all the way back to your truck."

The despair was flooding out of me now. "Are you kidding me? You decided to walk now?"

There was no response.

"Storrie, I left to come help you, but I was followed by a cop. I went through the light like you said. I'm in some sort of park with a lake, you've gotta come help me."

"Oh," he responded, "you must be in Adventure Land."

"What the heck is Adventure Land?"

"It's the park you're in. Dude, you're screwed."

He hung up the phone and stopped answering my calls. He did not come for me. I went to the back of my truck and grabbed my longboard. I figured if I could run fast enough, I could dodge the police through the bushes and shrubs. If I could somehow make my way back to civilization again, I might be able to outpace them on my longboard. With my longboard in hand, I weighed my options. If I ran and they caught me, I'd be in ten times more trouble. Not to mention that they would impound my truck again. Even if I did flee, they'd be able to run the plates and find out who the vehicle belonged to. Even if I ran and somehow managed to evade them, I would still have to explain to the cops why in the world my truck was stranded on the edge of some pond in the middle of a park called Adventure Land.

I knew that even if I didn't face the cops tonight, I would have to face them tomorrow or the next day. They might even put out a search warrant for whoever owned the vehicle. I reasoned that if I wanted to keep my vehicle, I would have to face them. I had the faintest bit of hope that maybe the cop hadn't followed me. Maybe I would be able to make it out of there after all. With that small gust of encouragement, I slowly set my longboard down in the bed of my truck and hesitantly climbed into the driver's seat.

I could see bright lights shining in the distance. Each minute, they got closer as they wound through the trees until, finally they arrived on the opposite side of the bridge. The vehicle came to a sudden halt, and its beaming lights shined across the bridge, causing my quarried truck to light up like a Christmas tree. Red and blue flashes of light with bright beams of white permeated the darkness, ricocheting off my truck and into my surroundings. My stone-cold eyes registered each flash, but my body sat paralyzed in fear.

"Because you despise what I tell you and trust instead in oppression and lies, calamity will come upon you suddenly—like a bulging wall that bursts and falls. In an instant it will collapse and come crashing down. You will be smashed like a piece of pottery—shattered so completely that there won't be a piece big enough to carry coals from a fireplace or a little water from the well." This is what the Sovereign Lord, the Holy One of Israel, says: "Only in returning to me and resting in me will you be saved. In quietness and confidence is your strength. But you would have none of it.'" —*Isaiah 30:12-15* (NLT)

***

It seems the more in compliance we are with the law, the less we need to fear it. The more we obey the law, the less likely we are to experience its negative repercussions. It seems the good citizens don't fear the law or its officers in the slightest. The law doesn't harm those who obey it; it cannot. The law only harms those who defy it. It took me the better part of a lifetime to learn this.

Chapter Seventeen

The Second DUI

I heard the door slam as a man emerged from the shadows and crept forward into the blazing gleam of his own headlights. I didn't know if he was shouting at me or into his radio for backup, but I told him to calm down. He looked a little puzzled, like he was a bit surprised I could hear him so clearly from inside my vehicle. For a few moments, he stood motionless, his jaw slightly gawked as his head bobbled up and down, gauging the bridge underneath his feet and the small path that led to my truck.

"How the hell did you get that thing over there?"

Before I could so much as attempt to answer, he seemed to catch himself from going off-topic and began to shout at me.

As he crossed the bridge, he yelled, "I need to see your hands. Stick your hands out of the window right now!"

I immediately stuck my hands out the window, and he lunged forward to shackle me in cuffs.

"What the hell are you doing here?"

I blinked a couple of times and said, "This is Adventure Land, right? I drove to this park to help my friend. He was out in the cold, and he needed a ride."

He looked blankly at me. "What drugs are you on, kid? What the heck are you talking about, Adventure Land? You must be tripping out of your mind."

"No, really, this has got to be Adventure Land..."

He cut me off again. "Cut the crap, kid, what was your friend's name? Where is he at?"

"My friend's name is Storrie. He needed my help, he told me to come to Adventure Land."

He replied, "What kind of name is Storrie? Is he supposed to be your imaginary friend or something? Stop bull crapping, kid."

"I promise it is! Here, look at my phone."

He jumped back cautiously as I reached for it with my cuffed hands.

"Please," I said, "we can even call him if you want, he's a real person. He wouldn't stop calling me, asking for a ride. I wanted to help him, he's my friend. He told me the name of this place is Adventure Land. I'm sure I'm in the right place. This must be Adventure Land."

I realized, in that moment, that I must've sounded like a total lunatic. Who on earth would name a park Adventure Land? Maybe Storrie just called it that in one of his mischievous plots to extract comedy from every possible situation. He was probably laughing hysterically, in eager anticipation of the conversation that would unfold when my own mouth fumbled such a ridiculous statement to the police. Despite the truthfulness in my claims, I realized I looked like an utter imbecile. There was no way for me to explain my driving through the forest, crossing this bridge, and somehow ending up on the teetering ledge of this isolated pond.

After examining the perimeter of the vehicle, the cop abruptly pulled me out and led me to the tailgate, commanding me to sit down. He beamed his flashlight into my hazy eyes, as if his headlights weren't enough. He held a small card up next to my head, and after his eyes shot back and forth several times, he mumbled something I couldn't make out.

"Stick your tongue out."

"What?"

"Stick your tongue out."

I laughed for a moment until I realized he was serious. "Wait, you really want me to stick my tongue out at you?" And then I obliged with glee.

He gazed for a long while, seemingly awestruck but didn't say anything. He quickly moved from examining me to excavating my vehicle. I sat in suspense, my thoughts racing. *I didn't have anything in my car, I didn't have any drugs on me, he couldn't arrest me just for being in a conspicuous circumstance, could he?* As all of these thoughts were racing through my head, my heart sank when, in the distance, another pair of lights emerged. I couldn't fathom the thought; it was all happening again. I was getting arrested again. Worse yet, I felt like this time I was getting arrested because I couldn't say no to a friend in need.

Like a vacuum, a distant voice sucked out my thoughts and sent me slamming back into the present.

"I'm gonna say it one more time, kid. What the heck is this?"

My vision centered, and the haziness cleared. The officer was holding an old Slurpee straw that he must have found in my vehicle. From his actions, I gathered that he was either trying to slam it down my throat or force me to claim it.

I stared blankly for a moment and asked him, "Have you never had a Slurpee before? It's a freaking Slurpee straw, dude."

He aggressively retorted, "Don't you play games, I know what this is!"

"Ah, so you have had a Slurpee before. Yeah, they sell those straws in every gas station in our country. I don't know how you found that one, though. I haven't had a Slurpee in years. You must have been digging real hard."

He thrusted himself forward with the straw in my face, his voice shaking with indignation. "I know what you did with this straw!"

"No crap, I drank a Slurpee out of it. What else do you do with Slurpee straws? I don't understand why you're so obsessed with that stupid thing, though."

He beamed his light in my face and lifted the straw into my field of vision so that I could see what he was talking about.

"Do you see it? What's that on the side of the straw? I have you now, kid. What is that, huh?"

After a moment of pause, I realized he was waiting for a response.

"Well, sir, considering that's a Slurpee straw, I would assume that that is a bit of old Slurpee residue."

This time he was outraged. He angrily marched back to my vehicle and continued his search. Now his accompanying officer stood by his side on full alert. After a bit of contemplation as to what in the world was going on, I realized these officers were so confident that I was guilty that they were going to make me guilty, even if it meant they had to fabricate evidence in order to do so.

I sat helplessly reflecting as they continued to scrounge through my truck until, suddenly, as if through a trapdoor, a realization broke into my mind.

It was the phone that had torn me from that sweet place of slumber and brought me to my current nightmare of reality. I could hear it ringing, buzzing, screaming, each blare symbolizing my friend's desperate need for my assistance, each blare beckoning me into this situation. Call after call, voicemail after voicemail, text after text, the jeer of my phone rang throughout my car, my dreams, and my lucidity. Without that stupid phone, I wouldn't have even known about the party, I wouldn't have been with Storrie, I wouldn't have that obnoxious ringing sound flooding my thoughts. Was this all just a nightmare? This was not what I wanted, but by demanding my phone back, it was exactly what I had asked for. Despite my best efforts to ignore it, shut it off, and turn it on silent, the phone was determined to taunt me. It seemed as if it were for this very reason that I had received it back in the first place.

The officers seemed unsure what to do with me. I was not drunk, and they were unable to locate any paraphernalia or other substantiating evidence. Other than the truck being parked where it shouldn't be and my bizarre statements about Adventure Land, there was nothing they could incriminate me for. That is, until they completed a drug test. As the officers ripped me from the back of my truck and forced me into the law enforcement vehicle, I began to regret my decision not to run when I'd had the chance.

During the past few weeks, I'd begun to feel that there might actually be an end to the endless cycle of penalties and fees. I'd spent an entire year trying to earn back my freedoms, but I now found myself stumbling through a set of revolving doors that would lead me back to square one all over again. Fines, counseling, court, AA, DT, probation, community service, licensing fees, impound fees, license suspension, countless hours walking and bumming rides back and forth between all these penalties. The weight of this mistake felt like a millstone tied around my neck, dragging me deeper and deeper into that pit of despair called hopelessness, the one from whence I'd come, the one I'd fought so hard to climb out of.

The officers brought me to the police station where they drug-tested me. Immediately, they could see that I had smoked weed, but they reasoned that a blood test was necessary to discover which drugs I was really on. I cooperated with them as they stuck a needle in my arm and drew blood. The blood test would be more accurate than the urine test, and I dreaded to think what they might find from the lab results. I felt a looming sense of despair, as I had the last time, I'd gotten a DUI. It was a repeat of what had happened before, except this time I didn't flip them off, cuss them out, and pee on the floor. I was too deflated to quarrel. As I sat there, I realized that this time I wasn't disappointed or angry with them, but with myself. To my surprise, I found myself telling them that I was sorry and that I wished none of this had ever happened.

My truck was impounded again, and my parents were in no rush to pick me up from the police station this time around. When they finally arrived, it was past four in the morning and I had just a few hours to sleep before having to go to work. There was no lecture this time. It was not worth the effort. They knew I would do what I wanted, regardless. When my mother dropped me off at work that morning, it was an unremitting reminder of my newly-found disposition. After eighteen months of waiting to get it back, my license was now in the hands of local law enforcement. I felt like a teenager who had once learned how to bike but had to be put back on his training wheels again. I floated through the day, emotionless and apathetic, unaware that I was also soon to be fired from my job. As my life burst at the seams, I had to fight with all my might not to burst into tears all that day.

"Godly sorrow brings repentance that leads to salvation and leaves no regret, but worldly sorrow brings death." —1 Corinthians 7:10

***

"Who is the one who condemns us? Christ Jesus is the One who died [to pay our penalty], and more than that, who was raised [from the dead], and who is at the right hand of God interceding [with the Father] for us." —*Romans 8:34* (AMP)

My parents decided to hire a lawyer to defend me and my case. They paid thousands of dollars for the lawyer. As they drove me to see him I was filled with grief. He told me since it was my second DUI, we were looking at five years of a suspended license and thousands of dollars in fines.

His heart softened as he looked at me again. "Michael, I'm going to do everything I can to help. I was a drug addict once. By God's grace, I got out of that lifestyle, and I vowed to help as many people as I could. That's why I became a lawyer, to defend people who struggle like I did."

He looked deep into my eyes and then continued, "I'm sorry this is happening to you, but it's never going to change until you decide that you're done with this life. As long as you think these things are the ultimate pleasure that life has to offer, you will keep seeking them. As long as you keep seeking them, you'll feel divided inside; you will also keep breaking the law. I know these consequences suck, but as long as you keep breaking the law, you'll keep bringing them on yourself. It won't ever stop until you decide to change. God helped me change my life, maybe He'll help you too."

A month later, we had our hearing. My lawyer showed up with an enthusiastic smile that was all but befitting for the situation. His grin spread from one side of his face to the other. He looked at me excitedly and beckoned me closer.

"Michael, something has happened. When we got the blood test back from the police department, it showed negative for every form of drug, even weed."

I responded, "You're joking, right? That's impossible."

He continued, "Since a blood test is more reliable than a pee test, that is the evidence they are required to use. The blood test proves you are innocent!"

I tried to hide the tears welling up in my eyes, but one betrayed me by dropping to the table.

My mind whirled, and the room seemed to spin. *How was this happening? I wasn't innocent, I had been high. This was impossible; blood tests don't show up wrong. Together, we smoked close to a half ounce. I couldn't have passed that test. Weed is detectable in the blood within seconds of inhalation and traceable for up to a month after that.* The lawyer's voice broke in, ripping me from my racing thoughts.

"There are just two obstacles that we need to face now. If the officers that arrested you decide to come here and testify against you, you could still be incriminated. The officers' report stated that your tongue looked completely green and fuzzy, like a little nugget of weed, due to overconsumption."

I laughed a little because I'd never heard such a thing before, and then I secretly hoped that the police would not show up. My mind flashed back to the gentle apology I had given the officers. Maybe it spoke to them. If they had a choice, maybe they'd choose not to prosecute me because I had been vulnerable, transparent, and relatively kind, aside from our dispute about the Slurpee straw. I thought, in contrast, about my first DUI, where I had cursed at and resisted the officers. I sighed with relief, grateful that things had unfolded differently this time.

"What's the second thing?" I asked, hopefully.

His response was hesitant. "This could prove to be the more difficult task. I need you to tell me what diphenhydramine and dextromethorphan are."

I responded coolly, "One is a cough medicine, and the other is an allergy medicine. They are both over-the-counter drugs that you can get in any grocery store. Why?"

He seemed surprised as he said, "Those are the only two things that showed up positive on your blood test. If what you say is true and we can prove it to the judge, your chances are more optimistic than we could've hoped. I'd like to pray for you before we head in there."

He folded his hands and bent over them in a posture of humility. "Father, I pray for Your favor today. I pray that You would give Mike a second chance. I pray that You would forgive him for the wrong that he's done and lead him in a new way of life. I pray that You would show yourself strong today on his behalf so that he knows it is You and that You are looking out for him. I pray that the police would choose not to come today and prosecute him, in Jesus' name. Amen."

He stood up and went into the courtroom.

Every time I faced a judge, I went in with a sense of impending doom. They always told me, "You're innocent until proven guilty," but I knew that was a bunch of rubbish. I wasn't innocent, period. It didn't matter what I told myself or how I justified my actions, I wouldn't be there if I was innocent.

And yet, my lawyer stood on my behalf, poised, prudent, and determined. He would not give up my case, and he would not fold without doing everything he could for me. I was not in this alone, I was not defenseless and hopeless anymore. Even though I knew I was guilty, my lawyer gave me so much confidence that, for the first time in my life, I entered the courtroom feeling hopeful.

The judge heard our plea, and none of the officers showed up to push the case. He lowered the charge to a DWI for driving while under the influence of cough medicine. Within a moment, my criminal charges were reduced from a felony to a misdemeanor. By some miracle, the city that I was arrested in fell under the jurisdiction of an entirely different court. The judge didn't even mention the charges that had been placed in the bank from my previous arrests. Instead of having to pay for them, all the penalties that I had accrued for myself were overlooked and forgiven. Instead of getting locked up and pulled out of school (as was previously outlined and agreed), I was given a small fine and required to voluntarily relinquish my license for six months.

When I realized that I had experienced a miracle, I couldn't help but think that the God to whom I had prayed must have orchestrated this whole thing. I demanded that He give me my phone back, and He did so in a way that made it obvious it wasn't just a coincidence. It led me directly into the clutches of the law. What I wanted led me to what I didn't want. What I wanted led me to what I hated. Getting my phone led to me getting arrested. I could choose whatever path I wanted, I could demand my own way, but there would be consequences. God wanted me to understand that every decision has consequences.

And yet even after letting me see where my own path would lead me, God bailed me out of the consequences that I had brought on myself. It seemed even if I chose things that led to bondage and captivity, He would be there to stand on my behalf and offer me a path forward. He removed the incriminating evidence against me and set me free. But what good was it when I couldn't change, when I just kept demanding my own way and getting myself trapped again and again?

"I am writing you these things so that you will not sin and violate God's law. And if anyone sins, we have an Advocate [who will intercede for us] with the Father: Jesus Christ the righteous... And He [that same Jesus] is the propitiation for our sins [the atoning sacrifice that holds back the wrath of

God that would otherwise be directed at us because of our sinful nature—our worldliness, our lifestyle]; and not for ours alone, but also for the whole world." —*1 John 2:1* (AMP)

***

Under the law, we never really know if we are ever going to be good enough or not. It is daunting and overbearing. If we break it, there are consequences; if we're obedient to it, we can escape its penalties. The most promise it could offer me was that if I was good, and changed my ways, and could prove it over a span of years by staying good, I could be forgiven. If I performed all the right steps, I could wipe my slate clean. Under the law, you have to earn forgiveness. Under the law, you have to constantly prove yourself, and the moment you fail, the hammer comes down hard. The gospel is the exact opposite. It states that Jesus has already stood in the place of judgement for any criminal or transgressor who would believe in Him. It states that He wipes our slate clean, even while we are sinners, even when we don't deserve it. Yes, we are guilty, but He is willing to take our penalty, to serve our sentence in full, and His guarantee is so sure that even when we mess up again in the future, He doesn't change His mind about us.

The "gospel," the "good news" that gives us hope, is the fact that God accepts us as we are, even before we've fixed up our lives or believed all the right things. His only requirement is what my lawyers required of me: to stop denying and hiding my faults so that they could help me. To admit I didn't have my act together. To believe that He wanted to help me. To plead guilty, not because it would benefit me but because I finally understood that my sin was killing me, destroying me from the inside out, robbing my precious minutes and hours, filling my mind with lies and delusions. For any who would trust in Him, Jesus stands before the judgement seat of God defending them against the evil one who flings accusations at them day and night, ever scheming to destroy them.

"The wages of sin is death, but the gift of God in Jesus Christ is eternal life." —*Romans 6:23*

Chapter Eighteen

Clean Slate

" At that time the Lord, the Lord of Heaven's Armies, called you to weep and mourn. He told you to shave your heads in sorrow for your sins and to wear clothes of burlap to show your remorse. But instead, you dance and play; you slaughter cattle and kill sheep. You feast on meat and drink wine. You say, 'Let's feast and drink, for tomorrow we die!'" — *Isaiah 22:12-13* (NLT)

Looking back, I think the reason I kept chasing quick fixes was because, for the briefest moment, the slight reprieve they offered helped me forget how messed up and broken I was. In my heart of hearts, I felt like the slate of my life was so scribbled and dirty, with so many arrests and broken relationships, that it wasn't even worth trying to clean up. Since I could not be cleansed, fixed, or cured, I simply learned to cope by covering the messy "whiteboard" of my life with pieces of white paper: a fling with a cute girl boosted my pride, an epic adventure with friends made me excited and confident; sports made me feel tough, while good grades and a nice job boosted my ego. While each distraction helped me to ignore the mess underneath, I never found anything that could erase it. So, I stacked up the distractions until they grew so numerous, they fluttered everywhere throughout the muddled chaos I called my life.

I was like a train, headed full steam, down an old set of tracks that would eventually drop me into oblivion. Instead of heeding the warning of the conductor, I annihilated him to remove my guilt as I passively and regretfully watched my life go slipping by. I considered anyone who tried to warn me of the dangers ahead to be an enemy: the law, the authorities, the police, my family, the educational institutions, God. I silenced all of them so I could live in the way I pleased.

In removing the conductor, I presumed that I did not need him, that I could do his job, that any set of whimsically concocted guidelines could replace his expertise. Without the conductor, there was no room for me to feel bad when I failed to meet any superimposed standards. There was also no guidance, no voice to inform me of imminent danger or to save me from it, no one to help me correct my path or understand what was going on around me, and why. I had no standards, and that meant there was no way I could measure the efficacy of my life. It turned out that meeting a certain set of definitive standards would have been easier than meeting an ever-changing list of my own subjective values.

I had been loved and supported and encouraged, and all I had done was take advantage of the people who gave me this help. No one likes to be rebuked, but sometimes we need it. At least, I did. I had been so callous that almost nothing could break through to me. I was like a corpse, and the rebukes I received were like a defibrillator, shocking my heart and forcing it to return to some semblance of normalcy.

One day, as I was trying to reconnect with one of my oldest friends, she looked me dead in the eyes and said, "You're not the same person I used to know. Before you started using drugs, you were caring and fun to be around. Now all you can think and talk about is yourself, your drugs, and what girl you're hooking up with. You're not Mike Heil anymore, you're a shell of who you used to be."

Around the same time, one of my friends who was mature, rich, and successful, reached out to me. We had dated in the past and she wanted to take things to the next level. We hadn't been in touch for almost two years, so I couldn't wait to catch up with her. When I finally found a ride up to Salt Lake City, I excitedly told her about what had been going on in my life.

After about an hour of talking, she looked me dead in the eye and said, "You need to grow up, Mike. Stop boasting about your stupid fights and telling all these stories about how you got arrested. It only makes you look like a criminal. In the real world, people don't care about that kind of stuff." She then told me to get out of her car. As she drove off, she said, "You can reach out to me if you ever do decide to grow up."

That conversation turned around so quickly that it made me dizzy. I not only realized how immature I was, but also how menial and pathetic my lifestyle and worldview seemed to other people. In my attempts to impress her, I repelled her. I may have been able to impress and attract drug addicts, but those who were successful, I could not. For the first time, I realized that other people from other classes of society or with differing worldviews saw my pursuits and lifestyle through a different lens than I did. What could impress one crowd could disgust another. I wanted to be accepted by both, not only accepted, but exceptional. I stayed in Salt Lake that night recoiling, calling every girl I could think of trying to rebound, trying anything I could to distract me from her words and my failure to live up to them.

Shortly after, my dad found a pile of needles hidden underneath the bathtub. He pummeled the punching bag for hours until he finally confronted me. When he did, he seemed desperate and despondent.

"Nothing gets through to you. It's almost like nothing can change you. Is there anything I can do? Nothing is working. If I stopped drinking, would you stop doing drugs? Tell me, what am I supposed to do? How am I supposed to help you?"

I felt so lost in my addiction, I believed that no one was capable of understanding or helping me. I thought I was uniquely broken, so messed up that no other human could possibly get me. Turns out most addicts feel that way. I knew he drank occasionally, but I had no clue how much he drank, how much it meant to him, or how much he was offering by his willingness to forsake it for me. To this day, I wonder what things would have been like if I would've opened up to him and let him fight alongside me instead of blocking him out. I can't count how many times I have wished that I could go back and take him up on that offer.

Somehow, through each of my arrests, my parents never gave up on me. They would sit and talk with me and ask me what was wrong. They would help me pay my fines when I couldn't. They were always kind and supportive. I couldn't understand why they didn't just kick me out or disown me. That's what I would've done. That's what my friends' parents were doing.

I knew I was wronging them and harming myself by doing so. Yet, I had no power to change my addiction; all I could do was curb its symptoms and manage its consequences. My rebellious pursuit to find meaning and pleasure in life had cost my parents — and me — so much money, time, and stress. At first, it seemed impossible to make amends for the trouble and pain I'd caused them, but when I discovered a program that would allow me to graduate high school with an associate degree in science, I committed myself to it. I was determined to turn my life around, but I was doing it in my own strength.

I started taking more ADD medication because the amphetamines helped me focus and do better at school. When I couldn't stock up on ADD medicine, I would use meth. After class one day, we were making our routine runs at the local supermarket. Despite having $150 in my pocket, I still chose to steal $10 worth of eyedrops and a certain type of glass makeup container that could be used to smoke meth. The highly trained security specialist watched the whole thing on video.

After years of doing this, we discovered that it always looked fishy to steal from a store without hitting the check stand. So, we stood in line to buy 99 cent iced teas with the more expensive products tucked safely away in our pants. As we bought our drinks, two male employees positioned themselves in front of us and stared us down. My friend got the jitters and ran. Turning like a gazelle, he evaded them both. I remained in line and tried to act as cool and calm as I could. I was eighteen now. In the legal system, that meant I was an adult, and all alleged crimes would be placed on my permanent record.

I finished checking out and headed toward the exit, trying not to look suspicious and hoping they hadn't connected me with my loony friend who had scampered off like Elmer Fudd with a bullet in his butt. I was the one who was on meth, after all, not him. As I stepped toward the exit, a police car situated itself directly outside. Another one followed, so that they were positioned in a V shape, blocking my way out.

The employee who had been glaring at us positioned himself in front of me and said, "I won't allow you to leave the premises. We have reason to believe that you've stolen from us. The cops are here for you."

I slowly moved my finger toward the receipt in my hand, saying, "Sir, I can assure you I bought this product."

He responded, "That's not what we're talking about, and you know it. The stolen items are in your pants."

At this point, I bolted to the left, hoping to brush past him, but as I did, I ran straight into the officer who had just come through the sliding glass doors.

He grabbed me and said, "Kid, you need to come with me. We're going upstairs."

I tried to shake his grip, but to no avail.

He started shouting, with his face close enough for the droplets of spit to splatter on mine, "If you try that one more time, I'm writing you up for evading arrest and disturbing the peace. If you want three citations instead of one, be my guest."

In defeat, I walked with the officers until we hit the staircase, where fear overtook me. I blinked, and then I found myself trying to rip from their grasp and run.

"Not again!" I shouted. "I can't do this again!"

By now, there was a small crowd staring at me.

"What had happened to my friend?" I asked.

"It's none of your business," the officer responded as he dragged me up the stairs into the security room for interrogation.

Additional officers arrived, and they took turns shining lights into my face and interrogating me, insisting that I was high. Eventually, they told me that my friend was in their custody and that they'd found a bag of meth on him.

They continued to question me until it seemed as if the process would never end. Finally, I spoke up again, "You've been doing this for hours, and you haven't proven or found anything on me. Can you please just give it up?"

The officer, pointing his light in my eye, responded angrily, "We believe you're dealing drugs, and we're not going to stop until we find our answer."

They knew my friend had drugs; they knew I was high, and they knew I was the one with all the cash. If they could just get me to confess to dealing, this misdemeanor would turn into a felony, and they could finally put Mike Heil where he belonged.

I looked up at them and tried one last half-truth, "I have a job; you can call my boss or even my family if you don't believe me, but I earned that money."

After a few more attempts, they finally conceded, dragged me down the stairs, and threw me in the back of one of their vehicles. I figured they were taking me to the station to drug test me again like they had last time. From there, they'd be able to prove that I was high, and that I had sold my friend his meth.

During the car ride, the officer looked back at me and said, "Why do you do things like this? You're throwing your life away."

I sat in defiance with arms crossed, but if he would've looked closely, he would've seen a single tear streaming down my face. I knew he was right, but I didn't know "why" I did things like this. When we arrived at the station, he sat me down and handcuffed me to a chair in the lobby while he looked up my file.

As he read the report, his demeanor hardened. "Kid, you've got one heck of a record." My pride inflated and I sat up a bit as he continued, "You're screwed. With a record like this, you're going to jail for a long time."

When he finished talking, he grabbed me, forcing me to stand up. My arm yanked against the chair, which pulled me down again.

"You're going into the holding cell," he said as he bent down to unlock my arm.

He yanked up again, this time moving my frail body with ease. When we arrived at the holding cell, he shoved me through the door.

"It could be up to seventy-two hours before we get you transferred over to the jail, but with a record like this, you better make yourself comfortable. You're not going anywhere."

As I sat on the floor in the corner of the concrete block, it felt as if the last domino had fallen in my crumbling world. For the first time in a long time, I starting weeping, and I couldn't stop. The impact of what was happening was steadily sinking in. For the third time in my life, my eyes shot heavenward.

I was on my knees now like I'd been when we set the forest on fire. I knelt there with tears streaming down my face and a hideous, hopeless wail escaping my mouth. It was over. I'd thrown it all away. I muttered something.

"It's all over, I ruined everything." My phrases were broken up between sobs. "I can't do this anymore. This life, it's empty. I don't know what I'm doing. Help me... Please help me."

I stayed there on my knees with slobber dribbling down my face as the tears steadily clouded my vision. "I'm sorry," I said, "please forgive me. I've messed up so damn much. I just keep failing. I fail my family, I fail my friends, all my relationships have failed. I'm a screw-up. I don't know how to change. I can't do this anymore. Please help me."

I wept without end until suddenly a comforting feeling washed over me. If I could have heard God speak, I'm sure He would've said, "Yes, you fail, your heart is deceived, and it endlessly seeks things that hurt you, lie to you, and tear you from Me, but My heart seeks you. I will never give up on you."

My endless sobbing slowed until my chest steadily raised and lowered. I didn't know what happened at that moment, but I knew I wasn't alone any longer, and I knew that whatever I had to face, I would make it through and be alright. I stayed there on the cold concrete for a long time until I heard the cell door open behind me.

The officer peeked in and stepped through the door. Before I had the chance to wipe my groggy eyes and resume my act of chauvinism and impregnability, he began speaking.

"I... I don't understand this exactly," he fumbled. "But you've been given a clean slate. I can't hold your previous crimes against you. Even though they show up in my files and merit detainment, I can't hold them against you."

I began to speak up, trying to ask him what this meant, but he interjected.

"Your record has been wiped clean. I have to treat you like this is your first offense... If you'd been in your buddy's shoes, you'd be a felon, and I could still hold you here just based on what you did today... But as it is... I have to let you go."

My mind turned to that moment right before entering the store, where I handed my friend the meth and told him to give me his money. If we would've waited until after our visit to the grocery store to do the drug deal, I would've been the felon, not him. I had no idea things would unravel like this; I felt bad for him, wishing that I could've taken his punishment for him. He had asked me for the drugs, and he was still 17, which meant he was a juvenile and his punishments would be lessened, but that didn't lessen my guilt.

The officer stared at me with condemnation in his eyes, giving me a knowing look that said, "I know you're high, and I know you sold your friend those drugs, but I have no choice but to let you go. A greater power is at work." Regret glimmered in his eyes as he reached for my cuffs and turned the key. After sliding them off my bony wrists, he led me out of the cell and sat me down in the waiting room.

He returned with a clear plastic evidence bag which contained all of my belongings, handed it to me, and told me I was free to go. Inside the bag, there was a citation with my name, the three crimes I'd committed, and a barely legible court date scribbled on it. I pulled my phone from the bag, and, after a moment of contemplation, I called my ex-girlfriend Adalyn, who had recently dumped me for Rogue. She had hurt me, but I didn't know who else to share this with. When she finally arrived to pick me up, she was with two of our friends, and they were on their way up to the city to score some black.

The whole way up, I shared with a captive audience everything that had happened. I told them about the officer, telling me that my awful record would land me a spot in jail for a long time. Then I told them how everything had changed in a moment. Somehow, in between the time when he first looked up my record and the time that I prayed, suddenly everything that condemned me was non-applicable and void. When I told them about how I'd kneeled on the ground and prayed, they started making fun of me. I tried to tell them how I'd felt God enter the jail cell, but when I said "God," it stuck in my throat like a canker sore, awkward and unfitting. I was afraid to sound phony or religious, but I had no other way to explain what had happened, and I wasn't phony, I was sincere.

I told them how, when I'd finally broken down and handed everything over to Him, something changed, and I felt like a different person. I suddenly had confidence that no matter what happened, I could face it and be alright. Even if they locked me up for years, I knew I'd be alright.

"I know it sounds crazy," I said, "but I'm not delusional. Think about it, at the same moment that I prayed, something happened, and my record was wiped clean."

In place of my record stood a God whom I had mocked, ridiculed, and despised, a God whom I had ignored and considered myself to be above, independent of, and smarter than. Against all logic, He chose to set an ungrateful and condemned man free... again! The officer spoke facts: I was a criminal. I was beyond my last chance. And yet, God seemed to see through those facts. Instead of listening to the accusations against me, which were all true, He didn't let my faults or failures define me; instead, He washed them away.

"In my distress I prayed to the Lord, and the Lord answered me and set me free. The Lord is for me, so I will have no fear... the Lord is for me; he will help me." —*Psalm 118:5-7* (NLT)

***

I didn't know how to explain what I felt until that summer when I took Philosophy 101. I felt like the figure in Plato's cave who had spent his whole life chained down and unable to move. His world consisted of the cave and the shadows on its walls. Throughout his whole life, he'd never looked at a real object, only the vague shadows of reality which danced across the confines of his insignificant chambers. Likewise, my understanding of reality had been restricted solely to my own intellect, emotions what I could feel, touch, and explain. I vehemently fought against the idea that there could be anything more than just the physical realm. I had no room for any concept of the supernatural.

In my existentialism and hedonism, I had stared at the shadows on the wall, convinced that what I saw was all that reality had to offer; I was defiant of the proposition that something could be creating the shadows, that someone could be operating at a level beyond my conception. Opposing every idea that someone could actually be responsible for making the world around me, I was determined to believe that the order around me came from a bang, not a being. My reality had always been limited to what I could see, deconstruct, and rationalize, but the miracles I had seen were breaking all of my paradigms.

There was something more than just the shadows on the wall, more than just the physical realm in front of me. It felt like God, the same being I had always denied, had broken my chains and released me from my precincts. Experiencing God felt as if I were escaping from the cave and seeing the outside world for the first time, the sun beaming down, the grass bright and green. It was more beautiful than anything I'd ever experienced before. I felt complete and total love and acceptance, a clean slate, a new start, a new hope, a new joy, all of it tangible and real. Why on earth He would give all of this to a wretch like me, I could not understand, but it was given nonetheless.

The difficulty was that I didn't know how to function in a world outside the confinements in which I had grown so accustomed. I did not know how to trust God; I did not know how to have a relationship with him, and I was not convinced that any church was equipped to help someone in my situation. So I kept running back to my cave, looking longingly at the shadows on the wall. I kept picking up the shackles that He had knocked off my wrists and running around with them dangling off me. I was stuck in between worlds, and I did not know what to do.

For a moment, I saw the beauty of this great and glorious new reality, but when we got to the city, Adalyn handed me some heroin, and I took a puff. Something had changed. I'd been let loose from the confines of my cave, but I was still carrying my chains around with me. Bound by them, I acted out of my habits, as I always had. Only this time, the high that had once been the climax of my existence seemed pitiful and empty.

"Truly, truly, I say to you, everyone who commits sin is a slave to sin." — *John 8:34*

***

When my court date arrived, it seemed as if the judge had no access to my previous record. For all practical purposes, it had been erased. In an act of mercy, he dropped two of the three charges levied against me, leaving me one Class B misdemeanor for stealing. Once again, I evaded jail time and was set loose with nothing but a warning and a hefty fine.

"I don't think the six months' jail time that you've merited will do you any good," he said. "I'm choosing not to treat you like a common criminal, and I am expecting you not to act like one any longer. I do not want to see you here again. Is that understood?"

After a brief pause, I responded, "Yes, sir."

He continued, "You're an adult now; any crimes you commit from this point forward will affect your aptitude for job acquisition. You still have a chance to make something out of your life. Don't waste it, Mr. Heil… Next case!"

I had spent months anxiously preparing for this day, anticipating that I would be immediately transferred to jail upon sentencing, as the arresting officer had predicted. I trembled, wondering why on earth a guilty man had just been set free. It seemed as if this God was as dead set on rescuing me as I was on satisfying myself. I couldn't help but reflect on all the poor decisions that brought me to this point. And yet, in each step, it seemed like God had been there working on my behalf. In the deepest, darkest moments of despair, when I felt totally forsaken, He had sent multiple interventions to show me that I was not ever alone.

He did not remove me from the situations I created and the path that I chose, nor did He nullify the awful consequences of those decisions. He let me choose my path, and He allowed things to unfold in their natural sequence so that I could see the fruits of my decisions, but He was there for me every step of the way. Who and what was this God? For a while, I acted like God was a girl at my school. I acted like God was a substance that delivered euphoria to my brain. I didn't ever think about God as an external being independent from me. Now it seemed like God (the Being) was trying to get my attention, but I did not know how to draw close to Him.

All I knew for certain was that somehow this God managed to see good in me when I could only see bad in myself. This God seemed determined not to give up on me, even when I felt like giving up on myself. To me, God had been little more than a fairytale. To me He was an abstract concept or set of ideas, not a living person who was all-powerful and real. And yet this fairytale was beginning to break out of its pages into the real world—into my life.

"For if while we were enemies we were reconciled to God by the death of his Son, much more, now that we are reconciled shall we be saved by his life." — *Romans 5:10* (ESV)

Chapter Nineteen

Spiritual Funk

"Who is as blind as my own people, my servant? Who is as deaf as my messenger? Who is as blind as my chosen people, the servant of the Lord? You see and recognize what is right but refuse to act on it. You hear with your ears, but you don't really listen." —*Isaiah 42:19-20* (NLT)

A desire for the spiritual had awakened inside of me, but I wasn't sure how to address it. Each time I experienced God, I realized that I wasn't alone, and that there was much more to this life, but because of my negative experiences with religion, I refused to seek God in any traditional setting. I decided that if I wanted to be on God's good side I better try to be a good person, so I spent the year trying to work to earn the favor, forgiveness, and right standing that God had (obviously) already given me. I traded all of my bad habits for good ones. I traded the negative influences in my life for positive ones. I became a spiritual seeker.

My experience in the jail cell had changed some things, but not everything. Drugs and hooking up both felt less satisfying now; wrong somehow. For the first time, I could see that both were façades and that neither truly satisfied, but throughout years of acting on my addictions, I had whittled these habits into my brain and life. Over time and repetition, these habits had become, like a river in a canyon, carved so deep into the confines of my mind that they were seemingly unchangeable. If I were to change, my mind would need to be transformed and reconfigured from the ground up. I had trained myself to be dependent on these things and now I needed to train myself to separate from them. It took years to get addicted and it would take years to get to get unaddicted.

I learned to replace much of my drug use with exercise, which also helped relieve stress and deliver dopamine to my brain. I stopped putting myself in environments that triggered me. Instead of going out with friends, I would spend time at the gym and enjoy the sauna. I smoked cigarettes since the buzz distracted me from my deeper longings and temptations. I went to support groups which gave me structure, accountability, and a sense of belonging. I needed to stop blaming others for my emptiness and shortcomings; I needed to stop hoping the emptiness would change without me changing. If drugs, partying, and relationships kept me continually feeling insecure while at the center of my being, then they needed to be surmounted and something else positioned in their place. I could not expect change to occur without changing what was at the center of my life or the purpose for which I was living.

It was easy for me to start good habits like taking advanced classes and doing more sports, but weeding out the bad habits was not as simple. I still went to class high sometimes, but at least I wasn't doing it every day. Before, I could not function without drugs, could not live a single day. Now, very gradually, I was changing the purpose for which I lived. Before, I was a druggie. Now I was a super studious, highly advanced student who was only on drugs sometimes. I was finding that sweet spot of balance and moderation. Maybe, at some point, the drugs and partying would be gone, and I'd just be a successful student, employee, and citizen. It seemed to me that the two most common paths for finding meaning in life were partying or prosperity, and I was excelling at both.

A heavy weight of guilt drove me in my success. I felt like I needed to make up for all the money, stress, and time I had cost my family. So, I pushed myself, trying harder and harder to be a good person and do well in school. I knew I had done them wrong, but without fail, they had always been there to bail me out and help me get back on my feet again.

Since school came easily to me, it was one way that I was able to get ahead, and I felt that by doing so, I would also make amends for some of the trouble I had caused my family. It was sort of an accident that I got placed in these advanced classes. A teacher who favored me suggested them and told me that I could save a lot of money. I took the classes for a year-and-a-half before I realized how valuable they were. When I started them, I was doing heroin almost every day, but I had still managed to slip by with Bs and Cs. I had gotten so far ahead, even while on drugs, that I only needed to take four more classes to finish my associate's degree. I would be getting my college degree just a few months after the other students my age were getting their high school diplomas.

The amount of money I'd saved by getting this far ahead was almost two years of college tuition, or about $10,000 dollars. It wasn't as much as I'd cost my family through all my arrests and fines, but it was a start.

Since I only needed the four classes, I signed up to take them that summer on campus at Utah Valley University. At the same time, I sent applications to other universities for bachelor's degree programs that would start in the Fall of 2010. I decided it was finally time to put partying behind me and pursue an elite education. I had "lived the good life" and now it was time for something more. I had become less satisfied with partying, and I could only hope the road to prosperity had something more to offer.

I made new friends, created new habits, and developed new hobbies. I tried moving to a new city, I tried starting from scratch with a new life in a new apartment, and I tried pursuing an education and a good career. What I found was that solving the puzzle of addiction was not as simple as refraining from certain substances, people, and activities, and replacing them with healthier ones. Physical and social changes like these helped and were a necessary part of my recovery, but they were not enough. They were enough to get me mostly sober and remotely successful, but I still felt little purpose in life. The only thing I could deduce was that since I was focused only on the physical, my healing was not holistic. I was neglecting part of who I was. If I wanted to heal both inwardly and outwardly, I needed to address the whole of my being, not just isolated parts.

I realized that human beings were not only physical and social but also emotional, intellectual, and spiritual. In response, I slowly started opening up to advice and ideas I'd previously closed myself to. Instead of belittling people when I heard them talk about spiritual things, like my friends and I had always done, I listened to them eagerly. I was open-minded about pretty much every form of religion or spirituality, except Christianity. I listened when others talked about meditation, centering chakras, prayer, positive affirmation, centering oneself, and connecting with the universe.

I was so eager to connect with my Higher Power, or the earth, or the universe, or whatever God was, that at the peak of my search for something more I went without shoes for almost an entire year. I kept hanging out with hippies who told me that I was one with the universe and I needed to open up to it more in order to find healing. They said when you don't wear shoes, you can feel the earth's energy and each solitary blade of grass. By connecting to it, they said that I could also connect with others.

I believed in every form of religion that I personally deemed inclusive and befitting, while rejecting and ignoring the ones I didn't like. For a while, I believed in and practiced principles from Buddhism and Hinduism. I liked the fact that they taught me about moderation but did not entirely dissuade me from drug use or hooking up. They gave me the freedom to live the life that I wanted to. If I wanted to try drugs occasionally, the wiggle room in these belief systems allowed me to do so. They empowered me to be who I wanted to be, while at the same time giving me religious rituals like meditation, balancing my chakras to fall back on, and karma to help me find a greater sense of purpose in things.

I would sit in the steam room for hours, trying to cleanse myself and focus my energy. I would balance my chakras and pray for others, pouring out everything inside of me so that they could take my energy and be healed. I would go to the drum circle as often as I could, twirl fire, and balance on slacklines. I would go to the Hare Krishna temple shrooming and worship love itself, dancing with glee, getting strange red dots placed on my forehead, while the rest of my friends tripped balls and cowered in fear in the restroom. I would go to the festival of colors where handfuls of chalk were tossed to and fro, like snowballs and thick clouds of chalk representing every color of the rainbow filled the air and covered our clothing.

Since loads of hippies, potheads, and drug addicts believed in these things, I often found myself in likeable company. These were the people I preferred to be around, the people who understood me, and those I understood. In a sense, these beliefs allowed us to do what we wanted, hook up, do drugs, whatever, all under the banner of spirituality. Yet each time I did one of these things, I found myself either regretting it or spiraling out of control. After a while, I realized that most of the people who believed in this stuff were still actively doing drugs and were just as stuck as I was, even though, like me, they pretended not to be.

At some point I got tired of justifying myself, finding beliefs that excused my actions, and doing the same things over and over. I decided it would make more sense to get advice from people who'd managed to overcome their dependence on substances, so I started opening up to friends who were in the Twelve Steps. They told me that addiction was not a moral or philosophical problem but a spiritual one. They told me I couldn't think or work my way out of it; only God could free me from it.

I told them I had been trying spiritual solutions and none of them were working. They encouraged me to not give up. They assured me that the Higher Power was real, that God was real, and that He could help me, just as He had helped millions of others like me. I was relieved when the Twelve Steps program allowed me to create my own interpretation about who and what my Higher Power was. I mixed together all the things people had told me and forged my own religion out of them. I called it spirituality, not religion.

I went to a few AA meetings and realized that, in essence, the Twelve Steps were supposed to teach me how to have a conscience, how to care about things other than myself, how to correct my mistakes and act with honor and integrity, as well as how to understand good behavior and taking responsibility for bad behavior. They taught me how to understand a sense of "good" that went beyond my personal feelings, lusts, desires, and opinions. These very basic concepts of good and bad gave me a concrete foundation; at the very least, if I could discern good from bad, I would be less likely to base my life solely on emotions.

The main thing people focused on in the Twelve Steps was sobriety. We went from glorying in our drug stories to deriding them. Still, we were always sharing stories about drugs. The difference now was that we shared how dumb drugs were instead of how awesome they were. Either way, however, we were constantly thinking and talking about drugs. Even though we'd successfully stopped taking drugs, all of our focus and effort was still concentrated on and centered around them, or rather abstaining from them. Sometimes the constant focus on drugs and drinking generated a sense of nostalgia. Sometimes we talked as if we would eagerly go back to the good old days, if only drugs and drinking didn't cause us (and our loved ones) so much harm.

For many of us, drugs and drinking were still our concept of the good life. Somewhere deep down we still believed these things to be the ultimate pleasure in life and regretted not being able to enjoy them. One day, a very wise woman listened to me rambling about how much drugs had cost me and how angry I was about getting deceived by them, becoming addicted, and wasting so much of life. She quoted Jesus and told me I needed to learn to turn the other cheek. "These things hit you," she said. "They punched you in the face and now you have a choice. You can keep focusing on them and judging people who do them, or you can turn your cheek and focus on something new. Before you were obsessed with loving drugs, now you're obsessed with hating them. Either way, your life is still ruled by them."

The Twelve Steps teach that the only way to be freed from addiction and restored to sanity is through total and constant reliance on a Higher Power. I guess this Higher Power is somehow supposed to replace drugs, pleasure, and whatever else we have placed at the epicenter of our existence and fill the gap that these things cannot. Since our Higher Power is independent from, separate from, and beyond us, a Higher Power can help us in ways we cannot help ourselves. If we cannot put our Higher Power at the center of our lives, then something else will be there, and it will not be so kind a ruler.

The best advice I ever got was, "Whatever you keep in the center of your life, that thing will always drive you. If it is your Higher Power, it will drive you to healing and purpose; if it is pleasure or any other thing, you'll dig your own grave and justify yourself while doing it." I was told that even if I had years of sobriety, I would always be an addict, and I believed it. *Since my identity was that of an addict, didn't that mean abstinence from drugs was contrary to my identity and doing drugs was in alignment with it?* This confused me because if I believed this philosophy, it meant I would never heal from my disease; I would only go into remission. It also meant that the harder I tried to abstain from drugs, the more I was fighting against who I really was.

I needed a Higher Power at the center of my life; I needed a power higher than myself to come and save me, but for the life of me, I could not figure out what that Higher Power was supposed to be. I refused to believe in the Christian God because of my negative life experiences, but every other type of Higher Power that I heard people talking about seemed to lack the necessary characteristics to be trusted with something as important as my soul and perhaps even my eternal wellbeing. I knew that a Higher Power could not be a significant other or a figment of my imagination. It couldn't be me, or my ego, or my toothbrush. It couldn't be my drug of choice. If the Higher Power were any of these things, it wouldn't be greater than me, and it wouldn't be able to offer me any real help.

As I sought out my Higher Power, I realized that rather than confronting me, or changing me, it attached itself like a glove to my worldview and enhanced it. About 90% of the time, it never disagreed with me. It was what *I* wanted it to be, it told *me* what *I* wanted to hear, it let me make *my* reality. I chose *my* own ultimate purpose and created *my* own worldview, and it was my assistant. It was always helping me accomplish *my* goals and *my* purposes. It let me keep myself at the center and build whatever type of subjective reality I wanted. It never gave me any laws, any rules, any external objective reality at all. Instead, it let me choose for myself.

For most of the year I wore no shoes. This Higher Power was my guide, but it seemed to be just as confused about the world as I was. Eventually, I realized that my Higher Power was an ethereal nothingness. It was a collection of lofty ideas that, although beautiful, were not capable of contradicting me, reshaping my paradigms, or defining reality for me. It was a god that appealed to my own sensibilities; it was as ever-changing and subjective as my own mind.

This Higher Power was the least offensive and most inclusive belief system I could find. I liked the fact that people found it agreeable because that meant they would also likely find me agreeable. My world was still about me, everything still revolved around me, what I thought about myself, and what I could get others to think about me. I was always changing in order to fit in, and after a while, I realized that my Higher Power was doing the same thing.

After doing psychological cartwheels with varying philosophies about Higher Powers for a year, I decided that all forms of religion were little more than positive psychology that served to help us rewrite the tracks that we played in our minds. I decided, in the end, that's all I had, my mind, and whatever track or CD I decided to play in it. On a good day, it would play cheery tunes, but as soon as I got triggered and my desperation for drugs kicked in, or as soon as I failed, or relapsed, the tune would change. My identity and self-worth would often change with it.

In moments of compromise and failure, my positive affirmations flip-flopped around in my mind like fish out of the water. In those moments, I could not remain positive, so the affirmations I tried to persuade myself with were empty and misleading more than anything else. In some moments, if I were to force myself to be positive, I would be lying to myself. I would be neglecting reality. Life wasn't always good, and I wasn't always happy. *Was something wrong with me because of that fact, or is that just how life is?* Positive psychology was good, but it was not enough.

I remember the book *The Secret* [40] being all the rage. It taught that people attract whatever they focus on. If I believed in good things, focused on them, and expected them, then I would get them. I tried doing this, not only believing in good things but anticipating them and expecting them. I tried to think and hope for the best, but it didn't change who I was. It didn't change my core, my desires, my actions, nor my life, for that matter. Did it matter how many nice thoughts I put out into the universe if I remained a self-centered prick? Did it matter how many "selfless" thoughts and deeds I had if the only reason I performed them was to benefit myself, or gain a better future for myself? Putting good things out into the universe didn't undo or negate the negative things I'd done. It also didn't negate the fact that every action has its own consequence. When my friends believed and expected that they would win over the hottest girl at the drum circle, they got her, but they also got STD's.

If karma was true and my Higher Power simply gave whatever I put into the universe back to me, I would be screwed; I would have spiritual STD's. If there was a scale to balance my good actions with my bad ones, I would cosmically fail, I would break the scale. There were so many occasions when I slipped up, when I thought, and said, and did stupid, awful things, when I took advantage of people and lied to them. If my eternal wellbeing was based on my ability to tip the scales or be a good person, I was eternally doomed. If I really believed in karma, I would constantly have to look over my shoulder. The universe would surely have some horrible fate coming for me. If I believed in karma, I would probably be a fly in my next life because of all the messed-up crap I'd done in this one.

At my core, I was seeking the wrong things. I did not even know what I wanted in life, let alone what I needed. What good was the law of attraction when all the things I wanted, desired, and attracted ended up being more harmful than they were helpful, and when all the things I longed for and sought did not satisfy me in the way I hoped they would? I needed to change. I needed to tip the scale. I needed to, but I couldn't. It didn't matter if I said nice things and put on a fake smile. It didn't matter if I pretended like I had things all figured out. The fact that I kept doing the same messed up things showed that I wasn't healed, I was stuck.

My spiritual pursuits gained me nothing. It was as if the Higher Power I was seeking was nothing more than the sum of my favorite thoughts and ideas. It could not answer my prayers, change my circumstances, or do anything objective at all in my life. It was basically a figment of my imagination. I was a part of it, and it was a part of me, but it was not beyond me, above me, or separate from me. At its very best, it could maybe help me to massage my own psyche, but I needed objective, concrete, and tangible help, love, and guidance. I didn't need an ethereal spirituality, I needed something pragmatic and real. I was tired of building my life on a flimsy foundation.

I needed to find the God I'd met in that jail cell, the one who didn't give me what I deserved. The one who gave me freedom when I deserved judgement. The one who gave me mercy when I deserved wrath. The one who gave me a clean slate after I had muddied it up. I needed Him, whoever He was; that was the God I needed for my condition. That God answered my prayers. That God was cognizant, independent from me, and powerful. Maybe it didn't matter so much *that* we prayed, as it mattered *to whom* we prayed. The God I'd met in that jail cell was a being who could listen and respond, not just through my subjective feelings or emotions, but objectively. He really changed things, which meant He existed outside of myself. He wasn't just the product of wishful thinking. He was real.

My reasoning was: If there is a God who created reality, then that God alone understands it fully and in its entirety. If this is so, that Being's voice and words are consistent, objective, and clear. They are the constructs that constitute reality itself. While my constructs of reality change like a shifting shadow does as the sun sets, God's does not. While my mind is always changing with the onset and accumulation of new knowledge, God understands all things perfectly and in their totality. If there is a Higher Power who actually made all things, it is this God's voice that matters and whose opinion counts. This Creator alone would not only know why we exist, but also for which purpose we were created.

I was still not sure about the whole idea of a Creator, but the alternative was believing that I was a living piece of stardust that counterintuitively built itself together in response to an explosion, the mathematical probability of which was an anomaly of cosmic proportions. If that theory proved true, then I was also a very sophisticated monkey who would soon return to being a lifeless chunk of dirt. On the other hand, the idea of some transcendent, all-powerful being speaking or sculpting me into existence seemed just as unlikely. The ramifications of the first world view were clear: eat, drink, and be monkey, for tomorrow we die. We die, and we are gone, and there is nothing more.

"Now the Holy Spirit tells us clearly that in the last times some will turn away from the true faith; they will follow deceptive spirits and teachings that come from demons. These people are hypocrites and liars, and their consciences are dead... Do not waste time arguing over godless ideas and old wives' tales. Instead, train yourself to be godly. 'Physical training is good, but training for godliness is much better, promising benefits in this life and in the life to come.'" —*1 Timothy 4:1-2; 7-8*

Chapter Twenty

Stranded on a Cliff Face

"The Lord is gracious and full of compassion, slow to anger and great in mercy. The Lord is good to all, and His tender mercies are over all His works." —*Psalm 145:8-9*

During my summer at the college, I met more than just pretty girls. In my business law class, I met a pretentious individual named Samuel. He seemed to see straight through me. After one twenty-minute conversation, he seemed to see me more clearly than did most people whom I had called friends for years. He examined my foundations and almost instantly discovered the faults and cracks that caused me to feel so unstable. Every week he would seek me out and talk with me. He did not have much tact and was as brash a man as I'd ever met.

"Look at the way you dress, kid. It signifies that you're desperate for attention. Why are you so desperate for women? Well, you're using relationships to affirm your self-worth. You pretend to think very highly of yourself, but you wouldn't need to draw attention to yourself like this if you actually did."

I felt almost violated by both the accuracy of his assessment as well as Samuel's forthrightness.

"Yeah, I guess so," I finally managed.

"Look, kid," he continued, "relationships are your center, they're at the core of your life. You always smell like smoke too, which is gross. But you probably use substances to sedate the pain when relationships don't go well. You claim to believe in a Higher Power, but you don't; you don't know God at all."

At this point, I started shouting at him. "Listen, dude, I grew up going to church. I know what all that crap is about! I'm sure I know more about religion than you do. I've met hundreds of religious suck-ups, and I think they're all a bunch of narrowminded hypocrites who lack understanding of real life and what it's like to really struggle." He listened calmly, and when I was finally done, he said, "If I've been right with everything else, will you please just hear me out on this one? I'm not talking about religion, and I'm not talking about how much you think you know. There's a big difference between knowing something and doing (or living) something. You might know about Christianity, but you're living for yourself. You are your own Lord, you might use God to get you out of trouble, you might use the name of Jesus when you're overwhelmed, but He is not your Lord. Even if you say you believe in Him, even if you call Him your savior, it's just lip service. You aren't living for or with God, you are living for yourself."

By this point, I retorted, "The reason I'm not a Christian is because of narrow-minded religious people like you."

Samuel responded compassionately, "I'm here because I care about you. I want you to have a bright life and future. I spend time with you because I see that you're hurting inside, and you lack guidance. When I was your age, someone sought me out and helped me tackle the lies in my life and fight my way through them and find hope again. I believe that there's hope for you and I want to help you get unstuck the same way they helped me."

I wanted to yell at him again, "What, so you're saying I believe in lies? You're saying I'm stuck and need help?" I wanted to yell, but if I was honest with myself, I knew he was right. Why try to deny it?

"If I can tell you one thing, it's this," he said. "You wouldn't be insecure if you actually knew God. If you had any idea how much He loves you, how much He sacrificed for you, how much He has already done for you, and how much He still has yet to do for you. God's love isn't conditional like ours is. God loved you at your worst. When you were at your lowest point, when you couldn't even love yourself, when you were groveling on the ground, when you were a criminal, even then, God loved you enough to give up His life for you. He loves you more than any human ever will, and His love is able to satisfy more than any human's love ever could. He loved you because He chose to, not because you earned or deserve it. His love is different than human love.

"We live in a world full of contracts. When someone fails to meet the outlined terms of the contract, we seek a better suitor. When the agreement stops benefitting us, we cancel it. God's love is different, it's a covenant. With covenants, there are no exit clauses, there are no grounds for termination of the agreement. Once you enter the covenant, there is no way to void it. The stronger party is committed to the weaker party and will uphold them, even when they break their end of the agreement. In other words, God's promises aren't dependent on us, He knows we'll fall short. His promises are dependent on Him. When we fail, He remains faithful. The only thing He asks is that we trust in Him."

After this conversation, I tried to avoid the man as much as possible, but he wasn't willing to just let me slip by. After class, he would make his way directly toward me to see how I was and pick up wherever he'd left off with his religious ranting.

Luckily for me I got to take one week off school for our family's annual trip to Lake Powell, which was as much of an innate contradiction as I was. Lake Powell was a massive 140-mile-long lake in the middle of an even bigger desert. The only thing that made the lake possible was a giant dam that blocked up one of America's mightiest rivers. I could not stave off my impulsive need for adventure. It was one of those sure, solid things that brought me joy, no matter the circumstances. Adventure and adrenaline had become my newest fixes.

The more I tried to refrain from drugs, the more important became snowboarding, wakeboarding, longboarding, skating, biking, hiking, bouldering, cliff jumping, and every other thing that got my adrenaline pumping. I realized these things couldn't balance me out inside, but they were good outlets. That feeling of insidious fear, the big "what if?" that pulsates through your mind while suspended in midair. The split second where everything seems to freeze before you go plummeting towards the ground like a bolt of lightning.

Better yet, this was the one vacation where my parents always loaded up on booze before heading out. By this point, I had significantly lowered my consumption of weed, hard drugs, and even cigarettes, but I still considered alcohol fair game. If my parents' stash was ever short, then my sister and her friends more than made up for it. They were four years older than me meaning they were all 22 and up, just above legal drinking age. My favorite thing to do was climb the rocks and boulders, jumping from one to the next, seeing how far and long I could fly. Whenever I did this, I felt like a kid again. I would scale the cliffs like Spiderman; the only difference was that my safety depended on technical abilities and innate skill rather than superpowers. In the mornings, we would wake up at six while the water was still smooth as glass to go slalom skiing. After that, we'd have breakfast and coffee. Then people would start breaking out beers, and the drinking would continue throughout the rest of the day.

As a eighteen-year-old, I wasn't technically allowed to drink, but in an environment like that, what else could an addict do? I would swipe the stuff when they weren't looking and store away small stashes of it in emptied plastic water bottles. One day I remembered to drink booze but forgot to drink water. We went on a long hike that day. At some point, we found the most delightful looking crag I had ever seen. I had to climb it. But as I was ascending, we realized it was too technical and difficult for my friend. She decided to turn back, and we agreed to meet at the houseboat later. I gulped down my tiny bottle of vodka and orange juice and handed it to her, since I needed both hands to navigate the climb.

At one point, I had both hands on one cliff face, and both feet on the opposing face, with my body spread between the gaps like Kuzco and Pacha from *The Emperors New Groove*. I loved doing this and had gotten pretty good at using pressure to climb up crags like this. At the top, I had to push hard with my feet to launch the rest of my body onto the opposing ledge. By now, I was at least 250 feet above the water, but much of that terrain had been sloped. Only the last 75 feet or so had been directly vertical. Each time I thought I was nearing the top, I would poke my head over the ledge to find another spectacular challenge awaiting me. When I finally got to the top, my torso and hands clung to the slick sandstone while my feet and legs dangled over the cliff.

The night before, it had rained hard and created flash floods and waterfalls that poured down the cliff face towards our houseboat. My throat was getting so dry that when I swallowed, it felt like sandpaper was grating it. The raging desert heat had eradicated any trace of last night's rain. If even a puddle remained, I wouldn't have hesitated to wet my mouth with it. A day in the desert with no water was a day too many. The top of the cliff was not flat but had rolling rocky hills, some of them stretching seventy-five feet upwards at a slant before curving back down again. My goal was to make it to the cliff where the waterfall had been the night before so that I could shout down to everyone in the boat, letting them know I was safe. From there, I knew of a route I could use to make it safely back to the houseboat. But before I could make it there, I hit an impasse.

One of the steep slopes curved in on itself, dropping straight down into a cavernous hole in the rocks. It was a forty-foot drop, and only after I dropped would I be able to work my way up another slope towards the houseboat. I turned left, hoping to find a way around it but found myself once again at the edge of the massive cliff I had ascended. I turned right, hoping to find an alternative path, but kept running into bizarre cliffs that dropped off into pits made of solid stone, similar to the one I'd found before.

As I walked, the remaining light faded from the sky. I kept pressing on, knowing that I needed to somehow make it back down the cliff before nightfall. My original path of descent had been foiled when I met with the unforeseen impasse. Now my only way down was to go back the way I'd come. Luckily, I'd brought a flashlight, but it was a piece of crap. It was an eco-friendly light that was self-powered and didn't use batteries. To power it, I had to rotate a small knob in continual circles. It made an obnoxious whirring sound, and the light it generated shined at a maximum of five feet. This was just enough to make the light hit the ground that immediately surrounded my feet without shedding any light on my surroundings. To make it shine this far, I would all but have to stop moving and focus on doing nothing but twisting the knob as fast as I could. If I tried to generate light while walking, the beam went about three feet.

As I walked down one of the steep slopes, my foot headed towards what looked like the shadow of a rock. But when it came to the point where it should have connected, it just kept dropping. The rest of my body followed, teetering until it hit the rock, and started slipping downwards. I pressed my body hard against the sandstone, hoping the friction would slow the fall. I slowed enough to grab hold of a piece of rock, and fortunately for me, it held.

I remembered looking down those pits earlier. The floor of each of them was solid rock, sometimes smooth and other times jagged. A thirty or forty-foot fall onto a solid rock in the dark was survivable, but I would need rope to get out and someone at the top to pull me. I wasn't sure whether anyone else in our group could even rock climb this high to retrieve me, even if they waited for daylight. If I did fall in one of these pits and somehow survived it, having to wait through the night with broken limbs would be torture. I gathered my strength and pressed on, all but crawling at this point.

Once again, I mis-stepped. My limbs fell through the air and I went tumbling downwards. As I fell, I dug my nails into the slippery rock, pushing my entire body down to gain friction as I clutched desperately to the nearly vertical ledge. I tried climbing up, but the flashlight in my palm prevented me from gripping the rock. I almost crushed it as my flailing arms shot forward to grab hold of the rock. In order not to fall, I had to drop the little light; it flung by a string that was attached to my arm, waving and dangling in the air, just as I was. As I pulled myself up, I found myself trembling, but whether from dehydration or shock, I do not know. Just a few more inches and I would have… Crap. I would've been dead.

Crap, crap, crap. Have you ever heard the expression, "That scared the crap out of me?" I always thought it was a silly expression. I had never been able to wrap my head around how on earth someone had managed to popularize such a bizarre statement. In this moment, however, I realized it wasn't just a figure of speech. It was based on a real-life phenomenon. Apparently, the amount of terror produced by slipping off the ledge and desperately gripping the sandstone while plummeting towards the black abyss, and realizing if I couldn't stop myself, I'd be a goner, was sufficient to give rise to the phenomenon.

In sheer terror, I hyperventilated, and then my body froze, and then this compulsion came over me. The adrenaline pumping through my veins hit me so fiercely that there was no other option. So, I pulled myself up and dropped my britches, and I left a memento right there on that cliff face. It was a primal sort of, "Hmpf, that's what you get if you mess with me, cliff." I didn't have any TP, so I pulled off one of my socks and, after using it, left it on top of the pile. It was a cairn erected in my memory, a commemoration of my utter shock, fear, and embarrassment.

Usually, this kind of adventure sent my spirit soaring, but the drunkenness, dehydration, and multiple close-calls zapped every bit of joy out of this excursion, making every step tedious and wearisome. If this is where demanding my own way led me, was it really worth it? I wasn't just stranded on a cliff in the middle of the desert with no water, my whole life was a compilation of intimidating jagged cliff faces impinging upon one another. This physical situation was the perfect representation of where I was at emotionally, spiritually, and intellectually. I was dangling from precarious perches, stranded, empty, and running on fumes. Nothing I'd tried so far, had ever worked. I felt as if the lifestyle I had chosen, the parties, the drugs, the girls, the status, including all of my accomplishments, my college degree, and my job amounted to nothing more than a steaming pile of crap that would fade away into the cold hard earth when I died.

I decided the best thing I could do would be to save my energy, spend the night on the cliffs, and navigate my way down in daylight. I found a small, flat overhang a considerable distance away from my cairn, and hunkered down. The overhang was roughly five feet long and two feet wide. I scrunched up on the rock with knees tweaked upwards so that my body could fit lengthwise. My eyes stretched to take in the starlit tundra. The moon was dark that night, and the stars shone like phosphorescent holes that broke through the veil, divulging fragments of heaven.

Looking up into the infinite splendor, I couldn't help but notice the stars dancing with light, as harmonious in their movements as an orchestra. The purple, black, blue, yellow, and golden streaks of light melted together into a glimmering pool so thick you could drink it. Each beam of light flickering through countless light years of time and space, each star shining so huge that it could fit tens, billions, or even quadrillions of earth-sized planets into it, so huge and significant and yet, at the very same moment, smaller than the point of a needle. I couldn't help but be in awe. I couldn't help but wonder if the God who had been answering my prayers, cleaning my slate, and erasing the evidence against me, even that which was entwined in my very blood, also made all of this. If He made it all, He must also be bigger than all of it. And yet, somehow, it seemed that this great Being was willing to be intimately involved in my life.

197

I thought about how puny humans are in comparison to the vast expanse of space and yet how much of our lives and wellbeing we base on one another. I thought about how human love has the power to make us feel on top of the world and send butterflies racing through our stomachs. How it also has the power to break our hearts, causing depression and overwhelming sadness. But if human love is that powerful when it's placed at the center of our lives, what could the love of God do? If a human who is inestimably small can make or break our world, what could the love of the God who created the infinite expanse of space do if it were placed at our core?

I looked up to the heavens and whispered, "If You're really out there, I need you. I need to know that you can hear me, and that you're real, and that you care. I need a miracle. Not just to get me down from this place, but with everything else, too."

I paused for a moment, trying to decide whether to continue or not.

"I don't know if You could actually care about someone like me, especially after all the messed-up things I've done, but if You do, please help me make it through the night and get down from here."

Teetering there on that little ledge, I clung to a handle in the rock, gripped it with all I was worth, and closed my eyes.

✳✳✳

As I forced myself to rest, I reflected on the last thing Samuel had told me. "If you really understood the gospel, you couldn't leave unchanged. Jesus ran the race in our place, He lived the life we couldn't live, and He died the death we couldn't die. When He rose from the dead, He didn't just give us hope, He promised anyone who believed in Him the gift of eternal life. You don't need to keep striving to prove yourself anymore. He is willing to pardon and forgive you already, just as you are, even though you're guilty and don't deserve it. None of us deserve it, Michael; that's the point. I don't deserve it any more than you and yet I know that I'm loved to the core anyway. You see, the gospel changes everything.

"God is willing to reach into your mess, not because of any merit you have or anything good that you've done, but just because He is kind, loving, and merciful. It's just what He does, He washes the people who don't deserve it clean and renews them.

"Religious people try to earn forgiveness, and religion often makes people feel as if they'll never be good enough, but that's not the gospel. If you only knew how much God loves you and were willing to accept what He's done for you, you wouldn't feel guilt, you wouldn't feel shame, you wouldn't feel insecure. You wouldn't need to desperately search for affirmation and value in all these places that can't satisfy. If you knew the gospel, you would be satisfied, secure, and confident."

For years, I'd seen the Bible as a book of fairytales, and yet he talked as if it would be reasonable for me to base my life and wellbeing on it. As I reflected on his statements, I realized my own life experiences testified that every word he spoke was true. The nature, heart, and character of the God He was talking about was indisputably the One who had been there in that jail cell with me and wiped my slate clean.

He continued, "If you want to follow God, you have to turn away from whatever it is you were trusting and instead turn to Him. What do you turn to when you're having a hard time to make you feel better and to give you relief, confidence, hope, or pleasure? Whatever you turn to, that's the thing you worship. That's the thing you love most. Whatever is at the core of your life, that's the thing you are actively turning to and trusting in to give meaning to your life and help you through the hard times. That thing is your functional god. If you put drugs or money or sex in the center, your wellbeing will be dependent on those things. In essence, they will rule you."

I remember looking at him impatiently and saying, "Everyone looks to those things for pleasure. Why would I give them up just because you tell me to?"

I remember Samuel smiling at me encouragingly, with all the patience in the world. "I'm not telling you to do anything; you can do as you wish. I just want you to know that those things will have negative consequences. I have a feeling that you can tell me more reasons why you shouldn't let those things rule your life than I can, but the decision is still in your hands. I just want you to see things clearly, not just for the initial thrill they might bring, but the whole picture, the long-term cost, and everything else. The more you indulge in these things now, the more tied up with them you will become, and the longer it will take for you to gain stability and heal. More importantly, trying to remove these things on your own will only lead to greater emptiness. Unless you replace these desires with something better and more fulfilling, you will always feel like you are missing out by abstaining from them.

"There will be times when your strength isn't enough, when you struggle, and relapse, and feel like a total failure. If you base your identity on Him, your performance doesn't have to define who you are anymore. You will know that you are fully adored, and wholly accepted in both good times and bad. If, however, you base your identity on your ability to abstain from substances you will be just as empty and unstable as you were when you based your identity on substances. Jesus offers a type of peace that the world cannot offer (John 14:27). The "peace" that the world gives is fleeting and never fully satisfies. The peace that Jesus gives is real and lasting. It's everything you've been looking for. I can promise you that.

"It breaks my heart to see the enemy stealing from you, killing you from the inside out, and destroying your life (John 10:10). You think you've been in control this whole time, but you've been letting darkness rule your life. It doesn't have to be this way. There is something better. Jesus isn't some cosmic killjoy; He is the only one who knows why you're here and what you were made for. He alone can lead you into true and lasting joy. As He said, 'I have told you this so that my joy may be in you and that your joy may be complete' (John 15:11). Just stop trying to play God and let Him call the shots for once."

My response to the man surprised me: it was anger. I remember a few solitary tears dripping down my cheeks, but when my head cleared, I had nothing but a determined resolution to prove him wrong. To prove that I could put my life together and figure things out by myself. I didn't need Christianity in order to get my life together. I had my own set of beliefs and my own worldview, and the Christian God simply did not fit into my paradigms. At the end of our conversation, I remember fuming with anger and throwing my cigarettes away, determining to never buy nicotine again. The last words I said to him were, "I'll change on my own; I don't need help from anyone."

***

"MICHAEL!!!" the shrill voice permeated the darkness.

"MICHAEL, WHERE ARE YOU?!"

I jolted upright, trying not to fall off my perch.

I tried shouting back at the darkness, "I can't get down, I'll try to find a way in the morning!" But the voices in the darkness could not hear me. At the top of my croaky lungs, I shouted again and again until my dry throat was too parched to keep it up any longer. I was screaming now, at the top of my lungs, angry that they were forcing me to yell like this, but no matter how loud I yelled, they still couldn't hear me.

I could see an echoed haze of a spotlight now; they were shining it everywhere in a desperate search for me. Even if they had Search and Rescue out looking for me, no one was going to make it up that cliff at night. As the spotlight beamed upwards through the dark night sky, I wondered why I could hear them so well when they couldn't hear me at all. Finally, I realized their voices must've been echoing up the canyon walls while mine was sifted away by the raging wind at the top of the exposed cliff face. After what seemed like hours of shouting back and forth, the voices finally quieted, and I lay back down.

The looming impermanent type of cold that can only be found in the desert in the dead of night descended upon me. I began shivering fiercely. The skin of my arms and legs pressed against the hard cold rock sandwiched between it and the cold air that blew fiercely around me. I scrunched my body into a ball under the tank top, hoping that it might dull the sharp cold or trap some of my escaping body heat. I closed my eyes again, hoping for sleep, but my shivering was interrupted by little drops of rain that pelted me, sending goosebumps across my body.

It began raining harder and my thoughts drifted towards the waterfall from the night before. I wondered if the water might work itself into a frenzy around me and drag me down the cliff with it. Flash floods were common in this type of landscape; they came every time it rained. It kept coming down, harder and harder. I cozied up closer to the frigid rock and buried myself deeper in my tank top. By this point, the rain was building into streams and flowing off the rocks around me. I sat there in the fetal position, wondering if the rain was going to sweep me from my feeble perch and down into the dark abyss.

I couldn't stand it anymore. "Please!" I shouted. "Please make it stop! You're right… I need You… I can't do this on my own. I'm tired of trying. I need help. I've needed help for a long time."

As if in direct response to my prayer, the rain let up, like someone turning off a faucet.

Apparently, the miserable rain had a purpose.

"Thank you," I said, and I resumed my shivering, gazing up into the sky until dawn broke through and the stars themselves started to fade. I couldn't sleep for even a minute that night. All that night I lay up shivering and thinking about the brevity of life. How one misstep can take any of us out of the game indefinitely. I thought about the style of life I'd chosen and where it had led me. I hoped with all my might that I'd be able to change.

I realized I'd been teetering on a cliff for a very long time now. I needed to find something stable to build my life on, something solid and reliable. I would need help, but after tonight, I realized I hadn't ever been entirely alone in this battle. At first light, the moment the hue of the darkness began to lift, I forced myself to get up and take my first wobbly step towards freedom.

I cried out, and He answered. He helped me, just like He had every other time. I thought of the Milky Way and those magnificent and grandiose beams of light, tunneling downwards. Then I thought about how the God who'd created all of that kept answering my prayers and inserting Himself, a Being more glorious and powerful than those incalculably massive stars, into my life.

I scoured the cliffs for an hour until I finally found a place where I could get down. It wasn't pretty, but it was my best shot. I grabbed hold of the ridge and lowered myself, knowing that by hanging off the ledge, I could shorten the drop by about six feet. After dangling there, I dropped about fifteen feet onto a three-foot overhang. When I peered over the ledge of this second overhang, I realized my next jump would be almost twenty feet down, even after lowering myself. I looked back up to see if I could turn around, but the ridge above me was far out of reach. With no way back, I committed to my path. Luckily, I had been doing parkour for years and had trained myself to jump off houses, trees, and balconies, without injury. Still, this was high even for me. I leapt, trying not to sprain anything on my landing, luckily this ridge was about seven feet in diameter, a landing ground that I needed.

The next leap was only 10 feet and the one after that 15. After a few more, I looked up at the soaring 100-foot giant that towered above me, grateful to be down. I traipsed across the rocky slope for about a mile before the rocks merged with the water and disappeared. I jumped into the water, shoes and all, treading, pushing, fighting to get home. I gulped down mouthful after mouthful of the murky water, never having been thirstier in my life. Not caring one bit that people I knew had personally used the lake as their own public toilet. I swam until I felt like I would drown as my waterlogged shoes pulled at me. It was just then that I saw a little rock overhang, just wide enough for me to sit on, cross-legged, if I could manage the strength to pull myself up out of the water. I sat there, breathing heavily, with my eyes closed, until finally, at 6:30 in the morning my parents' boat came flying around the corner to rescue me.

"But you are my witnesses… You are my servant. You have been chosen to know me, believe in me, and understand that I alone am God. There is no other God—there never has been, and there never will be. I, yes I, am the Lord, and there is no other Savior. First, I predicted your rescue, then I saved you and proclaimed it to the world." —*Isaiah 43:10-12* (NLT)

Chapter Twenty-One

The Cycles, Faith & Science

"I said to myself, "Come on, let's try pleasure. Let's look for the 'good things' in life." But I found that this, too, was meaningless. Anything I wanted, I would take. I denied myself no pleasure. I even found great pleasure in hard work, a reward for all my labors. But as I looked at everything I had worked so hard to accomplish, it was all so meaningless—like chasing the wind. There was nothing really worthwhile anywhere." — *Ecclesiastes 2:1,10-11* (NLT)

I knew that I needed to change, but the way I kept approaching it was centered entirely around myself. I was tired of a lifestyle that kept leading me to teetering cliffs and stranding me there, but I didn't know any better way, other than trying harder and doing more. Even if I wanted to, I did not know how to have a relationship with God. Even after seeing spiritual things happen, I wasn't able to simply drop the secular beliefs that I held dear and start believing in God. I wasn't willing to base my beliefs solely on my experiences, I needed to base them on logic, rationality, empiricism, and reality itself. If I wanted to find truth, I would have to open myself up to every answer and possibility, even the beliefs that I had always been biased against, like Christianity.

Now that I was in college, I was learning all sorts of interesting things. One professor taught me that the cause of humanity was a bomb, an explosion of cosmic proportions. When I asked my professor, "Don't bombs create chaos?" he just agreed and said that this was different because it was a very big bomb. So, I asked, "Wouldn't it create even more chaos in that case? Isn't expecting an explosion to create organisms, and structured society like dropping a nuke on a city and expecting it to reconstruct itself and build itself new buildings without any other intervening forces. What could those intervening forces have been?"

I wondered how on earth educated people could assume that accidental explosions created intelligent life, but the only answer I could find was time. But the idea that if you drop enough bombs over a long enough period of time, eventually one of them will defy the laws of physics did not make sense to me. According to Newton's third law (for every action, there is an equal and opposite reaction), if the reaction, the end result, the world we now live in is structured, organized, and intelligent, then the cause must have also been structured, organized, and intelligent. If the cause were a bomb, or an explosion, then the reaction, the world we now live in, would also be an explosion. Since Newton's third law is a law and the big bang theory is only a theory, I decided to trust the law over the theory, which meant someone intelligent must have created us.

By the end of the summer, I finished my associate's degree and was accepted into the University of Utah. I kept myself constantly busy with full-time college and three part-time jobs. I made sure I did not have a single spare moment of time when I could slip up or relapse. When I wasn't doing homework, I would go snowboarding. I tried not to leave any fragment of the day unaccounted for. In addition to helping me maintain sobriety, working like this also allowed me to offset some of my college expenses. I joined the National Society of Leadership and Success [42] and began implementing the principles I learned there toward seeking out truth, which by this point I was certain was a real thing. I switched my major four times during my first year and eventually ended up pursuing a bachelor's in psychology.

As I tried to enter into the world of prosperity and success, I saw that most kids were drinking and partying during the weekends. At first, I was extremely tempted to work hard during the week and party alongside them during the weekends; but I knew how empty it was, so instead, I just hid myself away in my studio apartment and worked. I'd get up at six each day and stay up until around midnight or one. Every morning, I'd brew and drink an entire pot of coffee. I would scurry from class to class and then job to job and then from one homework project to the next. After a while, it started to feel like my constant scrambling for success was just another coping mechanism, another tool to keep me busy so I didn't need to address what was going on inside.

Things were great on the outside; in all practical matters, I was thriving and excelling, so why did it feel empty? I was doing what society said a good, healthy college kid should do, but it was starting to feel just as meaningless and empty as drugs and partying had, maybe even more. I looked around at all the college kids who were getting away from their parents for the first time, all these kids ranting and raving about their first drunk or first high, acting as if they'd made the most remarkable discovery.

They looked like infant children to me, boasting about the mud puddle they'd found, urging everyone to come and play in it. I wondered how many years they would wallow in the mud before they realized there was something more to life than fleeting pleasures. Some would end up like me, throwing their lives away for the rush and thrill of it. I wondered how long it would take them to find out the best that drugs, alcohol, and partying had to offer was fleeting, temporary satisfaction that led to dependency and a compromised ability to find joy without those things. The more they turned to those things, the more their emotional, social, and psychological wellbeing would become dependent on them, and the harder it would be to be happy without them.

For about six months, I inwardly mocked the other students and judged them for just barely beginning to embark on a path that I had already thoroughly explored. As I worked my many jobs and aced my classes, I started to feel superior to my contemporaries. Then I started another semester and started doing the same things over again: Honor roll, dean's list, 4.0 grade average, leadership, first job, second job, third job, coffee pot, homework, hit the sack, repeat, flashback. After so many repetitions, I started to realize that the path of prosperity was not all it was cracked up to be. The pervasive emptiness started creeping back in.

School was starting to feel like yet another cycle, albeit a constructive one. At first, I told myself, *once I get into college, once I get a good job, once I get popular, once I get ripped, or recognized, then I'll be happy*. But after each accomplishment, I only experienced temporary satisfaction. Each time, I would reassess, set higher goals, and work harder, saying, *once I meet this goal, then I'll be happy. Once I get a career in my field, once I find the right woman and make a family, then my life will have meaning.* I worked rigorously. When I finally accomplished my goals, I felt proud and excited, but it never lasted long.

Each time around the cycle, we make slight modifications, adjusting our objectives, goals, and methods slightly, confident that this time, we will finally be satisfied.

We keep telling ourselves, *you'll be so much happier when you find something better.* And then we do find something better but still aren't any happier. We get the dream home only to be overwhelmed by the mortgage, the dream job only to find that we now have no time to have friends or a social life. We get so loaded we don't need to worry about money anymore, only to find that people are using us for our wealth, and our family is looking more forward to our death and their inheritance than they are to family time and our wellbeing. We realize that even after accomplishing our goals, we still have to face ourselves at the end of the day.

If you would like more information about the Cycle of Fleeting Pleasures or a free pdf download please visit www.michaeljheil.com/addiction-cycle-graphs.

It didn't seem to matter whether the goals I set were constructive or destructive, both led to cycles that felt like hamster wheels with occasional treats. The constructive goals like careers, vacations, degrees, adventures, luxury and status seemed just as futile as the destructive goals like drinking, drugging, sexing, relationships, and partying. None of them brought lasting objective and subjective meaning to life. At best, they gave a temporary blip of euphoria before they faded into obscurity.

If you would like free pdf downloads on constructive cycles, destructive cycles, and habit formation, or are reading the audio version please visit www.michaeljheil.com/addiction-cycle-graphs.

Ford, Rockefeller, and countless other millionaires, after expending the majority of their lives in the pursuit of money, came to the realization that prosperity could not satisfy. Rockefeller must've been keying into the futility of these cycles when he said, "I have made many millions, but they have brought me no happiness."

The most prominent example in history of someone reaching the apex of prosperity is Solomon, king of Israel. He lived the majority of his lavish life enjoying the things the rest of us endlessly strive to obtain. In regard to wealth, his passive income was 50,000 pounds of gold per year (1 Kings 10:24). He accumulated such a large percentage of the world's silver into his capital city that it was considered worthless and was more plentiful than stone (1 Kings 10:21, 27).

He ruled with such wisdom and insight that his fame spread throughout the known world. He built palaces, terraces, temples, and mansions of such glory and splendor they were unlike the world had ever seen or imagined. In regard to women, he had 700 wives and 300 concubines! He would have to sleep with a different woman every night for three years in a row just to cycle through all of the women married to him and start again! In addition, he was the CEO, president, and king of a million employees, international infrastructure with a $1,169,600,000 passive annual revenue.

Solomon is said to have been the wisest and wealthiest man who ever lived. He had authority, power, wealth, money, women, fame, and everything else a person could ask for. And yet, after experiencing, accomplishing, meriting, and obtaining all of this, he said, "I have seen all the things that are done under the sun; all of them are meaningless, a chasing after the wind." He writes that without God, human wisdom, the accumulation of possessions, labor, work, power, authority, competition, and success are all meaningless because when we die, they all amount to nothing. He even indicated that religion was meaningless; without God, there was no one to worship, and there was no reason to do good or avoid bad.

Without God, the end reward of the wicked is the same as that of the righteous; we all die and turn to dirt. By choosing to believe that the universe is meaningless, we free ourselves to live and do whatever we want, but we also doom ourselves to a worldview that ends in despair. If everything is happenstance, if there is no afterlife, no eternity, no judgement day, no God, then there is no ultimate hope or justice.

In an earthbound perspective that excludes all consideration of God, there will be no day of reckoning. The good will die young, nice guys will finish last, and the murderers, rapists, and warmongers will never be held accountable for their actions. Humans will continue to be free to act like animals, biting and devouring one another. If there is no God, or Creator (no one outside the cycle) all our greatest feats and accomplishments will disappear when we die. Like chasing the wind, whatever we gain, we will eventually lose. Not only will we be forgotten when everyone we know dies, but even the greatest legacies will equate to nothing on the day that the sun burns out and the human race is no more.

If there is no judgement day for the world, when all of humanity's evil deeds are accounted for and squared away, what hope is there for humanity? And yet, if there is a judgement day when each of us is held accountable to our own actions, what hope is there for us as individuals, since each of us has failed?

If God accepts each of us as we are, without holding us accountable to our actions, He would be choosing to allow the evil, bitterness, cruelty, injustice, lying, hatred, division, and oppression of humankind to continue unhampered. If He accepts us just as we are, what hope is there that the world will change? What hope is there for the world? The Bible, the biblical God, says He will square everything away. There will not be one unjust deed left unaccounted for. The biblical God says either you will pay for your own deeds or, if you trust in Him, my Son will pay on your behalf. Either way, not one unjust deed will be unaccounted for.

***

With access to the university libraries, I decided to embark on an intense journey of reflection, study, and introspection. As I did so, I realized that our beliefs and philosophies are the foundation upon which we build our lives and find our meaning. In essence, our core beliefs construct our identity. My belief that there was no objective right or wrong allowed me to justify drug use, sleeping around, and rebellion. My belief that there was no God allowed me to feel like I could do whatever I wanted and get away with it. The philosophies I believed in constructed my worldview and contributed to the sort of lifestyle I chose.

I kept getting angry at everyone who disagreed with me. I claimed that there was no truth, yet I got upset when other people disagreed with me or held a different perspective about my identity group than I did. If someone thought drugs were lame when I thought they were cool, I hated them and rebelled against them. This kept happening with my family, the police, and the authorities. If someone thought drugs were cool when I thought they were lame, I made fun of them. This kept happening with other college students. I realized that I was full of biases that were continually shifting and changing as I acquired more information. It wasn't until I looked past my biases that I could understand the biases of others. It wasn't until I doubted my biases that I could be free of them.

Doubt didn't help me grow, or heal, or progress, but asking the right questions and finding answers to those questions did, especially when I was willing to listen to answers, ideas, and philosophies that contradicted my inherent biases. I was biased against religion, morality, and all constructs of objective good and bad. I didn't want there to be a God, so I immediately discredited every philosophy surrounding Him. At the same time, since it seemed like my entire culture was saying there was no absolute truth, I decided the belief was credible without ever actually researching it. I didn't realize that the statement "there are no absolute truths" is an absolute truth claim. I also didn't realize that the more people say there is no absolute truth, the more offended they seem to get when someone challenges their particular set of truth claims.

The truth claims and belief systems that we adhere to make up our worldview. Each worldview makes claims about the beginning, middle, and end of humanity. In other words, our worldview explains our origin, our purpose, and our end destination. As I studied, I realized that all the various worldviews could be broken down into two categories: the humanistic group which claims that humanity is all there is, or the deistic group which claims there is a creator or some form of intelligent designer.

The secular/humanistic worldview teaches that the beginning or origin of humankind is a cosmic mishap. There is no Creator and no intentionality in creation, just chance. As the evolutionary biologist Stephen J. Gould put it, "We are here because one odd group of fishes had a peculiar fin anatomy that could transform into legs for terrestrial creatures… We may yearn for a 'higher' answer — but none exists" [27]. The end result of this worldview is that once we die, we exist no more. If our source is meaningless and our end is meaningless, would it not be logically consistent to say that the middle (the present) is also meaningless? What does this worldview teach about the middle? It teaches that after the first living organisms inexplicably exploded into existence, they went through evolution, natural selection, and survival of the fittest, otherwise known as Darwinism.

Darwinism teaches that we are, and have always been, animals competing with one another for dominance and survival. Charles Darwin in *The Descent of Man* wrote, "With savages, the weak in body or mind are soon eliminated; and those that survive commonly exhibit a vigorous state of health. We civilized men, on the other hand, do our utmost to check the process of elimination; we build asylums for the imbecile, the maimed, and the sick; we institute poor-laws; and our medical men exert their utmost skill to save the life of every one to the last moment…this must be highly injurious to the race of man… Care wrongly directed, leads to the degeneration of a domestic race; but excepting in the case of man himself, hardly any one is so ignorant as to allow his worst animals to breed" [28].

According to these theories, in order for our species to thrive, the weak must die out. It is not only okay for the weak to die, but essential. It is best for our species if the oppressed, the addicted, and the afflicted die, because it will rid our gene pool of the weak. Those at the top of the food chain can do whatever they want, even if it means harming and exploiting others, because as long as they reproduce their dominant genes, they will give future generations of humanity a better shot. This is what an existence looks like that is reduced to evolutionary biology and is void of morality.

If our end and origin are meaningless and, in the middle, we are hapless, competing creatures, then why do we grieve the prospect of death? Why do we care when people get hurt or suffer? Why do we long to be reunited with our lost loved ones? Why do we yearn for permanence? Why is there something inside of us that cries out for justice when this worldview teaches the strong should live, and the weak should die?

It wasn't just the fact that I desired some sort of meaning in life that drove me to God, it was also logic, empiricism, and science. "A growing number of respectable scientists are defecting from the evolutionist camp… these 'experts' have abandoned Darwinism, not on the basis of religious faith or biblical persuasions, but on scientific grounds, and in some instances, regretfully" [29]. Dr. George Wald, professor emeritus of biology at Harvard University and Nobel Prize winner in biology said, "There are only two possibilities as to how life arose. One is spontaneous generation arising to evolution; the other is a supernatural creative act of God. There is no third possibility. Spontaneous generation, (the idea) that life arose from non-living matter was scientifically disproved 120 years ago by Louis Pasteur and others. That leaves us with the only possible conclusion that life arose as a supernatural creative act of God. I will not accept that philosophically because I do not want to believe in God. Therefore, I choose to believe in that which I know is scientifically impossible; spontaneous generation arising to evolution" [26].

The biologist Ludwig Von Bertalanffy said, "The fact that a theory so vague, so insufficiently verifiable, and so far from the criteria otherwise applied in 'hard' science has become a dogma can only be explained on sociological grounds" [30]. The physicist H.S. Lipson said, "I think we need to go further than this and admit that the only acceptable explanation is creation. I know this is an anathema to physicists, as indeed it is to me, but we must not reject a theory that we do not like if the experimental evidence supports it" [43].

Even science was pointing me towards a Creator, if I would only lay down my biases and listen, maybe I could find Him. Fred Hoyle, the mathematician, astronomer, and cosmologist who developed the theory of stellar nucleosynthesis and coined the phrase "Big Bang" said, "Once we see that the probability of life originating at random is so utterly minuscule as to make it absurd, it becomes sensible to think that the favorable properties of physics on which life depends are in every respect deliberate....it is therefore almost inevitable that our own measure of intelligence must reflect...higher intelligences...even to the limit of God...such a theory is so obvious that one wonders why it is not widely accepted as being self-evident" [44].

The deistic worldviews that I had studied and entertained until this point had been confusing and ultimately unhelpful for my condition. For the first time in my life, I decided to study the biblical account, to which I had always held a subtle animosity. The biblical worldview claims that humans are the result of an intentional act, meaning we are here with purpose. It also claims that humans are made in the image of God, and therefore, each human life contains inherent value. Since this is our origin, humans are designed to love, care, serve, honor, and value one another. Regardless of whether we like each other or not, we are to see each human life as precious, and treat it as such. Though we do harm each other, sin, and act like animals at times, God has provided a future of hope for anyone who would turn from wicked things towards Him. This worldview claims that the beginning, middle, and end are all meaningful. It claims that human life holds value, not because of each individual's accomplishments, or ability to dominate and outpace others, but because of their composition; not because of what they've done, or merited, but because of who made them and what He made them for.

The Christian worldview teaches that we are more than an accident and there is more to our existence than biology and self-satisfaction. It teaches that every human is a complex and dynamic physical, intellectual, emotional, and spiritual being who has been intentionally created for a purpose, and who is loved deeply by their Creator. If I believed in this worldview, I would turn to God for my purpose and satisfaction instead of trying to find value in drugs, friendships, relationships, money, success, prosperity and other fleeting things. I would understand these things aren't capable of meeting all my needs (spiritual, emotional, intellectual, and physical) and would therefore stop spending my time and energy seeking them. I could stop flitting around the cycle like a moth around a light. But would trusting someone outside of the cycle and beyond myself really make that much of a difference?

I never liked religion, but I also never knew exactly what it was. As I studied various definitions of religion, I found that its main objective was to provide people with beliefs and practices that help them find meaning, purpose, and beauty in life, as well as to help them process and deal with death. Religion gives people a narrative, an answer to the question of where they came from and where they are going. Our narrative helps us understand how and why we ought to live a certain way. Religion provides the why to our existence. Even atheists have a philosophy or belief system that explains where they came from, where they are going, and why they exist.

Religion is just a fancy word for a belief system. Belief systems, by nature, demand exclusive devotion to their particular set of "truth" claims. Once we latch onto a set of truth claims, we are almost required to start rejecting alternative truth claims, and therefore, alternative religions. Each belief system has rules, rites, and rituals that are designed to build on one another. My whole life, I was taught evolution. I did not know that it was a religion, but since it told me the purpose and nature of my existence, where I came from, and where I am going, it fit the definition perfectly. It was the meta-narrative that I based my life on and fit my life into.

Evolution ultimately tells us the "why" and "what" of our existence. Since it is taught by the education system as fact, and the education system is supposed to be unbiased and objective, then whatever else we choose to believe must first be viewed through the lens of evolution if it is to be true. If we want to be considered intellectual, the acceptance of this theory is our only way to do so. Additionally, we are taught that all forms of religion are subjective and unscientific. Phillip Johnson, in the PBS documentary *In The Beginning: The Creationist Controversy* said, "Darwinian theory is the creation myth of our culture. It's the officially sponsored, government financed creation myth that the public is supposed to believe in, and that creates the evolutionary scientists as the priesthood."

It really doesn't matter what we think of evolution, the fact is that all American public-school systems teach it. Starting in sixth grade science and through college, this theory demands increasing devotion. With this type of education, it's difficult to take any set of religious truth claims seriously. Not only does evolution meet all of our religious needs, but it is also presented as the only logical and empirical option.

In many first world countries, school systems teach several explanations for life on earth, and they present each of them as theories, not fact. Evolution is one of the many theories and so is creationism. They present the evidence for both belief systems, as well as the areas in which the evidence is lacking. And they investigate all the reasons why both theories are viable explanations for life on earth. My education was different. I learned that evolution was the only viable explanation and I came away with the impression that it was the ultimate truth that I needed to sculpt my reality around. I didn't mind this because it enabled me to justify the reckless lifestyle and actions I wanted, but if I'd had the choice I would have preferred an unbiased education where I could've learned about each viable theory.

George Kocan, in *Evolution isn't Faith But Theory* wrote, "Unfortunately many scientists and non-scientists have made Evolution into a religion, something to be defended against infidels. In my experience, many students of biology – professors and textbook writers included – have been so carried away with the arguments for Evolution that they neglect to question it. They preach it… College students, having gone through such a closed system of education, themselves become teachers, entering high schools to continue the process, using textbooks written by former classmates… High standards of scholarship and teaching break down… Education becomes a fraud" [31].

The constructs through which evolution is taught and dispersed are what give it so much of its authority. Since it is a belief system that falls under the scientific label, we don't think of it as a belief system but as a scientific theory. And yet, it is both; it is a scientific theory and a belief system. It is a belief system on which people base their existence and identity.

214

We are taught separation of church and state and told that the classroom is not a place for religion, but somehow Darwin's ideas are the exception. Those who go to public school but not church are exclusively taught the evolutionary metanarrative. Those who go to church and school are taught two exclusive metanarratives that inherently contradict one another, yet they are not taught how to hash these ideas out.

It's no wonder so many of my contemporaries mocked religion. It's no wonder Western society is leaving deistic religions in droves and becoming increasingly secular. How could we not, under these paradigms? Still, my journey was forcing me to address these things. When I met a professor from the Faraday Institute for Science and Religion out of Cambridge University, he taught that evolution does not disprove, discredit, or contradict Christianity. Rather, in his lectures, debates, and presentations, he showed countless examples of how there is more science supporting Christianity and creationism than there is supporting evolution.

"Still," he said "I know many Christians who believe in evolution too." "Sorting these things out is the journey of a lifetime. Just because you don't understand everything right now, and you have been taught to focus on the differences, doesn't mean you should let it destroy your faith. And then he introduced us to dozens of books that would help us along in our journey. Science is one of the most limited fields in the sense that it can only study the physical realm. While other disciplines allow us to create things and bring them into existence, science can only observe that which has been created and try to understand it better.

He did not stop there, however, but taught us the history of science. To my surprise the entire field of science was created by Christians who believed that by studying the laws of the universe, and creation itself, they would be able to learn more about the Creator. Newton, Galileo, Kelvin, even Kepler, the father of empiricism himself, and countless others, all studied science because it agreed with, supported, and substantiated their Christian faith and belief in God. Every bit of order, structure, intentionality, and design they saw in the universe helped them better understand the Creator. Since science was created by Christians, people who use science to discredit Christianity are cutting off the root of their own tree.

For some reason, it was important to me to find out all the ways in which Christianity and the Bible lined up with reality: How it taught about crop rotation, diversification, and resting the land over 3,000 years before agricultural science discovered these techniques in the 16th Century, and how the Bible taught extensive hygiene practices that prevented the spread of sickness and disease, such as washing before meals, quarantining when sick, and much more. It taught tall of these thousands of years before the discovery of germs in the 17th Century. It even taught how people should go to a designated area outside the camp to poop, bury it, and cover it up, instead of deucing around town where others can step in it. This may seem like common sense to us now, but it was cutting edge back then.

In 600 BC, one of the biblical prophets even wrote about how the earth is a curved, circular object, that moves and rotates. He recorded this hundreds and even thousands of years before Socrates, Aristotle, Eratosthenes, Galileo, or Columbus were ever even born. If "the church" is ever credited for having believed in a flat earth (like the rest of the world did), it is only because they disbelieved God's Word.

"All who make idols are nothing, and the things they treasure are worthless. Those who would speak up for them are blind; they are ignorant, to their own shame. Who shapes a god and casts an idol, which can profit nothing? People who do that will be put to shame; such craftsmen are only human beings. Let them all come together and take their stand; they will be brought down to terror and shame." —*Isaiah 44:9-11*

Chapter Twenty-Two

Eudaimonic and Hedonic Happiness

"The reason I was born and came into the world is to testify to the truth. Everyone on the side of truth listens to me." — John 18:37

I believed the only way to find truth was by asking questions and analyzing the evidence. If this God really did create all things, then I should be able to find evidence of Him in all fields of science, sociology, history, anthropology, psychology, physiology, philosophy, and reason itself. Thousands of years ago, the Greeks figured out that there are two different types of happiness. Hedonic happiness happens when we feel good and get the things we want. Eudaimonic happiness, on the other hand, refers to having a meaning for our life or a purpose for our existence. Even the creators of hedonism knew that we must find a purpose for our existence that goes beyond simply making ourselves feel good.

Aristotle said that people who only live for hedonic happiness are reduced to an animal-like existence. If the main purpose of our lives is to make ourselves feel good, we are like the animals, chasing our next meal, solely fixated on short-term gratification. Yet we live in an era when hedonism is at the center of every advertisement, every billboard, every app, and interaction, and consumerism makes the task of pleasing ourselves increasingly more convenient and important. Many of our cultural beliefs, teachings, and practices revolve around temporary pleasure and satisfaction.

Our culture is good at finding hedonic happiness. What we are not so good at is finding eudaimonic happiness. We live in an era of secularism where, for the first time in history, the widespread belief is that there is no ultimate hope or purpose for our existence. Hedonic pursuits are enjoyable, but they are not a sufficient purpose for which to live. Without eudaimonic happiness, it doesn't matter how hedonistic we are, or how much we satisfy ourselves, it will likely be void of purpose and meaning.

I was beginning to think there was no adequate reason for our existence. I realized that so long as the main pursuit of my life boiled down to hedonism that I was more like the hamster on the wheel than I cared to admit.

As I watched the people around me chase different things, I realized I wasn't the only one on a hamster wheel. Many college students think that partying on the weekends and filling their lives with one-night stands is the path towards satisfaction. Many adults think that education, success, luxury, vacationing and wealth are better paths. I had hoped so as well, but they were proving to be just as empty. The harder I ran towards success, the more burnt out I felt.

It was at this low point, when I was growing increasingly convinced that human life was futile, that a group of Christians broke through to me. At first, I was annoyed with them and I wanted them to stop pestering me. Pepper, Gerry, and Jam. They were the first three people I met at the University of Utah and I met them my first night on campus. They sat with genuine smiles spread across their faces. Their eyes were lit up with joy as they told us about Jesus until three in the morning. I had met quite a few church-goers before, but I hadn't met born-again Christians who were my age. If I had met them, I'd always judged them. I'd never been willing to get to know them. Now that I was, I found them to be the most peculiar creatures I had ever encountered.

After that first night, I expected not to see them again, as the campus was massive, and none of us had the same major. None of us lived near one another and all of us were in different grades. Yet, everywhere I went, I kept running into these same three individuals. Even though there were well over 30,000 students on campus, these same three popped up everywhere I went. At first, it seemed like an uncanny coincidence. My whole life had been void of these types of caricatures, now they were everywhere. In reality, God was pursuing me; He refused to let me slip through the cracks. I thought once I'd

218

gotten my associate's degree and moved away from Samuel, that obnoxious man at UVU, that I'd left the Christians in my dust. I was wrong.

I was busy enough between my various jobs and classes to justify brushing them off and ignoring them, but every time they saw me, they ran to greet me. When they asked me how I was doing, I could tell they cared. They listened to my answers carefully and poured encouragement into me when they could. Each time they saw me they'd invite me to a Bible study and I would politely decline. They would smile and say, "No problem, let us know if there's anything else we can do for you. Hope to see you around!" I had spurned their invitations enough that they should've known I wasn't interested, but they seemed to see past my calloused outer shell.

After several months of seeing these same three individuals everywhere, one of them finally convinced me to join their study by telling me that there would be girls and food there. *Girls and food*, I thought. I decided to join him, and he wasn't wrong. The biggest problem for me was that I wasn't sure how to connect with girls who had morals. I found it very alarming that they managed to "kindly" spurn all of my advances. I mean, who knew that you could be rejected with kindness?

They didn't seem to need alcohol or drugs to be happy, or confident, or to have a good time. They seemed to get high off life itself and frequently delighted in the simple things. They were generous and would offer to buy my meal whenever we went out. In the end, it was their kindness that drew me back, not just the girls, but all of them. I was used to friends keeping me around because I could get them drugs, get them invited to the trendiest parties. I was used to friends who would lie to me and sleep with my girlfriend. I was used to friends who always measured me and compared themselves to me, friends who discarded me as soon as they realized I wasn't game for whatever it was they were scheming. These people were so kind that it confused me. They actually cared about me, who I was, my past, my problems. And they wanted the best for me.

I was always comparing myself to others and scorning those I thought I knew better than. First, I scorned religious people in favor of partying; now I was scorning partiers in favor of prosperity and education. It was not until I met the Christians that I learned how to love others and stop judging them. They taught me where true security comes from. They taught me to be satisfied in God so that I didn't need to use other people or compare myself to them.

They taught me to have one focus, to live for an audience of one, and that no one else's opinion mattered. They taught me that God loved others as much as He loved me. They taught me that my own reservoirs of love, patience, and forgiveness were not enough, but that I could draw from God. They helped me to forgive Rogue and Graham and Denny and Adalyn. They taught me how to move on and stop letting the past interfere with the present. They taught me how to trust again.

My new friends took me on road trips, too. During spring break, we hit seven national and state parks in seven days. These weirdoes spent every morning studying the Bible and prayed all throughout the day. They stopped on top of the most epic cliff you could ever imagine, just to praise God for it and talk about the mystical process that had created it. Gerry was fascinated with geology and loved telling us gruelingly specific details about the rock formations. The part that intrigued me the most was when they shared their stories and shared about how they came to be Christians. These Christians were not like any I'd ever met before. I soon learned that not everyone who bears the label "Christian" is the same. Up to this point, I had thought that they were all brainwashed fanatics, but very nice, brainwashed fanatics. I presumed that none of them had a clue what the real world was like.

When Jam spoke up and started sharing his story, he told me how he'd been a stoner. At this point, my eyes lit up with anticipation. He shared about how he would deal heavy quantities of weed until one day he got detained in Las Vegas. They caught him with a half-ounce and wrote him a ticket for peddling that would likely put him in jail for two years. When he went back for the court date, he decided to take a homeless man to breakfast while he waited for the courts to open. During that breakfast, the homeless man started ministering to him about Jesus. My friend broke down and shared his whole story, and the homeless man prayed for a miracle, asking God to forgive him and give him a new path forward. Despite Jam's feeling that things were a little backward, he thanked the homeless man and headed to the courthouse, ready to fess up to his crimes and face whatever penalties lay ahead for him.

"Give me your name," the lady at the front counter shouted at him condescendingly.

After telling her his full name, she said, "You're not in our system."

He froze, anxiety hitting the roof.

"There must be a mistake," he responded. "Look, here is my citation."

Puzzled, she checked the system again, using the citation to check the proper spelling.

"My God, this must be your lucky day, son. Someone's sure looking out for you. You're not in the system; you've got no business with the court."

Flustered, he said, "C'mon, if I miss my court date, they'll lock me up for even longer. You've got to find my info. It's got to be in there."

Getting impatient now, she looked him straight in the eye and said, "You are not going to court. Your crimes have been erased. Now get out of here."

In a manic episode, he searched the city for the homeless man who had prayed for him, but to no avail. Overflowing with gratitude, he wanted to thank the man and tell him about the miracle that had happened in response to his prayer. Unlike me, he maintained his enthusiasm for Jesus with an inextinguishable passion from that day forward. Upon hearing his story, I realized that at one point, some of these Jesus freaks had once been cool, too. I wondered what had happened, but I decided that my new friends weren't as lame as I initially thought.

The surprising thing was that they didn't care what I thought about them; they cared about me. Even though I'd inwardly made fun of them for their Bible studies, sharing their life stories, and praying, I couldn't stop thinking about how joyful they were. How utterly different they were from any other people I'd ever met. We went on many adventures to Zion, Arches, Canyonlands, Bryce Canyon, Capitol Reef, Grand Canyon, Monument Valley, the Petrified Forest, and more. Each time I was with them, we laughed until we cried and then some more. But each time I came home, I would experience a sense of emptiness. A void that I tried to distract myself from through incessant work and study. I knew it was God who made all the difference in their lives, but I didn't know how to trust in Him like they did.

"I am the way and the truth and the life. No one comes to the Father except through me." —*John 14:6*

Chapter Twenty-Three

Something More Than Chasing the Wind

By this point I was 19, and by some miracle I'd managed to not get arrested for a full year. Although I was no longer using drugs, my inner hippie could not resist the temptation to stand out and make a name for myself. College was the chance to redefine myself, I thought. So, I called myself Mac and really started flaunting my shoelessness. I kept telling myself that I wasn't doing it for attention, but because I liked the way the bare ground felt beneath my feet. That perspective quickly changed once the winter months hit, and I found myself trudging around the steep mountain campus barefoot in the snow. By that point, I'd committed myself so much to the idea that I wasn't willing to give it up. Instead, I just drove as close to my class as I could and bore the cold the rest of the way. Now that my identity was no longer in my drug stories or rebellious accomplishments, these attention-seeking quirks were all that distinguished me.

When scattered blades of yellow grass started sticking up out of the snow, we knew that spring break was near, and our group planned another road trip. When Gerry stopped by my place to pick me up, I threw my bag in the back and hopped in the passenger seat. He looked down at my feet to double-check my status.

"Mike," he said, "where are your shoes?"

"C'mon Ger, you know I don't wear shoes."

"Mike, we are going to be hiking the Grand Canyon, climbing through slot canyons, and traversing mountains. You need shoes."

I rebutted a half dozen times until finally, he said, "Either go get your shoes or get out of my truck."

I went back into my house and dug through my closet for a while until I finally located an old pair of sneakers that I hadn't worn in almost a year. I carried them out begrudgingly and tossed them in the back of the truck.

"You happy?" I asked.

During the drive, he refused to let us listen to anything other than Christian music. He later showed us an eleven-hour documentary called *They Sold Their Souls to Rock N Roll* that explained why. I thought he was a total nut job. We made several stops along the way for potty breaks, stopping at a few rest stops and gas stations. I went in barefoot without thinking twice. Gerry was appalled and took on the role of my mother, explaining to me how unsanitary my behavior was.

"You're going to get yourself sick," he said.

I told him that my feet were so calloused that it was basically like wearing shoes; I just used my own leather instead of someone else's. I guess bacteria is insensitive to things like that, however, because I was starting to develop some wicked indigestion.

We drove through the towering walls of Zion National Park and shimmied our way up the beautiful cliff face on the far end. The route lead us through a majestic tunnel carved into the heart of the red rock giant. The tunnel was pitch black except for a few holes engraved like windows in the belly of a beast. The first thing that Gerry did was turn his lights off so we were cloaked in total darkness. He honked erratically as we floated through empty space towards a singular pocket of light a few hundred feet in front of us. As we passed the solitary opening, he slowed to a stop, and we were surprised to find a clear view of the cliffs opposite us.

He flashed his lights as if to give us a glimpse of how long the tunnel was before returning us to a state of total darkness. A pair of lights appeared, looking like a glowing speck in the distance. He continued to drive with his lights off as our two vehicles gradually approached one another. When we were close enough to differentiate the single golden speck into two approaching headlights, he flipped his lights on. The beams of light met in a collision of color, and the illuminated tunnel seemed to open up. The two vehicles crept past each other at a slow crawl until, finally, the tunnel dropped us on a winding road in a barren desert.

Our first hike was through Water Holes Slot Canyon, a majestic canyon on sanctioned Native American land just outside of Page, Arizona. I had successfully managed to not wear my shoes this far into the journey, but my luck was about to run out. As soon as we stopped, Gerry told me that I could either put them on or wait in the car while the rest of the group hiked the canyon. It had been so long since I'd worn shoes that I hadn't even thought about bringing socks. I wasn't sure whether I owned socks anymore.

I wrestled with the shoes, trying to pull them over my cold sandy feet. They felt awkward and uncomfortable. I clumsily ran after the rest of the group as they hadn't bothered to wait for me while I dug my snow embossed shoes out of the back of the truck and put them on. Plop, plop, plop. I felt like a duck out of water. However, the moment we descended into the canyon's steep, glowing rock walls, my insecurities melted away, and my jaw dropped. The walls looked like waves of the sea, frozen in time and imprinted with chunks of sunshine. The walls ran parallel to one another, twisting and turning, but somehow always managing to do so in perfect tandem.

Rays of sunshine beamed through the narrow slit at the top of the canyon walls and straight down into the deep shadows of the caverns. It pierced the darkness and, in some strange, fantastical way, the two seemed to make one another more beautiful. The dark and light complemented each other, not in the way that the right shoes complement an appropriately suited outfit, but in the way that life complements death. Without one, you simply can't have the other. Maybe God was doing something like that in my life, too? A deep sense of awe and gratitude for life was beginning to pierce through the shadows and into my heart. It had not dawned on me until this moment (as I watched distinct rays of sunshine breaking into the darkness) that without a shadow, the details of each sunray would be virtually imperceptible.

In the darkness, every ray that broke through was not only noticeable but absolutely brilliant. Although this cavern surely did nothing to make the sun's rays more brilliant than they already were, it did serve to elucidate their existing beauty. In the same way, my chronic brokenness and failures didn't hinder the beauty of what God had done for me. Instead, my mistakes reminded me of the extent He went to in order to forgive me, heal me, and free me.

We went as far as we could until finally the canyon ended at a soft, smooth wall of sandstone that shot abruptly skyward. I immediately took my shoes off, gripped my hands and toes like a chameleon into the porous sandstone wall and began scaling the slippery surface. As I climbed, I turned my gaze upward and fixed it where I wanted to go. At that moment, and from that particular vantage point, I could see the hole in the ceiling through which the light entered the canyon. I smiled as I realized that the walls of the shaft curved up into the shape of a heart around me. As the sun glistened down the column, it beamed like a heart made of sunshine. It was God's heart, and it was enveloping me.

No picture could have more aptly described the feeling of transcendent peace that I felt that day. I was beginning to grow fond of these little love nudges that God kept sending in my direction. I used to be completely incapable of seeing these things, but I was starting to see signs like these more often. Each time I did, I felt like God was winking at me. Not in an attempt to get my attention, but as a reminder that He was near, that He would remain faithful even if I were not. I wondered how many times He'd displayed acts like this before to a blind audience?

My toe slipped, and I slid clumsily down the sheer rock surface. That big sheepish grin didn't fade from my face until we got all the way back to the car. By now, the sun was setting, and we needed to find a place to camp, but first, it was grub time. We hopped in, drove off, and headed to a Mexican restaurant in town. When walking in, a big sign welcomed us, saying, "No shirt, no shoes, no service." At that moment, I looked down at my feet and realized that I left my shoes back in the cavern at the end of our hike. I shrugged and walked in without them.

When I requested of Gerry that we turn around and go back for the shoes, suddenly he decided that maybe it wasn't such a bad thing after all that I preferred to go around barefoot. But he remained insistent that I buy another pair of shoes at the first possible opportunity. That night we were camping at Lone Rock Campground, a small beach on the southern tip of the great Lake Powell. The four of us set up the tent and climbed inside. Jam had told me his story, and now it was time for Gerry to share his and Pepper to share hers. We shared stories and laughed until we all faded into a deep sleep.

By now I was surrounding myself with Christians all the time because of their kindness, intentionality, and joy. I was going to Intervarsity and Campus Crusade meetings weekly and cherishing the wisdom they gave me. I surrounded myself with Christians, but I wasn't one. I didn't have faith, I just had reason. I could see that they had something that worked, and I wanted to benefit from it, but I couldn't bring myself to commit to it.

It took another full day before we made it to an outdoors store that sold shoes. In the meantime, I developed a sickness that crept through my body like a puppy going to town on its owner's slippers. I should've known that something was wrong when I found small fragments of my stuffing sprawled everywhere, but that was quite a bit before the fever, chills, and aches set in. But I'm getting ahead of myself again. In the morning, I awoke to an empty tent. The sound of heartfelt laughter was coming through the tent walls from outside. When I emerged, I saw them all sitting with their foldable lawn chairs erected in the shallow waters just offshore. They had their Bibles open and were engaged in intense conversation. "Come join us," Jam said as he waved excitedly.

"I'll stay here," I said as I thought about how weird they were. "Do you guys do this every day?" I asked. It took a moment for my voice to float across the water and carry to their ears.

Jam jumped up, traversed the distance in just a few seconds, grabbed a chair in one hand, and said, "Let me set this up for you!"

I looked at him skeptically until finally, he said, "You don't have to join if you don't want, but there's no better way to start your day than by reading about the Creator of the universe while thoroughly enjoying His creation!"

When we hit the water, it had a sharp, brisk edge to it. The fever I was developing didn't help. *Is this the only thing these guys do?* I thought to myself. *It's great that they take advantage of every moment, but do they have to do so by reading their Bibles, singing Jesus songs, and sharing edifying stories?* I mean, it was definitely constructive; these people were all top-rate individuals and exemplary students. On top of that, they all packed their schedules full with meaningful extracurriculars. *Maybe I shouldn't be so judgmental towards them,* I thought, as I begrudgingly embraced the moment.

It was nice that this type of peer pressure wasn't going to get me arrested. I'd become so used to getting manipulated and talked into things, it took me a while to realize this was different. They weren't pressing their ways on me at all. They were just grateful to live in God's promises in the present and to be free from the binding ways of their own pasts. They cut time out each morning so they could slow down, be intentional, study an impactful life lesson, rest in God, and put on the right attitude before setting out on their day. By spending time with God each morning, they were not only inviting Him into their day, but they were tuning into His frequency. That meant throughout the rest of the day, no matter what happened, they didn't need to worry because they could trust God to be in it. These routines didn't put them behind schedule, rather they eliminated ruthless scurrying, rushing, and worrying from their schedules.

Every inconvenience, every setback, every trial, every obstacle, was not an occasion for anxiety and stress, but an opportunity to trust God to show up, teach us a lesson, or bring a divine appointment. Since they were always tuning into God's frequency, they would often be on cue to contribute a harmonic note to the Creator's beautiful melody. I realized that although my friends were still normal people prone toward impatience, stress, and anger, these healthy rituals of worship kept them from letting those tendencies and temperaments control their lives.

While my previous friends had always talked constantly about girls, parties, drinking, and fights, this group invested considerable quantities of time looking out for the wellbeing of others. They made the world a better place, and they taught me to do the same. Since we were looking out for what God was doing, we would often find ourselves in the right place at the right time. Previously, I had always found joy in doing stupid things like bashing someone's mailbox with a baseball bat, or throwing eggs at nerds, or making fun of losers. We thought that we were being rebellious, but most kids do stupid stuff like that. We're all trying to make a name for ourselves and stand out. It wasn't rebellious at all; self-absorption and self-advocacy were the norm. What I was doing now was true rebellion, truly unique, and meaningful in every way.

My friends were teaching me to transcend that cycle and care for others. We didn't need to prove ourselves anymore. Instead of going out of our way to beat others up, we were building them up. This was truly outside the norm. We would find ourselves in the line at the grocery store in front of someone who was just diagnosed with cancer and was in dismay, and we would pray for them and encourage them. We would find ourselves running into someone who was thinking about committing suicide that night and spend time with them, listen to them, love on them, and give them our number so that they would know they weren't alone. We would help addicts rehabilitate, let them stay in our own apartments, and eat our food. We would pray for the sick and the demon possessed and walk alongside them.

We weren't just looking at how we could help others; we were looking into our own lives as well. Whenever we were together, we would talk about what was preventing us from honoring God, what things were keeping us stuck, or holding us captive. They would share portions of God's Word that gave me clarity on why I had become stuck in certain areas, as well as how God could help me heal and move forward. I had tried many times in the past to create accountability partners but, without fail, they had just made me feel worse about myself and my problems. Each time I had to call them and explain how I'd messed up yet again, I would feel utterly shameful. This was different, this was exciting and lifegiving. I had never seen accountability implemented with such genuineness, patience, precision, and care. Having God's Word to rely on, rather than just sharing random opinions and biased advice, made it like surgery for the soul.

They shared about the beautiful and unique plans that God has for each individual. Up until recently, I hadn't had many hopes or plans. My life had been like a car stuck in a snowy ditch in the middle of the night. I knew I was stuck, but I didn't know how to get out of it. When these guys came along, they had a tow truck, chains, and a spotlight that shed light on all the problem areas. They didn't make me feel guilty about my problems; instead, they jumped out into the cold and helped me start digging. Not only that, but they were teaching me to see the hopes and plans that God had for others, they were teaching me to jump out in the snow and start digging as well.

As we packed up our tent, we all got down together on our knees, excited and ready to see what the day had in store. One of our first stops when we hit civilization was the shoe shop. The pair of shoes I settled on were Vibram's that were shaped like feet, with toe sockets and everything. I don't know if I bought them in spite of or because they fit my quirky preferences with pristine exactness, but they were truly the ugliest set of kicks I have ever seen. When Gerry saw them attached to my feet like a glove to a hand, he had to use all of his willpower to refrain from bursting out in laughter. They cost me nearly sixty bucks, which had been half of my budget for the whole trip, but they seemed to appease him. I never did have the guts to wear them on campus when I got back. For the majority of their life, they remained in the furthest confines of my closet.

We made a routine bathroom stop at one of those gas stations with a burger place in it. At this point, I still wasn't quite aware that anything was wrong with me yet. I ran into the stall and jumped on the toilet. I was in my own little world until Gerry peeked under the stall, this time not bothering to hold in his laughter.

"Mike is that you?!" he spoke in a squeaky voice, drowned out and nearly unintelligible beneath his raucous giggling.

I realized at that moment that it sounded like World War Three in there. Machine guns, bazookas, the whole deal. He laughed hysterically for fifteen minutes straight. But that's not why he was laughing.

"Mike," he said, with the same squeaky pitched voice and tears streaming down his face, "you chased out a little boy and his dad. They were standing at the urinal when all of a sudden, pew, pew, bam, whompf, you started unloading. The little kid looked at his dad with the biggest eyes I've ever seen. He was so terrified he nearly ran out before he'd finished. In fact, I think he did. The dad grabbed him by the shoulders and pushed as quickly as he could. They both were looking back as they scrambled out the door. You'd have thought they were running for their lives."

He continued, "I couldn't help but look to see if it was you. When I poked my head under the stall, I saw your little toes scrunched up in a ball, going white because they were clenched so tightly. As soon as I saw the two bare feet, I knew it was you."

He stopped, trying to remember to breathe while laughing. By now, both of us were laughing so hard that the few people who did try to enter the restroom turned directly around and waited outside. The smell may have also been a slight contributor to their hesitancy, but we were laughing too hard to be embarrassed. It wasn't my fault that I had somehow contracted the plague. From that point forward, the sickness set in posthaste, and I was reduced to nothing more than a vegetable in the back seat of the truck.

Whenever the others would stop for a hike or to look at a scenic spot, I would lie in the back seat of the truck, bent with exhaustion. Luckily for me, our next stop was at the house of a friend. I got to sleep on the floor, which was considerably warmer and more comfortable than my sleeping bag in the tent.

From the moment my sickness began to manifest, Jam was filled with enthusiastic compassion. He wrapped his arms around me in genuine embrace and began praying. "Lord, heal my brother. Jesus, give me his sickness, and make him well again."

Gerry looked at both of us with slight disgust. I bet he was thinking, *Jam, if only you'd been in there with us at the gas station, you wouldn't go within ten feet of that monster.*

Jam, however, wasn't phased in the slightest. His only focus was on helping me and making me feel better. He meant every word of his prayer, and it filled me with joy to be around these funny Christians.

Our next stop had a quarter-mile hike, and I figured even in my sick condition, I could manage a meager jaunt like that. I had never heard of Horseshoe Bend before, but as we approached the towering cliffs, I realized the famous tourist stop overlooked one of the mighty Colorado River's most majestic features. Because of the great height at which we were extended in the air, everything below looked as insignificant and small as drops in the ocean. It took me a while to realize that there were tiny boats floating on the river below. My stomach did a flip, and I shivered in awestruck wonder as I looked down from the great height. *Did God really make this*, I wondered as I soaked in its beauty.

It seemed that after pushing its way through countless tons of thick red sandstone, the river encountered something it didn't want to mess with. So it flipped a hard left and pulled a model U-turn before proceeding on its intended course. The result was a near-perfect horseshoe engraved more than a thousand feet deep into the steep red rock. There wasn't a railing along the edge of it, or anything else, for that matter. One gentle nudge or slight misstep would send even the most able-bodied person flailing through the air to their imminent peril. As I stood leaning over the side of the cliff, Jam jumped from behind me, startling me half to death. He grabbed onto me as he did so, preventing me from rocketing into the air like a scared cat. I didn't think it was funny, but at least he was kind enough to not let me launch myself straight off the cliff while assaulting me.

From that point, we pressed on towards the Grand Canyon. Gerry had arranged for us to stay with some of his friends in Flagstaff for a night, and we were ecstatic to have somewhere warm to lay our heads. I suppose that this refuge was God's grace to me in my sickness. The ultimate sign of His goodness was the fact that the house where we stayed was filled with cute girls.

By this point, the viral infection was giving me a fever with chills and aches and also wreaking havoc on my gastrointestinal tract. Previously mentioned symptoms were suddenly being compounded by uncontrolled vomiting. In the small house, I was aware that my every move and sound could be easily monitored not only by the group, but also by our female hosts. It was terribly embarrassing, but for the first time in my life, I didn't really care what the cute girls thought of me or what my friends thought of me, for that matter. God kept winking at me this whole trip, so I figured that even in my sullied state, He must still find me pretty desirable. After twelve hours of embarrassment and rest, we finally embarked to survey the Grand Canyon.

The crew was considerate enough of my state of being to eliminate any big hikes from our schedule. We ended up taking little excursions from the vehicle to various viewpoints and overlooks. After a picnic, we were set to start heading north again; our journey was coming to a close. By this point, Jam's prayer to contract my sickness was very clearly being answered. He was getting a fever too, and although he didn't have quite the mountain of tissues that I did, he was steadily getting there.

On our way back, we stopped at Sunset Crater, a massive protrusion that leapt out of nowhere into the deep blue sky. Down the entirety of its rocky slopes lay limitless piles of magma rock. The rock was buoyant and layered so that anyone who wanted could use it like a trampoline to bounce down the side of the mountain. Like astronauts in space, each of the members in our group climbed up the rocky slope and bounced down its sides. Since the hill was so steep, each step could carry them five to ten feet. When hitting the loose magma rock, they could slide another five to ten feet down the hill in a single stride. I looked out of the vehicle with jealousy until I could no longer manage the strength to hold my head up. When they returned to the vehicle, Gerry decided to drug Jam and me with a generous dose of NyQuil.

Jam fell into a coma-like slumber as the rest of us shared memories and laughter over the events of the past few days. Before long, a horrendous stench began to permeate the vehicle. It smelled so raunchy that tears began to fill my eyes. With an accusatory glance, Gerry looked at me and said, "Mike, what is wrong with you? It smells like we ran over a dead skunk." By this point, I was laughing so hard that I wasn't capable of forming words to respond. The tears were now streaming heavily down my bright red face.

"It's Jam," I said, as I finally managed to fumble the words out of my mouth. "I think he shat himself."

I couldn't help but have compassion for him as he lay there, stinking up a storm. I thought of him wrapping his arms around me and praying for me. Asking to take this sickness from me, that I might be well. *What kind of friend does something like this*, I wondered. To my surprise, I was feeling better now. As I reflected, I realized that there is only one man who has taken up the entirety of our stench, embarrassment, and shame. He might let us journey it out for a time, but like Jam, he shows up when we need Him most, intercedes on our behalf, and is with us every step of the way.

I couldn't quite understand what was at the root of this whacky Christian love or what about it empowered people who were acting in faith to be so selfless. When Jam hugged me, he knew what he was doing. Yet, he was genuinely willing to contract my sickness in order to show me brotherly love. I know that my sickness was minor, but the Christian faith has always produced a people group who were able to conquer fear in order to serve, love, and care for the sick. This is the same type of love that caused Christians to stay in cities suffering from the bubonic plague. While everyone else was fleeing, they stayed to help the sick even though they knew it meant almost certain death. The same love that caused monks, nuns, and clergy in the Medieval ages to welcome ruffians to sleep in their cathedrals, homes, and monasteries and share food from their personal reserves. Something otherwise unheard of.

It would take me decades of research and study to find out that Christianity, the religion based on charity and love, was the very belief system that created what we call hospitality. Not only that but Christians created hospitals as well. So much of the good that we take for granted in our culture and world is rooted in Christianity. Where would we be if this movement centered around loving, serving, and praying not only for our neighbors and friends, but also our enemies, had not come into and impacted our crumbling world?

"Let me give you a new command: Love one another. In the same way I loved you, you love one another. This is how everyone will recognize that you are my disciples—when they see the love you have for each other." — *John 13:34-35* (MSG)

Chapter Twenty-Four

Adventures That Last

"I will sprinkle clean water on you, and you will be clean; I will cleanse you from all your impurities and from all your idols. I will give you a new heart and put a new spirit in you; I will remove from you your heart of stone and give you a heart of flesh. And I will put my Spirit in you and move you to follow my decrees and be careful to keep my laws." —*Ezekiel 36:25-27* (NIV)

I had hashed out the Christian faith empirically and scientifically and I'd found answers to most of my questions. I had seen God step in and display His love for me on many occasions, but I still had a hard time bringing myself to trust Him. It was hard for me to exchange my paradigms of reality for His. It was hard for me to trust His rules, His words, His laws, His version of things, and to surrender my own. Even though I knew beyond a shadow of a doubt that my own perspective, desires, and passions had deceived me, led me astray, and made me miserable on countless occasions, it was still difficult to muster up the faith to do things His way.

I wanted what my Christian friends had: a peace that wasn't derived from a limited source, a joy that wasn't dependent on circumstances. I knew it came from God, and that it was tangible and real, but I didn't know how. It didn't matter to them if they ran out of gas and got stranded in the desert, they would make a grand old time out of the whole ordeal. They had God in their lives. They had His peace and joy at their core. They didn't need anything else. It was perplexing. When I returned home after our road trips, I would ask myself, *how can I get what they have?*

One weekend, instead of our normal adventures, we went to a Christian camp and that was where it all finally began to make sense to me. They drew a picture of a wagon wheel with spokes and said it was a picture of the foundation of our lives; it was an image of the things that our lives centered around and the things we functionally relied upon to keep our lives moving forward. In each section they asked us to write the five things we spent the most time doing. I wrote school, work, homework, family, friends.

Since I knew it was a Christian camp, I thought I better erase one and add God in there somewhere, too. I decided to erase friends since it was really the only fungible option. They asked us how we thought God fit into everything. I haughtily answered, "Well, we just need to implement Him into all these things, then we'll be happy." They were too kind to tell me my answer was wrong, but it was. I couldn't have missed the mark by a bigger margin.

When they finally told us the answer, it seemed obvious. In the center, at the hub, was me. It all revolved around me. Everything I did was centered around *my* life, *my* goals, *my* plan, and *my* agenda. Even when I went to Bible studies or church, I did so in order to acquire new knowledge and friendships that would benefit *me*, help *me* do better, and make *me* feel better about *myself.* They said a Christian is someone who has deposed themselves from the throne of their lives and placed God there; a Christian is someone who has placed God at the center and the foundation of their lives.

I suddenly realized the goal of Christianity was not merely to implement God into my life and schedule, but to give Him my life. To be a Christian means I willingly surrender my identity to Him. To belong to Him means that my life does not belong to me any longer. If I wanted to reap the benefits of belonging to Him, He needed to come first now, not me. His words, His decisions, His guidance, His person, and my relationship with Him needed to be placed above all else. I needed to stop demanding my own way and start following His.

I thought that by constructing my reality so that I always got what I wanted meant I had authority over my life. However, the truth was that my feelings were dictating my life.

I suddenly realized that I was in the center of my world, and my emotions were at the center of me. They were the basis of my identity. Emotions had been my center point, the lens through which my reality was dispersed and regulated. The desire for pleasure, satisfaction, approval, and recognition had ruled my life. I'd based too much on my feelings, biases, opinions, and preferences. I'd based too much on what my feelings told me I needed, rather than what I actually needed. I didn't even know what I needed. Emotions are incoherent, unintelligible, and often conflicting, and yet in my life, they were the ones calling the shots.

When I experienced pleasurable emotions, I was at peace; when I lacked them, I felt anxiety. When I experienced positive emotions, I felt my life was meaningful. When I lacked them, it felt void of purpose and meaning. My emotions had led me to refute logic on countless occasions and enter into idiotic feats, relationships, and situations. In some ways, emotions had not only replaced common sense, but also spirituality in my life. I had expended all concepts of balanced physical, psychological, social, and spiritual wellbeing in exchange for a fleeting pleasure.

Emotions had been the primary factor in my planning and decision-making. Most of the time, they made my life feel like a roller coaster ride that ended abruptly with a broken piece of track. After watching how eagerly my Christian friends studied the Bible, I realized I wasn't going to have what they had unless I took it seriously as well. I saw the hope they derived from its pages and how much reliable guidance it gave them. I saw how much joy they got from applying it, and I realized it was the key. By this point I was growing convinced that my everchanging, ever evolving opinion was less sophisticated than a monkey's. My emotions were not a reliable foundation upon which to base my well-being. My opinion, and everything it was built on was about as solid as tapioca.

For years, I acted as if I were all knowing but that only prevented me from obtaining knowledge. Since I thought I knew everything that mattered, I wasn't willing to learn anything new. How ignorant I was! There are roughly 5,000 years of recorded human history. In those 5,000 years, roughly 129,864,880 books have been written. If I lived an average lifespan, I would have to read over 4,744 books a day and learn every human language. That does not include reading any of the roughly four million new books published each year. Yet, the sum of all human knowledge would still be nothing in comparison to that of the eternal God. If God is the eternal one who made and knows all things, those 5,000 years of books and knowledge are child's play to Him, less than a speck in the span of eternity. His mind is never changing, it is constant, and He knows all things.

The baffling reality of this whole ordeal was the fact that the more knowledge I obtained, the more my mind changed. The more I learned, the more I realized how little I knew. The more I sought to understand things, the more they baffled me. Furthermore, my finite human brain could only contain so much information. The more I learned, the less I was able to recall. Worse yet, each year there are new scientific breakthroughs, many of which contradict the old ones. Blinding myself by becoming set in my bigoted, limited perspective was equivalent to an ostrich burying its head in the sand at the threat of encroaching danger. When I finally acknowledge my finitude and let go of my biases, my world exploded with awe and wonder.

If the Bible is His instruction manual for the human race, it contains everything we need to navigate through the hardships of this life. Learning and applying the knowledge in it would be more valuable to us than reading all the books ever written. I needed to see if it was little more than an ancient historical account, or if it was as they said it was — "the living Word of God," whatever that meant.

I went to my parents' house and found a dusty Bible on one of their basement shelves. I grabbed it and randomly flipped it open. The title read Titus, Chapter 3. "At one time, we too were *foolish, disobedient, deceived,* and *enslaved by* all kinds of *passions and pleasures*... But when the kindness and love of God our Savior appeared, He saved us, not because of righteous things we had done, but because of His mercy. He saved us through the washing of rebirth and renewal by the Holy Spirit, whom he poured out on us generously through Jesus Christ our Savior, so that, having been justified by his grace, we might become heirs having the hope of eternal life" (*Titus 3:3-7* NIV).

When I read this scripture all I could think about was the God who had busted me out of my jail cell. I had enslaved myself to all kinds of passions and pleasures, but God's kindness and love broke through. I didn't earn it, I didn't deserve it, but He washed my slate clean, gave me a fresh start, a new chance. Not because of anything I'd done, nor because of anything I could ever do. He gave me something no one else could: forgiveness, hope, freedom, and joy that would stretch into eternity.

All I could think about was how, when I chose to set fire to my life by doing drugs, God sent a fire chief to forgive me and let me go. I'd blocked out God for years with constant drug use, until He finally got hold of me on my cell phone. I'd ignored Him and got a DUI, and He sent a Christian lawyer, along with a couple of miracles, to show beyond a shadow of a doubt that He was defending my case. How He sent the police to call me out on my actions, to call me to a higher standard. How they represented His law and His authority and called me to see beyond myself. How I blatantly ignored them and brought condemnation on myself in so doing. How He showed me mercy through the judges who withheld the consequences I'd merited. How, when I was groveling on the ground in that jail cell, looking up to heaven and pleading for help, He erased my record and forgave me of my past. He gave me what I couldn't earn and didn't deserve.

I saw how, when I ignored the clean slate God had given me, He sent Samuel to remind me who had set me free. I'd ignored Samuel to seek more trendy forms of spirituality, and stranded myself on a cliff, but He directly answered my prayers. I saw how I tried to earn His forgiveness, tried to be a good person, tried to seek superior knowledge and intellect, but none of it was enough to tip the scales in my favor. My very best efforts were not enough. Nothing I did brought me closer to healing, or freedom, or Him. All these things were alternative ways to retain control over my own life. I saw how I'd refused to surrender my life to Him, insisting instead that I could do good, and be good, and turn my own life around. I saw how He sent me Jam, Gerry and Pepper, the three Christians, to seek me out in love anyway.

I started weeping out loud as the scenes of my past replayed through my head. I'd always seen God's interventions as freebies, as nice gestures from an all-powerful genie-like figure. I was finally beginning to see not only what it meant to have a clean slate, but also how much it cost Him to give me one. I'd been so used to the court system and thinking of myself as a criminal. I'd been so used to pleading in abeyance, proclaiming my guilt and unworthiness and asking the judge for mercy. But God's love went beyond anything I'd seen in my lifetime. He wasn't just giving me mercy by overlooking my sins, He was giving me justice by paying off every debt I'd ever created and bearing every damnation I'd ever deserved.

He wasn't just telling me, "If you're good, I'll forgive you. If you do this and that and follow my protocol with excruciating exactness, then I will forgive you." No, He had *already* forgiven me. Just like the lawyer had stood on my behalf after my second DUI, so Jesus had stood before the judgement throne of God. Although I was 100% guilty, he had erased all evidence against me. When the eternal God looked at my record and said, "Michael is found guilty, the penalty of his crimes is death and his crimes must be paid for in hell," Jesus didn't just sit there pleading for my forgiveness saying, "Please forgive Michael. Please have mercy on him." No, He made a case for me and got a verdict on my behalf. He took the penalty on Himself and fulfilled everything that the law required.

I was not in the system any longer. I didn't need to perform an endless list of deeds to keep myself out of jail and in the judge's good favor. I'd been completely forgiven of my past, present, and future sins. In His book, next to the name Michael Heil was a signature that read: "Paid in full," signed Jesus.

"You, who were dead in your trespasses… God made alive together with him, having forgiven us all our trespasses, by canceling the record of debt that stood against us with its legal demands. This he set aside, nailing it to the cross." —*Colossians 2:13-15*

***

If justice is to happen, each sin must be accounted for. If God allowed our sins to continue without interference, without ever correcting or addressing the corruption, our sins would echo into eternity and He would not be just. Either the transgressor bears the penalty, or Jesus bears it on their behalf.

He took the wrath of the whole world's sins upon His shoulders. He took the wrath that was stored up against every single one of these acts of evil, and He bore the flaming, searing, scorching, penalty for each. God could not overlook the plight of the orphan or the widow, the victim of genocide, war, or rape; He could not turn His head away from any singular hurt, sin, or pain. He strapped Himself to our judgment seat to ensure that every evil act would be accounted for, and to ensure that justice would reign in eternity, He strapped Himself to my cross.

The cost was the life of the eternal, immortal, invisible God, the One who created everything, made us, and gave us His word to guide us. This was the God we rejected in order to do our own thing, and each go our own way. He who is a trillion times bigger than us entered knowingly into our shoes, although we are a trillion times smaller than a speck of dust in comparison. He made Himself like us, weak, frail, and puny so He could die in our place. He did this to give us hope for our future, an eternal hope that extends even beyond the veil of this life. This hope is not rooted in wishful thinking, but in concrete, tangible acts of the most sacrificial love that anyone has ever seen or lived.

Chapter Twenty-Five

Trusting Truth

It became a ritual, whether for spring break, fall break, summer break, or winter break, our motley crew was ready for adventure. Different individuals came along with us each trip, and every time the route of national or state parks we visited would vary slightly. Even when we visited the same places, new seasons blanketed them with unrecognizable characteristics, making each place look brand new to our childlike eyes, which viewed things with increasing awe and wonder.

These friends were secure; they didn't need to make a name for themselves because they already had all the confirmation and affirmation they needed from God Himself and their relationship with Him. Unlike me, they weren't desperate for the right girl or partner, they were firmly rooted in Him, and therefore satisfied with their lives. Gerry was the first person who taught me how to apply Christian principles. He lived at the Christian house on campus, which was always buzzing with activity. There was always an intellectual debate about science and religion going. The doors were always open, and swarms of students would come through the house. We'd pray for them, listen to them, feed them, and spend hours encouraging them. Gerry took me under his care like a baby wolf, nurturing me in the faith but never hesitating to put me in my place when I needed it.

Because of my past, I could not refrain from trying to attract and appeal to women. One day, Gerry took my phone and started deleting the number of every female he could find. He told me I needed to grow up and learn how to respect both myself and women. He gave me some strange, unanticipated Christian version of "the talk." It went something like this: "Christians don't think with their dicks. Everyone around you is trying to get laid; that's college. It's actually immaturity and hormones, but most college students are being ruled by those two things.

"Mike, if you want to be a Christian, you've got to learn how to consider others as better than yourself. We should respect women, not because of what we can get from them, but because of who they are. They are humans whom God loves. They deserve to be acknowledged and appreciated.

"Both men and women can treat each other like objects. They do this when they use sex and use each other's bodies to meet their own inner need for acknowledgment and appreciation. Until they get married, the partners are on audition, and they can be thrown out at any point that one partner finds a better suitor or gets tired of the other. When used in marriage, sex is a celebration of the fact that you've given one another everything and are committed to one another irrevocably. Since you've already given each other your time, trust, money, income, home, bank account, schedule, and everything else, giving each other your body is safe, natural, and enjoyable. Since you've committed to one another 'for better, for worse, for richer, for poorer, in sickness and in health, until death do you part,' you know that the other person will cherish you and will not just throw you out when you fail to perform to their standards. You've not only earned each other's love and trust, but you can give yourselves fully to one another, celebrating what you have, knowing that you're not being used."

For a while, I just ignored these concepts, telling myself that these thoughts were merely Gerry's opinion. I didn't want to give up sex and sleeping around. But when God brought a complete stranger into my life who said almost the exact thing same, it was hard to ignore.

"If you use sex whenever you want with whomever you want, you're treating it like trash, like it means nothing. Imagine a piece of duct tape. It's got a purpose, it's designed to stick to something, but if you stick it to the dog and rip it off, then the floor, the wall, the toilet, the neighbor's pit, after that, it just won't work right anymore. When you finally find your spouse and try to connect with them, there will be all sorts of crud in the way. It might be a physical STD, or it could be an emotional one that spreads through your relationship and life like an infection.

"If you use sex outside its proper context, it will hijack your emotions, get you into a bunch of stupid situations, and eventually control your wellbeing. I'm sure you've been hurt by all sorts of relationships in the past, and they've probably torn you up, caused you to get into fights, ate away at your self-worth, made you sick to your stomach. Well, that's why. Acknowledgement and appreciation are legitimate needs, but sleeping around is not the way to meet them."

These Christians always seemed to consider long-term holistic wellbeing. None of their answers were easy or quick but took grit and determination. Every "do" and "don't" had a reason and purpose behind it. I was finally beginning to understand the *why* behind things. I hated it when someone told me to just do something without explaining what, why, or how. Previously, I had based all my decisions on the fact that someone said that it felt good, but there was no real reason beyond that. Previously, the "why" had always been lacking. Previously my why had been about as sophisticated as that of a monkey. When my Christian friends taught me about the gospel, they didn't talk about the law or morality or doctrine or any of those things. They simply loved me and encouraged me. They accepted me and guided me. The more time I spent with them, the more I realized that I knew nothing about the gospel, despite growing up going to a Christian church. The more I spent time with them, the more I wanted to spend time with them.

Their answers seemed to work. I was tired of malfunctioning and following fleeting pleasures that seemed to lead in endless circles. What if there was something that could guide me with 100% accuracy? What if there was an instruction manual for the human race? Instruction manuals are not intended to restrict or diminish an object's functionality, but to ensure that it functions as it was designed, at its optimal capacity. The manufacturer of a car knows every piece of the vehicle. The manufacturer not only understands the functionality of each part, but also when and how it ought to be maintained, repaired, or replaced.

They put gauges and warning lights that let us know when the oil is low, the battery is weak, the coolant is low, and the gas is almost gone. They even program vehicles to pop out specific codes to tell us what is wrong. By following these gauges and codes, we can keep our vehicles running at optimum capacity. If we ignore the gauges and refuse to put gas in when it needs it, the vehicle will shut down. If we put milk inside the tank instead of gas, the same will happen, or if we use water instead of oil. In sum, it doesn't benefit us to ignore the instructions. The reality is that the engine functions in a certain way, and if we ignore the instruction manual in order to do whatever we please, things will break.

Humans are much more complex than vehicles are. We have one-billion cells per square inch that each have a nine-billion-digit DNA code written into them. Somehow, all of these cells function seamlessly together to heal our bodies when they are wounded and perform a countless number of other tasks. We might not break down as quickly or as obviously as a vehicle does, but we do break. If God really did create everything and the Bible is God's decisive word about everything, then that means it's not an opinion but an instruction manual. That means it not only can help us understand our error codes, but also address and heal the mental, physical, social, emotional, and spiritual hurt in our lives and in our world.

If God's Word is true, then its purpose is not to restrict us or prevent us from having fun, but to help us detect defects and fix anything that needs repair, to show us our intended purpose, and to ensure we function at optimal capacity. The manufacturer always knows how to fix the mess, even with the most complex problems. He never uses shortcuts, cheap fixes, or temporary solutions that cause more problems in the long run; he gets to the root of things and addresses them at their core. In the same way, if we were designed, then our manufacturer understands us entirely, and is able to address and heal every single one of our vast array of intimate complexities. If God is who He says He is, the Bible is the instruction manual for the human race, and He is the manufacturer. If the Bible is God's Word, then it expounds the objective laws of the universe. If it is not, it is just like all the other disputable theories, sometimes consistent with reality, and sometimes not.

As I started to deliberate whether I could trust the Bible or not, Bible verses started popping up everywhere. Whether it was my friends quoting them to me at precisely the right moment, a Bible study, a piece of paper on the ground, or a pop-up on my phone, each one seemed to hit the bull's eye of my soul precisely when I needed it.

After exactly one year of staying clean off heroin, I relapsed. I smoked enough to make me puke, went to my classes strung out, then to work. The next day I did the same thing again, but at the end of the day I went to my Bible study. The verse they were studying that night was "God is faithful in our unfaithfulness" (2 Timothy 2:13). I knew it wasn't a coincidence, and I sobbed silently, thinking of all the times God had been faithful to me in my unfaithfulness. I thought of the time I slit my wrist and should've bled out, but He sent my loving father to nurture me back to health. I thought about when I overdosed and he removed just enough of the drug so it didn't kill me. I knew He was faithful each time I drove drunk, high, blacked out, or into steam rollers, and came away unscathed, faithful in the single fact that I never hurt anyone else while being so reckless.

I remember, after trying so hard to refrain from hooking up, the first time I gave myself over in compromise. When I woke up and saw her black hair strewn over my arm, I nearly vomited. There wasn't anything wrong with her. It's just that for the first time in my life, I knew what I'd done was wrong. I went outside trying not to wake her, and I wept. I felt God's presence and kindness all around me, and yet I did not hesitate to betray Him, turn from Him, and pursue other lovers. I wondered if He would give up on me since I still kept choosing to sin and do the same old things, even now that I knew better. I felt utterly sinful and insignificant, like a reprobate, an incurable failure. I felt like, by this point, God would be crazy not to throw me out with the trash.

I remember opening my Bible and reading 1 Corinthians 1. The text read, "God *chose* the foolish things of the world to shame the wise; God *chose* the weak things of the world to shame the strong. God *chose* the lowly things of this world and the despised things—and the things that are not—to nullify the things that are, so that no one may boast before him" (1 Corinthians 1:27).

Then I realized God chose me, baggage and all. God chose a drug addict, a kid who had chosen to sleep on the street in a blizzard to get his fix and get laid rather than go home to his family. A kid who lied, stole, and manipulated others. God chose someone virtually worthless and considered me valuable enough to lay down His life. He took a kid who only cared about himself and put me first. He took someone broken and loved me through my brokenness. He never gave up on me, even when I ignored His advice and got myself into trouble. He stayed by my side challenging me with truth, even when I was a biased, naïve, and arrogant scoffer. He would love me into wholeness, through each step of the mess and mire. He took all the self-confident, self-righteous people who have all the right answers and look down their noses at others off their pedestals of perfection and placed the lowly, foolish, and weak in their place. It was only when I realized I was nothing, that I found I could be something of true and lasting value.

I read about how God leaves the ninety-nine-well-put-together-sheep in order to seek out the lost one and about how Jesus came not for the righteous and the healthy but for the sick and the sinner. I read verses about how God sends the sun, the rain, the crops, the harvest, to both the righteous and the wicked alike. He not only gives life to both but sustains the vital life functions of both. I could see dozens of ways in which He had been seeking me out and sustaining me, even as I'd rejected Him, and then I realized something. While the law condemns those who fail to adhere to it, God is a different entity altogether.

While the law condemns anyone who breaks it, God loves sinners, even those who actively reject Him and disobey His laws. God's moral law is much like the other laws that He created to govern the universe; it is inherently true. Even if someone wears a bird suit and hops off a balcony, they will not fool gravity. God's laws are indisputable and irreproachable, they simply *are* the way of things. Those who obey God's law will be blessed, while those who deny it will be cursed. If we build our lives on it, we will experience stability, health, and goodness. If we go against the law, we will struggle, we will feel empty, unstable, insecure, and void of meaning. And yet, God is different than the law; God is faithful to us, even when we curse ourselves by rejecting and being unfaithful to His law.

The wicked are like me, they take it all for granted. They ignore Him, and drive under the influence. They get themselves into car accidents, and He, in His grace, keeps them alive. They know the consequences but do it anyway. They get themselves arrested by intentionally breaking the law and opposing those who enforce it. By ignoring the law and defying God, they bring hell upon themselves, but what they find is that God has not given up on them yet. He is pursuing them and intervening on their behalf. Even as they damn themselves, He is providing a way out, a path forward, for any who would turn to Him. Their actions nearly kill themselves and those they love, yet each time they are protected it is solely because of God's grace stepping in to give them another chance.

God could've rightfully condemned me and let me rot in jail like my crimes warranted, but when I turned to Him, He forgave me and stood at my defense. Though I condemned myself repeatedly, He kept breaking me free. He kept giving me new opportunities to be made right with Him. I could choose to go to my grave denying, rejecting, and refuting Him, but He would be there intervening and interjecting Himself every step of the way. He would not let me recklessly shove my way into hell unwarned.

"Then everyone who has eyes will be able to see the truth, and everyone who has ears will be able to hear it. Even the hotheads will be full of sense and understanding. Those who stammer will speak out plainly. In that day ungodly fools will not be heroes. Scoundrels will not be respected." —*Isaiah 32:3-8* (NLT)

***

Though we quote the words of Plato and Aristotle, and teach of Caesar's Gallic wars in our history classes, we have only seven manuscripts recording Plato's life and works with the first copy written 1,200 years after his death; there are 49 for Aristotle, the earliest written 1,400 years after his death, and 12 for Caesar, with the earliest written 900 years after his death [21]. Yet we quote them with uniform certainty. Compare those to the 23,986 manuscripts that record Jesus' life and works, many of which were written within 35 years of His death and resurrection [22]. In addition to these manuscripts we have writings from over twenty historians, philosophers, and governors, who wrote about Jesus in the first and second century [23]. No other ancient text on earth has this volume of manuscripts, nor this many texts written this close to the actual events [21]. If you take just the Greek manuscripts, the language the New Testament was written in, there are over 2.6 million pages of text [20].

This person Jesus undoubtedly existed, and whatever He did turned the world upside down, creating an uproar unlike the world has ever seen before or since. And yet, despite His life being the most documented in world history, we find ourselves disbelieving, doubting, and discrediting it. Why? The events wouldn't have spread if they were historically incongruous. Fake news doesn't fly, it pisses people off. It would be like me trying to convince the world the Twin Towers fell because of an earthquake or tornado. All those who saw the event, and were personally affected by it, would go their graves refuting the lies, proclaiming the truth, and writing articles about what really happened.

As it is, we have 25,000 documents supporting Jesus' life, death, resurrection, and miracles, and we do not have one single historical document that tries to refute or dismiss them. It was common knowledge, with so many witnesses it was virtually indisputable, when hundreds of people are running around shouting, "I saw Him, I felt His scars, I heard Him speak, I saw His miracles, I saw Him die, and now He's back!" It makes sense that the news spread so fast across the known world that it almost put modern media to shame. And those were hand-written letters.

Two thousand years later, the majority of the world still acknowledges the day these events unfolded. We call it Easter; the day death was defeated. In the same way that He had shown up in the lives of billions of others, Jesus had made Himself known to me. I could testify with unwavering certainty that the resurrected king was still very much alive. Soon, He would hold me in His arms.

Chapter Twenty-Six

The Accident, Facing Him

The road trips partially satisfied my craving for adventure, but they were far too infrequent. So, I supplemented my adrenaline fix by escaping to the mountains with my board every chance I could finagle a few hours off work or out of class. Whether by myself or with friends, I made every minute count. I would fly like a shooting star, sending streaks of white into the gaping jaws of others loafing down the slopes, making a game out of dodging them as I flew past. There was nothing quite like floating down the mountain on a fresh sheet of powder, each turn feeling as if you were excavating a cloud.

One day, after shredding for hours with my sister, her friends reported a sweet spot of unclaimed powder. The location was slightly outside of the ski resort's boundaries, so we were required to traverse backcountry to get to it. The dangers of being in the backcountry were self-evident, but we felt reassured by the fact that my brother-in-law was an avalanche training instructor and backcountry guide.

As soon as we reached our destination, I rocketed down the mountain with reckless abandon. My competitive nature compelled me to go faster than was reasonable, but that was half the fun. My favorite sensation was when I went so fast that the buildup of wind caused my eyes to water. Those were the moments when I really felt alive.

In front of me, a stand of trees were grouped closely together and I carved skillfully, weaving myself through them like yarn through a needle. The slope steepened, and for a moment, it looked as if I were flying off the face of the earth. I balanced myself by lowering my center of gravity, using the sharp decline to boost my speed even more. The steep slope began to narrow, forcing me inwards towards the center of its gulch-like features.

On a groomer, I could go as fast as lightning and still maintain control with hundreds of feet to slow myself down and an unimpeded view of the mountain in front of me. Here giant rocks, boulders, and trees shot up out of the earth every few yards. The incline again turned sharply downward, and the slope pulled away from my board. I tried digging into the snow with the edge of my board as I'd always done before. This time, however, instead of slowing me down, my board skipped across the surface like a rock ricocheting off the water.

In front of me, a massive shard of rock breached my path. Again, I pressed down, trying to force my board to grab hold of the surface. It clutched onto the snow once, then twice, but my weak cuts did nothing to slow me down. By this point, I was shooting down the crevice like a ball launched full speed from the hand of a professional pitcher.

The boulder protruded onto my path as if it had been waiting there for me since the day of its conception. I used every bit of might I could muster to slow myself down, but it was drawing me in like a magnet. It was as if there was nothing I could do to avoid it. In the blink of an eye, my flailing body smashed into the boulder like a motorcyclist ramming into a truck in full-on collision. The impact crushed the bones of my left leg, but I was going so fast that even the rock could not stop me. The force of it sent me sprawling through the air with limbs flailing.

One spin, one and a half, two, and my body hit the ground before continuing to cascade down the slippery slope. When I finally stopped sliding, I laid lifelessly, and then I smiled. I'd never pulled off that many spins before. When I finally sat up, adrenaline was pumping through my body, causing my vision to blur. I tried positioning my board so that I could stand up again, but as I triggered the muscles that should've made my leg contract, nothing happened. I grabbed my leg with my hands, moving it into a standing position. As I placed my weight on the board, trying to stand up, pain shot through my leg. The bone shot to the right, and my leg hung limply.

I realized at this point there was no way I would be able to board down, but I still had no conception of the extent of my injury. I only knew that with each passing moment, the permeating pain pierced deeper. My boot had frozen stuck to its binding; I couldn't stand up, and I couldn't get the board off. At that point the pain seized me so fiercely that I began to choke. I started crying, and I couldn't stop. Screams of pain bellowed up in between sobs as I realized that my femur bone had split in half.

At this point, my sister had caught up to me. Assessing the situation, she asked me if I could stand up. With my mind unable to register anything but the all-consuming pain, I kept reaching for my ice-trodden boot, trying to remove it, hoping if I could remove the weight of the board that some of the pain would go away. In the midst of my incoherent death-screams, I managed a few meager words "Help Sis, please help me! IT HURTS SO DAMN BAD!"

She reached into her pocket to grab her phone. Once again, she found herself calling for help on behalf of her messed-up little brother. She tried ringing her husband, but there was no phone service. She rustled through my pockets, trying to locate my phone. As she did so, she jostled my leg, and my deafening wail somehow grew even louder. When she finally found it, she moved around with both phones held high in the air, praying for a signal, until one of the phones finally rang through.

When her husband picked up, she filled him in and asked for his professional advice. A pause... And then he responded, "You're in the backcountry," he said. "Ski patrol aren't obligated to come and rescue you guys. You're outside of resort boundaries. If he can't move and you can't find another way to get him down the mountain, your only option is to have him life-flighted. You need to call 9-1-1." She talked to me patiently, trying to walk me through our options. By now, the fierce pain was causing me to convulse.

I felt absolutely helpless. I screamed and screamed as the pain deepened. I couldn't focus on a single word that she was saying. Eventually, she couldn't handle it anymore. She grabbed my head and shook it, saying, "You need to calm the f*** down." My screaming was so out of control that cursing at me was the only thing she could do to break through the hysteria.

"Stop this! You need to calm down!" As she screamed at me, my eyes crossed with pain, and I seemed to see straight through her. I'd broken several bones by this point in my life and had a couple of surgeries on my arm for torn tendons. On a pain scale of one to ten, all of those events combined ranked at two. This ranked at one hundred on a scale of one to ten. The pain was transcendent, beyond what I'd imagined was possible for a human to experience. As I lay there, a verse filled my mind. It was something I had read earlier that morning, but it hadn't made sense to me until this moment. "My grace is sufficient for you, for my power is made perfect in weakness. Therefore, I will boast all the more gladly about my weaknesses, so that Christ's power may rest on me" — *2 Corinthians 12:9* (NIV).

As I lay there consumed by the pain, I grew increasingly convinced I was going to die. There was no way I could make it down from this place. I was close to passing out from the pain, and in the dark tunnel of my departure, various moments of my life flashed by me. I saw all the selfish things I'd done, all the lies I'd told, and I realized I would be seeing God face to face soon.

In light of that realization, I looked up to heaven and started praying. "God, I know that You can save me if you want to, but if not, thank you for my life." As I whispered the words my life continued to flash before my eyes. I saw all the horrible and selfish things I'd ever done, as well as all the wonderful gifts and experiences I'd ever had. "Thank you," I finally managed to mumble, as the tears streamed down my face and I prepared to meet my Maker. "I know you can save me if you want to Lord, but if not, thank you for everything." Everything went black and my consciousness streamed towards a brilliant and blinding light.

Thirty seconds later two white crosses bathed in blood descended upon me. My sister flailed her arms, screaming with vengeance. Screaming at me to stay awake and screaming at someone else I couldn't see. The two ski patrolmen had made a spur-of-the-moment decision to go backcountry, during their one-hour lunch break. Because of that decision, they just-so-happened to be skiing down the mountain, exactly where I was, at the moment I needed them.

They saw her and headed towards us. My vision cleared as my sister shook me, narrating what was happening. "There's help Mike! Help is coming! You're going to be okay," she shouted as tears streamed down both our faces. As they drew nearer, the large cross emblazoned on their clothing became clearer. "Jesus," I mumbled, "I knew you'd come..."

He had dispatched them to save my life even before the accident had taken place. They came when He sent them. They came when I needed them. They bore His symbol. They were there during the golden hour; without their help, I would not have made it down. They were the answer to my prayer. Without them, I am certain I would have died on that cliff face.

As soon as they reached me, they bent down to cut off my snow pants and get a look at the damage. I protested at first because my snow pants were expensive and I was a college student, but they ignored me. When the medic saw my leg, he told me we needed to call a helicopter immediately. But I couldn't stand the thought of costing my parents another twenty thousand dollars on top of the nearly twenty grand I had already cost them through fines, arrests, counseling, and impound fees. "Please," I begged, "just carry me down."

The bone was disconnected from the rest of my body. While it did not protrude outside of the flesh, it hung sideways in a most unnatural position, as if it were about to pierce through at any moment. As the medic stared at it, he warned me, "Mike, there are two main arteries that go in your leg past your femur. If either of those is cut, then you *will* bleed to death in the next five-to-ten minutes."

I already thought I was dying. It felt like I was dying. In fact, by this point, I would've chosen death over the uncontrollable muscle spasms that sent unfathomable pain pulsating through my body with each heartbeat. The medic merely confirmed my suspicions. As my dislodged leg tremored mercilessly, I thought of the verse I'd read that morning, and I clung to it as if my life depended on it. Jesus promised to give me power and grace in my weakness. I saw His grace as I stared at the white crosses in front of me, and I could feel His power filling me as I somehow found the strength not to scream with the echoing throb of each heartbeat.

"Jesus," I said, and the pain lifted just a little bit. I was delirious now, but the name seemed to give me just enough strength to breathe through the pain. I couldn't stop. I kept mumbling His name over and over, as I sat half-naked in the deep, cold snow. By now, my fingers were frozen stiff, and the snow just kept piling on my exposed skin and extremities. More than an inch had already accumulated on top of me. The ice caused me to shiver. Each time I shivered, the severed muscles triggered and created additional spasms of pain. The sharp pain from my leg seemed to permeate every cell of my being.

When would the backup arrive with the necessary gear to remove me safely from the mountain? The ski patrolmen had called for backup over an hour ago. Where were they? As we waited, I kept saying His name: "Jesus, Jesus, Jesus, Jesus." Every time His name flowed from my mouth, the pain lifted just a little bit. If I stopped saying His name, it would increase.

One of the ski patrolmen turned to my sister and told her, "The femur is the most painful bone break a human can experience. Usually, someone with a broken femur will scream continuously until they pass out." He chuckled before continuing, then he said, "Your brother's different though..."

He had no idea how, only moments before, I'd been screaming like a mother who'd lost her only child...until my tongue stumbled upon that "Oh-so-powerful name." He had no idea how much help that name was giving me, how much strength was being infused into my body by the simple pronouncement of it. As we waited, they dug a trench around me, a place where the toboggan could fit without sliding down the cliff that we were dangling on. I was beginning to black out again, but no state of unconsciousness could rip me from the unrelenting pain that held me in its grip. The objects in front of me became blurry as my vision was saturated by darkness. Someone was holding me in their arms. Suddenly a bright figure in gleaming light contrasted the darkness, sending it sprawling as He embraced me.

As eternal security wrapped its arms around me in a bear-hug. I tried turning my head upward to catch a glimpse of His face. I couldn't see anything except His eyes fixated on me in a burning gaze. They gleamed like flames of fire. More love and passion than the whole universe could muster danced across those eyes. It was Jesus. His grasp soothed me immensely. His steady grip over me was no longer just wishful thinking, it was a reality now. I clutched His robe and drew my face closer to His chest. As I did so, the ski patrolman began to lift me in his arms, clutching my broken and mangled body and forcing it onto the toboggan that had finally arrived.

***

Charles Spurgeon once said, 'I have learned to kiss the waves that throw me up against the Rock of Ages" [45]. Life is inconsistent, the planet itself turns infernally. The waves of time beat against the rocky shores of our lives, as we age to sand through every fleeting trial and experience. The only constant is change. And change, by definition, means inconsistency: highs and lows, good times and bad ones, safety and accidents, tragedy and triumph. On this earth, hope, joy, and peace are temporary things. They come one moment and recede the next, battering the shores of our lives with taunting impermanence.

If this accident were a wave, I did not think there would ever be a way I could learn to kiss it. Yet it was in that very place of peril, as I was dashed against a rock, that I met face to face with the Rock of Ages. Hardships can take from our life or they can add to it. Usually, they do both. Hardships produce the inky grey and black pigments which contrast upon the otherwise blank canvas of our lives. The dark, black, empty moments of life are very rarely enjoyable, but they are not worthless. In the hands of a loving God, they can and will serve a purpose.

Why? Why would God hold *me* in His arms? Why save me? If there was anyone, He could've rightfully left there on that cliff to die, it would've been me. I had always been a prodigal, one ruled by darkness, one who wandered, drawn in by wickedness and controlled by corruption. Yet, in the same way the father ran to enrapture the prodigal son in his loving embrace, God was now enveloping me. The father gave him life, breath, food, a home, safety, wealth, a future, and he told that same father, "You are as good as dead to me, give me your wealth and get out of my life." His father gave him what he wanted, and he became such a radical drunkard that he squandered an entire fortune on boozing and sleeping around.

His story was my story. We had both spat in the face of our Father, to whom we owed not only our lives, but every good thing we had ever experienced. We exchanged our Father and His all-sufficient love for money, sex, inebriation, and eventually emaciation. We both were bled dry by a world that cannot satisfy. And we both ended up in the arms of the same God and Father whom we had battered and blasphemed. Even at the very end, the son didn't come home because he had a sudden bout with virtue and decided to get his life together. He came home because he was starving and needed food. He came home because he was pragmatic, and it was the only practical option. He came home to benefit himself.

His lifestyle made him weak, sick, and famished. His decisions drained his virtue, his hope, and his future. And yet, the father had been waiting day after day for this child to come home. The moment the father so much as glimpsed him, he ran to embrace this stealing, slighting, self-absorbed, whoremongering, drunkard. The story was never about the magnitude of the son's sins. There is nothing impressive about sinning. The focus of the story is, and has always been, on the love of the father, and on His willingness to restore those of us who do not deserve it and cannot earn it. It was this same Father who now held me in the undying steadfastness of His love.

With His arms wrapped around me, I knew He was not willing to let me go. Undeserving and stubborn as I was, His love was greater than my rebellion, greater than my brokenness, greater than my hurt or hatred. In an instant, I suddenly knew it was all true. He was real, and in Him was the life I'd been longing for, one of purpose, meaning, and hope. I could lean on Him. Whatever I might face, He would hold me through it all. He would lead me in a dance that would free me from all the weights holding me down, from all the sin eating me up. He would show me true joy, peace, and delight. He would lead me out of death and into life.

I had failed more times than I could count. I had turned from Him both intentionally and unintentionally. Yet He kept coming at me, saying, "I'm not giving up on you. Your failures will never define you, nor will your successes. You are not hopeless, nor will you ever be, because I am with you. I will not leave you nor forsake you. I will not let you slip from my hands. You can ignore me, you can defy me, you can be unfaithful, but nothing will deter my love for you."

To be known wholly and completely by the Creator of all things; to face the reality that He sees our every thought, deed, and idle word, and still wants us and He is willing to look past who we are and what we've done, and die for us, to be valued like this is the greatest feat in life. This promise is not *only* for those who have gotten their act together, but for *any* willing to trust in Him. The most vile, vulgar, and pathetic of creatures can receive this gift, if only they will get on their knees and turn to Him, hand Him the reins and let Him oust the darkness from the throne of their lives.

Without God, whose arms I was in, all of life was nothing more than a rat race to find pleasure, wealth, and approval from others. One glorious rat race, and then we're gone. But I was not limited to an empty life like that anymore. I was His.

***

Two jagged spears of diagonally cut bone jostled back and forth, tearing everything but artery, as they worked to reposition me onto the toboggan. They were shouting at me now, their voices pulling me back into consciousness. "We need you to work with us here. We've got to get you in the right position to prevent further damage." I looked down to find that they'd managed to chisel away the ice that had previously bound my foot to my board. Even without the extra weight of my board, I still could not move the detached leg. Trying to do so sent tremors of pain pulsating through me.

The only way for me to move was by pushing myself forward with shaky hands. As my weight hit the toboggan the man who clung to the other end slid a few inches down the almost vertical slope. He braced himself and tightened his grip, trying not to slip off the ledge and into the frozen white abyss. Each of us gazed intently down the cliff, my vision hazing in and out. When I was finally situated, the medic inched his way skillfully forward, dropping five to ten feet with each turn. As we worked our way down the snowy terrace, and I fought not to slip from consciousness, I continued to whisper that oh so powerful name.

***

Perhaps, one of the most terrifying things in life is to face the prospect of our own death. And yet, no matter how cautious, careful, healthy, and discerning we are, death comes for each of us. Roughly 60,000,000 people die every year. Statistically speaking, 10 out of 10 people will die. It is one of very few things that remains 100% constant with no alteration. We are all called to go to a place we do not know. It is appointed for every human to die once. When we drop through that trapdoor, we will either fall into the hands of the transcendent creator God or into eternal nothingness.

Jesus made a series of the most radical claims that have ever been spoken. "I am the eternal God who created everything. I have power to do anything. I have gained victory over death. I will give you eternal life if you believe in me." He promises to anyone willing to trust in Him that death will not be their end.

As I faced the prospect of my own death, I could not think of any offer more relevant.

With each turn the sled ricocheted slightly. The straps tied around my body kept me fixed to it, but the bouncing triggered enormous pain. "We're going to get you out of this. You're going to be okay," the medic shouted over his shoulder.

"I love the Lord because he hears my voice and my prayer for mercy. Because he bends down to listen, I will pray as long as I have breath! Death wrapped its ropes around me; the terrors of the grave overtook me. I saw only trouble and sorrow. Then I called on the name of the Lord: 'Please, Lord, save me!' How kind the Lord is! How good he is! So merciful, this God of ours! The Lord protects those of childlike faith; I was facing death, and he saved me. Let my soul be at rest again, for the Lord has been good to me. He has saved me from death, my eyes from tears, my feet from stumbling."—*Psalm 116:1-9* (NLT)

Chapter Twenty-Seven

The Crux

After a lengthy descent, we finally arrived at a snowmobile, which had been positioned at the foot of the mountain to transport me from our location to the nearest road where the ambulance was waiting. Another lengthy period. The only thing anchoring me to reality was the pain, which never quite enabled me to slip fully from consciousness.

When we finally made it to the ambulance, they began pumping my body with opiates. After three doses of morphine, two doses of dilaudid, and one of fentanyl, my body tremored. The intensity of the pain did not relent. They had maxed out on opiates. They couldn't give me anything else, so they talked to me as the drugs gradually took effect. I groaned in agony as I whispered His name until we'd made it halfway to the hospital, when I finally passed out.

Before I knew what was happening, my body was being twisted and turned, my broken bone forced into tragically inappropriate positions.

I screamed, "Stop, please stop!"

The contortionism continued, and a voice spoke firmly in my ear, "We need to get these x-rays for the surgeon. I know it's painful, but we have to do this. We won't be able to help you until we get these done correctly."

I worked as hard as I could to hold my dislocated bone in the proper position. I blacked out from the pain. They continued jostling the shattered shards of bone back and forth across the table, forcing me awake with each jolt of pain.

When they finally finished, they forced my mangled body onto an operating table. Before they could perform surgery, they had to reposition my seized muscles and collapsed bones. They put me on an experimental medication to complete the pre-op. They pumped a mixture of ketamine and propofol (the drug that Michael Jackson overdosed on) into my system. My vision blurred as the surgeon grabbed a drill and began drilling a hole through my shin bone. As soon as he was finished, he placed a metal rod through the hole in my bone and connected it to a pulley device.

The weights that were racked onto the pulley slowly forced my muscles to extend, pulling the separated bones into alignment. The weights hung from the end of the hospital bed, suspended in the air. Even though the contraption looked like a middle school physics experiment for a pulleys lesson, it performed its job well. In a matter of minutes, the agonizing muscle twitches and seized nerves were forced into cooperation. Now we just needed to wait for the drugs to wear off so they could put me out, cut me open, replace my bone marrow with titanium, and drill bolts through my bones. This was beginning to feel like a repeat of the night when that stupid couch ate my phone. Ketamine and opiates pulsed through my veins, reality slurred, and my pulse faded in and out.

When I awoke, my mother was stroking my face like I was a long-lost pet. I fell in and out of consciousness several more times over the next few hours, and each time I awoke she was there, stroking my face and telling me everything was going to be alright. Each time she saw my eyelids flicker, she would initiate conversation.

This time she was talking quickly, "Look at this pretty nurse here. She has been helping you through this whole process. Isn't she beautiful?"

I looked upwards, attempting to gaze at her fine beauty, but my vision was too blurry.

"She looks like a static blob," I said, too intoxicated to realize the crudeness of my remarks.

My mother gasped and turned to the lady, "Huh... How rude! He doesn't mean that, sweetie pie, you just ignore him, he's not thinking straight," she said with encouraging decisiveness. And then I blacked out again.

When I woke up, there was frantic discussion about me. When they saw I was awake they rushed me into the operating room.

"Count backward from ten," the man in the mask told me as he realized I was gazing at him. "ten, nine, eigh…"

I do not know how many hours it was until I finally emerged back into the land of the living, but when I did, my leg was securely reattached to the rest of my body. When the surgeon briefed me on my prognosis, he said it would take roughly three months for my bone to heal. I'd be bedridden for a few weeks and then be on crutches for the remainder of that time. He asked me to follow up with him in a month and told me not to put weight on it between now and then. Without further ado, he prescribed me a plethora of oxycontin and percocet to subdue the pain.

I stayed in the hospital a few more days until I was fit to return home. My dad took almost a full week off work to spend time with me and single-handedly clean the same apartment he'd helped me move into less than a year before. He negotiated the details with my landlord, moved all my belongings, and cleaned the place so thoroughly he got the full deposit back despite the fact we'd had to end the lease early. As was his nature, he gave it entirely to me.

The first thing on my to-do list was to reach out to my professors explaining why I had missed class. A note from the surgeon helped greatly in my correspondence with each of them. They were impressed by my determination not to give up, even against such overwhelming odds. My parents had paid over four thousand dollars for the semester and I'd already completed over half the work; I was not about to give up now. I told my professors I was willing to write weekly emails to demonstrate that I'd read the text and do any extra work they might require. My only request was that they please allow me to work from home as my current condition made it difficult for me to reach even the bathroom, which was no more than five feet outside my bedroom.

Hobbling on my crutches caused so much pain I couldn't even shower without my dad's help. Climbing over the tall edge of the tub seemed as terrifying an act to me as a toddler taking his first steps. My dad would set up a crate in the center of the tub and wait for me to unclothe. Then he'd pick me up and lift me over the ledge. As he did so my eyes would cross with pain and fear. It felt as if just one wrong movement or misstep could cause the metal bolts, rods, and screws that held my fragmented leg together to be jolted out of place. Once he'd gotten me situated, he would reach up and grab the shower head for me, making sure the temperature was to my liking.

My father's love and kindness during this time astonished me. It was not because he and my mother hadn't always been this way, they had; but because now I was finally capable of realizing how blessed I was to have them. My parents had remained steadfast and loving, not just *after* I put them through hell itself, but every step along the way. I spent the next three months in the sunless, dreary basement of my parents' home. After being independent and going to college, finding myself here again felt like winding back up at square one. Not only living in the 'rent's basement, but once again, dependent on opiates, albeit this time, not by choice.

The pain would wake me in the middle of the night, surging through my body. If we missed one single dose of oxycontin, my body would surge. I largely stopped eating so that the painkillers would have a stronger effect, so that they would help me more, but also so that they would give me more of a buzz. I shrank down to an almost skeletal size. I finished out the semester in this fashion, stuck in my bed, drugged up on oxycontin, unable to move or eat.

Sometimes I would have flashbacks; I would see myself crashing up against the rock and feel myself dangling there, in-between there and oblivion. I would shake and tremble, seeing the accident in my mind's eye as if it were happening again. I suppose the opiates helped with that too, numbing not only the physical pain but the mental and emotional pain as well. I had a massive hematoma where my entire thigh and upper leg were swollen twice their normal size. The area was black, green, and blue, and was disgusting to look at. It took several months of healing before it looked normal again.

The doctor prescribed me a regimen of syringes with anticoagulants I was to inject in my belly to prevent blood clots. I tried so hard not to abuse them. I tried so hard to take the pills as prescribed. We thought that by hiding the pills upstairs where I could not reach them that I'd be alright, but we were wrong. I kept telling myself I was not the same person anymore, but I kept doing the same stupid things. Every four hours, I would be handed another dose of oxycontin to mitigate the pain. For the first couple of nights, I was able to take it as prescribed, but before long, I was lying and abusing it. I would pretend to swallow a pill but instead save it for later. I would endure the agonizing pain for a few hours just so that I could take two or three pills at once and get a buzz.

The more I took the pills, the more desensitized I became. After a while, I started chewing the pills, which still wasn't enough, so I started snorting them. The fact that I had been clean from opiates for so long did nothing to prevent me from sliding into addictive tendencies now. The pain was a realistic and adequate excuse to use the drugs, but it was getting out of hand. Each day, the needles full of anticoagulants looked more and more enticing. Each week, after injecting them in my stomach, I'd clean and save one or two of them and hide them in my nightstand.

Maybe it was the need to feel a stronger buzz, maybe it was built up residual fear and trauma from the accident, maybe it was the lack of other more adequate coping mechanisms, or maybe it was just the fact I'd trained myself to act on these habits for years and hardwired my brain for failure. Whatever it was, having the drugs readily available and prescribed to my name was enough to tempt me into abusing them. It didn't seem to matter how many boundaries I'd put in place or how much I'd grown in self-discipline. As I found myself acting in a way that grieved me to watch, I had to admit that I wouldn't be doing this if part of me didn't want it. The very fact I was doing it showed this is what I really wanted. How could I both hate something and want something at the same time?

On the first day that I fully relapsed and started shooting up, I waited until both my parents went to work. I'd been fighting the idea for weeks. It kept coming to my mind and I kept battling it out. No matter how hard I fought against it, I found myself veering towards that which I despised. When the chance arrived, each action happened nearly of its own accord. Without intellectually acceding to what I was doing, I found myself hiding a spoon and a lighter, seeking a cotton swab, storing up some extra pills. When I finally took the leap and shot up, I felt drowned in regret, sorrow, and shame.

Previously, I had always done whatever I wanted, without thinking twice about it, almost as if I didn't have a conscience. Now my conscience was screaming at me, "Don't do this to your parents again." "Don't do this to yourself again. YOU CAN STOP!" Each time I shot up, the voice would fade to an incoherent whisper, saying, "You don't need this." Even though I could clearly see what was good, I was still not capable of doing it. When you hate the things you are doing, and yet you still keep on doing them, you slowly begin to hate yourself.

I was breaking inside. A part of me still wanted drugs, even after all they had done to me. This was me when I relied on my own devices. This was me in my purest form. This was the sum of my own strength. This is what I amounted to on my own. This is who I was without constant, sincere, impassioned reliance on God. I was a backslider. I kept choosing sin, which was empty, and rejecting God, who was not, and I did not know why. I was a helpless living contradiction. Choosing to backslide was like choosing to jump into a pit of sorrow, guilt, and shame that I could not climb out of.

For a moment I thought I could pull myself off the painkillers, but when I tried, I couldn't function with the overbearing pain. I even tried using weed to get myself off the opiates but when I snuck out on my wobbly crutches and took my first puff in over a year, I found it surprisingly repulsive. It felt like that scene in *The Lord of the Rings* where Frodo puts the ring on his finger, and the eye of Sauron narrows in on him. It was like the veil in between the physical world and the spiritual world was lifted, and that huge flaming eyeball was blazing straight into my soul whispering to me with the voice of a thousand overlapping shadows. The darkness waiting eagerly to latch hold of my soul and drag me away again.

The power and intensity of that experience made me shake and tremble with fear. The reality and tangibility of God in that moment was so jarring that I threw the rest of the weed away and decided to just stick with the opiates. I knew that using drugs to get off drugs was stupid. I knew that classifying one drug as better or more tolerable than another was stupid as well. Weed was the reason I had become an addict in the first place. It had always been one of the main substances that kept me stuck, and one of the main excuses that kept me returning to this empty lifestyle. I just had so many years of bad habits that my very best and most genuine efforts to thwart addiction were not enough. I was the dog that returns to its vomit—the sinner who can't help but return to his sin.

After the accident, my mom got in the habit of coming straight home after work each day to cook me a meal, feed me my prescriptions, and sit at the foot of my bed, just the same as she had done for my sister. The second or third time she did this, I asked her if she would be willing to read to me from the Bible. Her heart must've melted to see her child, after so many years of obstinate defiance, finally hungering for more of God. The first text that she read when she randomly flipped the Bible open was from the book of Romans. It struck me so powerfully that it took all my might just to hold back my tears until she left the room. The text read, "But God demonstrates his own love for us in this: While we were still sinners, Christ died for us" (Romans 5:8 NIV).

If He saw me at my very worst, when drugs, sex, and other fleeting pleasures ruled every portion of my heart, mind, and life, and still chose to die for me, He must still love me now. If He was patient with me when I was living solely for rebellion, He must also be willing to be patient with me now that my heart was softening and I was actually trying. I was still failing, but at least my heart wanted to honor Him now.

Tears dripped down my face as I realized He died for me when I was at my worst. He didn't die for a good, well-put-together man, He loved and died for a junkie kid who was selfish. Not only did He die for me when I was snorting ketamine off a girl's butt and being a sleaze bag, but He made sure she sat on the ketamine so that when I snorted it, there wasn't enough to kill me. When I was driving drunk, He sent the police to make sure I didn't hurt anyone. When I was evading the police, selling drugs, and causing chaos everywhere I went, He corrected me when I needed it, let me off the hook when I needed it, and loved me through the whole process. His love wasn't just some abstract idea or feeling; He was there with me in each of these moments.

Each time I failed, it may have surprised me, but it didn't surprise God, who sees and knows all things, even before they happen. That's when it struck me. God knew I was going to stab Him in the back. God knew that if He saved my life, I was going to abuse these drugs. He knew that I was going to turn away from Him toward all the other things I loved more than Him. He knew I would relapse, yet He still chose to save my life. He knew that if He were to save me, I would let Him down, but He saved me anyway. He was there every time, providing a way so I could walk through it without losing myself to it. Even as I actively defied Him, even as I stabbed Him in the back, even as I abused my prescriptions, He loved me just as much now as He ever would. Even though He knew I would let Him down, He loved me enough to trade His life for mine. He had already paid for the worst that I could possibly delve out.

He loved me as I was; He had reached into my darkness and sat with me there. He didn't blame me for my faults or struggles. He hadn't grown impatient with my endless cycles of failure, and He wasn't going to. He didn't show me this kindness because of my good qualities or characteristics, or because I had potential. He didn't save me because of my track record, but in spite of it. That's when it finally hit home—God is not a pile of bricks or a collection of outdated rules—He is a living, breathing, Being. No church, no building, no collection of people would ever *be* Him. He was God. He was love. He is the greatest being in the universe. Nothing—save Jesus' death on the cross—could ever fully represent Him or His love for the human race.

"What can I offer the Lord for all he has done for me? I will lift up the cup of salvation and praise the Lord's name for saving me." —*Psalm 116:12-13* (NLT)

Chapter Twenty-Eight

The Boulder On My Path
& Plans Erased

"Lord, you will grant us peace; all we have accomplished is really from you. O Lord our God, others have ruled us, but you alone are the one we worship." —*Isaiah 26:12-13* (NLT)

Every day I'd think about the three miracles God used to save my life: How the moment I had prayed for help, He had sent it; how we'd been struggling with our phones and screaming on the side of the cliff when all we needed to do was use His direct line, and how the ski patrol were on their break and there to have fun, but they'd been sent directly to us, before my accident even occurred, before I ever knew I needed them. He timed it in such a way that the moment I finally turned to Him for help, two large white crosses descended upon me.

The second miracle, I only discovered later in the hospital. It takes 1800 pounds of pressure per square inch to break a femur bone. It takes three psi to cut an artery. Somehow, 1800 pounds of pressure had obliterated my leg, tearing through my bone, muscle, tendon, and ligaments, yet not even three of those 1800 pounds had touched my artery. It was as if His hands were wrapped around the artery, preventing anything from touching it. If even three of those 1800 pounds of pressure had been exacted on the artery, I would've bled to death. Adding to the improbability of it all was the fact that my bone was cut diagonally like two spears inside my leg, jagged and ready to tear through anything in their path. The fact is, the spears of bone did cut through everything in my leg, except the arteries.

The third miracle was still beyond my ability to explain. Jesus had held me in His very arms. He tangibly lifted my pain. He had given me help and strength, just like He had promised He would do through the Bible verse He had given me that very morning. Even though He knew I'd stab Him in the back, He'd still done all of this to save me.

The first verse my mother had randomly flipped to in Romans was so powerful we decided to read the whole book together. The next verse that stuck out was Romans 8:38, which said, "…Neither death nor life, neither angels nor principalities, neither the present nor the future, nor any powers, neither height nor depth, nor anything else in all creation, will be able to separate us from the love of God that is in Christ Jesus our Lord."

God's promise is that no power, nor principality, including death itself can separate us from His love for us which is in Jesus. No present fault nor future failure can separate us from this love. It never was, nor has it ever been our production of good qualities that merit God's love, it simply is who He is. He loved me, even when I despised myself. Brennan Manning once said, "God's love is a love that is so deep, so wide, that we can no more contain it than a teacup can contain Niagara Falls" [48]. If we get even the slightest glimpse into a love this great, there is no response other than to hand ourselves over to it.

I needed a new love. Not only a new place and person upon which to set my affections, not only a source that wouldn't deceive me, but I needed a source that would give back. I needed a source that could win over my heart and steal away my affections, a source more pleasurable than drugs and less deceitful, a source more constant than a significant other, a source whose faithfulness and consistency came not because I earned it, but because it was. I hadn't done anything to be rescued, nor could I do anything, but He rescued me, nonetheless. I had failed on more occasions than I could count, but He hadn't ever failed, and wasn't going to. For years, I had chosen to espouse addiction, sex, and success, rather than espousing the one who actually, truly, fully, cared about me. I had to live in lavish indulgence of my sin for years, before I was able to realize that it couldn't ever fully satisfy. I exchanged a love that would set me apart, heal me, and free me from dependence, for a pimp that kept me like a slave, locked in a hotel room, unable to escape. I traded freedom for vices. I traded fulfilling love for inanimate objects and idolatrous relationships that controlled and exploited me. But the whole time, He was waiting there, waiting for His prostitute beloved, ready to break me free. He interjected Himself in front of the bullet flying straight towards the heart of the one who had just stabbed Him in the back.

He was ready to take a pothead, alcoholic, heroin-addicted, whoremonger, a bulimic, cigarette smoking womanizer, and form the deepest type of bond that could be made and had no exit clauses or reversals. He had pursued me when others would've given up a thousand times. He made a covenant with me, signed by a pen dipped in His own blood, a covenant forged by His love, *in* His love, and *through* His love. It is a love story written by the Author of the universe.

Though I had drowned myself in guilt, sorrow, and shame, God drowned me in His love.

Why are we so moved by a good love story? Why does it touch our hearts so deeply when a hero willingly takes the fall on behalf of others? These stories touch us because they are wired into our hearts and modeled after the greatest story ever written, the story of God's love for His creation. Though we as a people pillaged this beautiful earth with acts of war, rape, terror, and molestation, He washed our sins with His blood. Instead of letting us damn ourselves unimpeded, He sowed a destiny of hope. Instead of shaming us for our many awful ways, He drown us in His love.

Once I understood this love, I could not let Him slip to the periphery. Once I accepted Him, I could not forget Him. I still struggled, but I woke to thoughts of Him and went to bed with those same thoughts. I was never lifeless or hopeless again. There were seasons of compromise when I struggled. Times I chose sin instead of choosing to trust God. In those seasons, I felt stagnant and faced great difficulty, but by the grace of God, my trust in Him became stronger through the trials. Over time, those transgressions became less frequent. Sometimes I would do good and walk in victory for a year, sometimes three. Sometimes I would struggle for a minute, sometimes I would struggle for six months on end. Yet God, in His grace, never let go of me, and never let my faults or failures define me again.

I never became a drug addict again and by God's grace I never shot up after that either. I smoked weed three times after I was saved, and each time I grew more repulsed by the substance. By God's grace I was able to break free from it completely. I never became a bulimic again, although I did puke at times, even after being saved. I wrestled with cigarette smoking on and off for over a decade, quitting for a year and starting again and quitting and starting. I wrestled with alcohol and used it as a crutch through several very hard seasons. And I struggled with lust in the same way. While some people are freed overnight, for me it was a very hard, very slow, very intentional process that has taken over a decade. There was no quick fix or magic solution, but there has been a lot of healing over time and one day my healing will be complete.

As my mother continued reading to me from the book of Romans, we grew closer than we ever had been. We both knew that God had saved my life and we were both eager to learn more about Him. He had answered her many prayers on those dark and desolate nights when sleep eluded her and she stayed up praying for her prodigal child. He had intervened in the way that only He could.

Neither of us had read the full book of Romans, so when my mom read the following verses, we were dumbfounded. "See, I lay in Zion a stone that causes people to stumble and a rock that makes them fall, and the one who believes in him will never be put to shame" (Romans 9:33 NIV). All I could think of was the rock that I had crashed into, the stone that made me fall. As I ripped the Bible from her hands and tore through its pages, I found that Paul had been quoting an ancient prophesy from Isaiah.

'God spoke strongly to me, grabbed me with both hands and warned me not to go along with this people. He said: 'Don't be like this people, always afraid somebody is plotting against them. Don't fear what they fear. Don't take on their worries. If you're going to worry, worry about The Holy. Fear God-of-the-Angel-Armies. The Holy can be either a Hiding Place or a Boulder blocking your way, The Rock standing in the willful way of both houses of Israel, A barbed-wire Fence preventing trespass to the citizens of Jerusalem. Many of them are going to run into that Rock and get their bones broken, Get tangled up in that barbed wire and not get free of it.'" — *Isaiah 8:11-15* (MSG)

Don't be like *this people…*

Don't take on *their worries…*

The Holy can be either a hiding place *or a boulder blocking your way*...

Many of them are going to *run into that rock and get their bones broken*...

Get tangled up in that *barbed wire* and not get free of it...

Flashes of the accident replayed themselves in my mind. Flashes of the news feed when I was young, the reporter standing next to the barbed wire fence, my sister absent from the frame, her blood showering the background. Flashes of my past: always going along with crowd, always doing what I thought would make me cool, always afraid, worried, insecure. Always refusing to make my hiding place in God. Always turning to the world, it's lies, and all the wild things, never being satisfied. Running, running, running, into the rock... The deepest part of my being, exposed by the eerie accuracy of this text. It had all happened. This text was my life and He was the boulder. My sin was the barbed wire. I'd gotten so tangled up in lies.

He was the stone that stood stubbornly between me and my oblivion.

He was even more unmovable, unyielding, and unbending than the means He'd used to reach me: His unfailing love, more unchanging than the nearly ageless boulder I'd crashed into. His words, more consistent and reliable than the laws of the universe themselves, His character, more faithful than the rising and the setting sun, His laws and guidance, more persistent than the police at rooting out my selfishness and calling me to be more, His ability and willingness to restore me, were and are more evident and guaranteed than the lawyer who'd defended me. His nurturing care was more persistent than my parents who'd refused to give up on me.

> Grace strikes us when we are in great pain and restlessness. It strikes us when we walk through the dark valley of a meaningless and empty life. It strikes us when we feel that our separation is deeper than usual because we have violated another life, a life which we loved, or from which we were estranged. It strikes us when our disgust for our own being, our indifference, our weakness, our hostility, and our lack of direction and composure have become intolerable to us. It strikes us when, year after year, the longed-for perfection of life does not appear, when the old compulsions reign within us as they have for decades, when despair destroys all joy and courage.
>
> The moment comes when a wave of light breaks into our darkness, and a voice says: "You are accepted. You are accepted, accepted by

that which is greater than you, by One whose name is above every name. Do not try to do anything. Do not seek for anything; do not perform anything; do not intend anything. Simply accept the fact that you are accepted!" When that happens to us, we experience grace.

After such an experience, everything is transformed. In that moment, grace conquers sin, and reconciliation occurs. The lost are found—the weak are made strong, the blind see, and there is nothing but acceptance. Nothing is demanded of this experience, no religious or moral or intellectual presupposition, nothing but acceptance. That is God's Amazing Grace.

~ Paul Tillich, *The Shaking of the Foundation* [41]

Grace had struck me even harder than the rock that had almost taken my life. Its impact had dislodged more than just a femur bone. Grace had —and would— dislodge all sorts of crap from my life. Though I was still a college student and had no idea what I was supposed to do with my life, though I still struggled and failed, I was not on my own any longer. Grace struck me, and I would never be the same. My first chance at life had been spent pursuing misdirected longings that couldn't satisfy. For all these years, I thought I knew what needed to be done in order to craft a life of meaning. I followed the various leads that people gave me and pursued those paths with reckless abandon. They were empty, but now I had something that wasn't.

I don't know how on earth I had managed to miss it this long, but joy, true joy, was in God. The joy and fulfillment I had always longed for was right in front of me. He wasn't only the greatest friend, or the fiercest lover. He wasn't just capable of creating meaning and purpose through the pain and hardships. The joy I found in knowing Him was beyond circumstance. The peace I had as I walked with Him could face down every fear and anxiety. Best of all, He wasn't fleeting or temporary, He was solid and reliable, and whenever I acted on what He told me, I always found hope and healing, even when I was facing really hard times.

As I got to know God more in that dark basement, I realized He was everything I'd ever wanted and needed. My whole life, I'd wanted to escape my hometown. I'd always wanted to get out and see the rest of the world, to see what "normal" looked like. Since I couldn't physically escape it, I did so mentally, using drugs to dull the fact that I couldn't fit in. As I got to know

Him, however, I realized that He was more than enough. I didn't need anything else. I didn't need to escape to another place. So, I made Him a promise: "God, I would be dead if you hadn't saved my life. I spent my first chance at life on myself, but this chance is for you. I'll do whatever you ask. I'll go wherever you want, even if that means you want me to stay here, as long as you promise to be with me. You are everything I've ever wanted and needed. Now that I finally see You, I know You are more than enough."

When God's love finally broke through the stone-cold calloused shell that barricaded my heart from His, I couldn't keep walking or living the way I had been. My life was no longer my own. It belonged to Him. When your heart is captivated by love, you cannot keep selling yourself to a prostitute. When your heart is captivated by God you cannot keep selling your soul to worthless idols. This is not another story of some street rat getting sober or "putting his life together." I didn't put my life together, God did. Every time I tried to put my own life together, I made things worse. No, I am not the protagonist of this story—God is; from page one, until the day I die. He has always been the hero, He has always brought the hope. My story was written by and centers around the God who restores, redeems, and makes all things new.

Happily-ever-after is not adequately summed up in the hero's journey. Even if you do ace every quest, defeat every foe, and obtain your magic castle, it will never be enough. Even the accomplishment of our dreams will not satisfy for long, and even our dream girl or guy is going let us down. But God's love never fails. His power and His plans don't only echo into eternity, they define it. If you want a happy ending, don't look for it in this life, and don't make yourself the center of the story. There is a God who is a real hero, who has fixed His attention on you, who wants to wrap up your story within His own and pour out His affections on you. It does not matter how pitiful, powerful, majestic, or frail you or your story may be. He is the God who takes the things that are nothing but foolish and weak, and calls them His own. He alone can transform our stories into something lasting and utterly beautiful.

In many ways this book is written for all my friends who never could break free; it is for those who still call the streets their home, those who have rejected their families and abandoned their children, all for just one more high. It is for my precious friends who tremble and shake and must drink one liter of vodka a day, just to survive, whose kidneys and livers are failing them though they are only in their twenties. It is for those friends who spent the last decade in prison and are better off because of it, my friends who were less fortunate, who kept evading the law, who acted on their addictions without hindrance, and whose hair and teeth and brains have rotted to mush.

Without the help and hope of God, I never would've recovered after my relapses. I never would've had anything better to exchange drugs for. I would've kept relapsing into oblivion. There are no heroes in the life of an addict, there is only the one who is rescued, or the one who never breaks free. In many ways, this book is for my friends who are still fighting, but are doing it alone. I am so proud of you. It is a miracle you have made it this far. Now come, lay your burdens down, and let your Maker set you free.

"God made my life complete when I placed all the pieces before him… Now I'm alert to God's ways; I don't take God for granted. Every day I review the ways he works; I try not to miss a trick. I feel put back together, and I'm watching my step. God rewrote the text of my life when I opened the book of my heart to his eyes." —*Psalm 18:20-24* (MSG)

Epilogue

"So if the Son sets you free, you will be free indeed." —*John 8:36*

Since I couldn't walk or move for three months, I decided to sign up for summer classes. I figured since I couldn't do anything else, I should at least get another semester ahead in school. I remember when the day finally came for me to take my first step without crutches. It was one of the most pathetic and delightful things I have ever done. Pathetic because I nearly toppled over, and delightful because I could feel the proverbial wind in my hair and the bright, warm sunshine on my face. I hadn't ever truly appreciated the ability to walk until after I lost it. When I realized how special walking was for the first time, I also realized that I hadn't ever truly appreciated the ability to breathe, smell, taste, or smile, either. I felt like the luckiest man alive, just to have two legs again, even though I still couldn't use the one very well.

As pitiful as it was, I was proud to be hobbling. My goals were lowered, not because my standards were lower, but because I'd been through trauma. It took me a long time to realize that my soul had been through trauma too, not just because of the accident, but also because of my past. My addictive lifestyle had damaged me mentally, physically, emotionally, intellectually, and spiritually. The trauma I'd experienced had not only wreaked havoc on my body, brain and life, but it had also stunted my development in each of these areas. It would take time to heal, and I might only be able to hobble for a while. Some would've called it pathetic, heck, I even called it pathetic, but my God did not. He could clearly see what I couldn't: My negligible efforts and goals were suitable for my circumstance.

Because of the distance education and advanced placement classes I had taken while still a drug addict, I was two-and-a-half years ahead of my contemporaries. By the time I finished the Spring and Summer semesters from my parent's basement, I was on track to get my bachelor's degree at age twenty. From there, I planned to get a master's degree at twenty-two, but God made it quite clear to me that the reason He'd helped me get so far ahead in school was for one purpose only, that I might serve Him. When I finally surrendered my will to Him again, God flung me out of the state and catapulted me like a wrecking ball through thirty-five different countries. Serving Him has been crazier and more profound than all my wildest drug stories combined.

I'd spent my entire life trying to be enough, to be good enough, to fit in, to be attractive enough, popular enough, smart enough, sober enough, stable enough. It turned out I'd been enough the entire time. According to God, the only One whose opinion matters, even at my worst I'd been enough.

Now I was defined by the only One who could ascribe definite, concrete, objective value to an object, the only One whose opinion wasn't subjective and fleeting, the only One whose existence wasn't slowly passing away, and the only One who wouldn't ever let me down. His words had always been true; the only difference was that now I trusted them enough to build my life on them.

My trust and wellbeing aren't placed in my own abilities any longer but in the God who fights on my behalf. He empowers me to stand each time I fall. I didn't just win because I got to go to heaven when I died, I won because I got to bank on God being here with me in the rat race of life. I would still struggle and fail, but I would never be alone in the battle again. The shortcomings and insecurities could no longer define me in the way they once did. As a Christian, I may still lose as many battles as the next person, but I won't lose hope.

Perhaps life's simplest and most frequent mistake is to take who we are for granted in our anxious anticipation of who we might be. He loves us as we are. Why can we not rejoice in that love? Can you imagine, for a moment, what would happen if we were to stop trying to find love in all the wrong places and start spending our efforts trying to cherish His love for us? I was finished being someone who called myself by His name, yet turned to all the empty things of this world to satisfy my innermost needs. I was through fabricating solutions of my own devising, crafting makeshift concoctions that never hit the mark.

I was done trying to pull love and meaning from the meager reserves of other people and my accomplishments. I was His beloved now, which meant I could soak up meaning and purpose from the limitless reservoir of the God who made me. The deficits which had always marked me were melting away. My identity was being rewritten. My shame was being erased. The inward feeling of lack that I strived to mask with so many things was being replaced with a complete confidence, a wholeness that I had never thought possible.

I was no longer missing a piece. Jesus had taken all my insufficiencies, washed them away, and filled the very core of my being with His approval. Just like the day that He had given me a clean slate and released me from jail, now He was doing that same thing internally. He was washing away the belief that I was an inadequate failure who was unworthy and incapable of ever changing. He was making me into a new creation and it was going to be a thoroughly delightful process.

What did it mean to be a Christian? It did not mean to be a good person, to be more Christ-like or to get my act together. It meant the king of the universe was at the center of my life. I got to trust in His wisdom instead of my own. He was my Lord and I was His disciple, His chosen, His beloved. Everything on which I had previously built my life inevitably crumbled beneath me like sinking sand. It didn't matter how many years I spent constructing my empire, or how well I built it, when the foundations I'd chosen were unreliable.

He was the solid foundation I'd always been looking for. The One who made me, saw me; He saw me reject Him again and again. And yet, here He was pursuing me, stepping in to rescue me. Because I wouldn't go to Him, He came to me, the God of creation, pursuing an insignificant speck with unparalleled devotion.

I finally found something more stable than myself, my emotions, and fleeting pleasures to base my existence on. I finally found something, solid, stable, and reliable. God was more permanent than the looming mountains that molded me to their will. Though my life is like grass that grows one day and withers away the next, God is so permanent, so unbending, so eternal, He makes the rocks look like vapors in the wind, the earth itself look like a drop in the ocean. So vast and immeasurable, He makes the boundless depths of space and the endless lengths of time look meager and insignificant. And this Being, Creator of all, set His love on me. This Being chose to make me an object of His eternal love. This Being chose to rip me from a fleeting and insignificant life in which I was decaying into dust, and give me life eternal, making me an object more immortal, more imperishable than the rocks themselves.

Somehow, God turned the worst thing I could have imagined into one of the things that I'm now most grateful for. Somewhere in between a rock and a hard place I met the Rock of Ages. Somewhere in between life and death, He saved my soul. Without that bone crushing boulder, I would have gone round and round, always changing my mind, my friends, my goals, my actions, never getting anywhere except the next hard place. Somewhere along the way, my world of rebellion and prosperity clashed with the spiritual world and I met God. Somewhere in your journey between this life and the next, I pray you will meet Him, too.

"Everyone who comes to me and hears my words and puts them into practice… They are like a man building a house, who dug down deep and laid the foundation on rock. When a flood came, the torrent struck that house but could not shake it, because it was well built. But the one who hears my words and does not put them into practice is like a man who built a house on the ground without a foundation. The moment the torrent struck that house, it collapsed and its destruction was complete" —*Luke 6:46-49.*

"If you declare with your mouth, 'Jesus is Lord,' and believe in your heart that God raised him from the dead, you will be saved." *Romans 10:9*

Bibliography

1. Centers for Disease Control and Prevention. (2021, November 17). *Drug overdose deaths in the U.S. top 100,000 annually*. Centers for Disease Control and Prevention. Retrieved November 20, 2022, from https://www.cdc.gov/nchs/pressroom/nchs_press_releases/2021/20211117.htm

2. National Institute on Drug Abuse. "Overdose Death Rates | National Institute on Drug Abuse (NIDA)." *National Institute on Drug Abuse*, National Institute on Drug Abuse, 20 Jan. 2022, https://nida.nih.gov/research-topics/trends-statistics/overdose-death-rates.

3. "Fact Check: Do Overdoses Kill More in US Than Guns, Motor Vehicles?" *The Daily Signal*, 27 Oct. 2017, https://www.dailysignal.com/2017/10/27/fact-check-do-drug-overdoses-kill-more-americans-than-gun-homicides-and-motor-vehicles/.

4. American Addiction Centers. Alcohol and Drug Abuse Statistics. (2022, October 21). Retrieved November 19, 2022, from https://americanaddictioncenters.org/rehab-guide/addiction-statistics

5. U.S. Department of Health and Human Services. (n.d.). Alcohol Facts and Statistics. National Institute on Alcohol Abuse and Alcoholism. Retrieved November 20, 2022, from https://www.niaaa.nih.gov/publications/brochures-and-fact-sheets/alcohol-facts-and-statistics

6. Grisel, J. (2020). Never enough: The Neuroscience and experience of addiction. Anchor Books, a division of Penguin Random House LLC.

7. DinaGusovsky. (2016, April 27). Americans consume vast majority of the world's opioids. CNBC. Retrieved November 18, 2022, from https://www.cnbc.com/2016/04/27/americans-consume-almost-all-of-the-global-opioid-supply.html

8. List of narcotic drugs: Examples of opioids & other narcotics. American Addiction Centers. (2022, October 20). Retrieved November 18, 2022, from https://americanaddictioncenters.org/the-big-list-of-narcotic-drugs

9. Newport, F. (2021, August 20). Provo-Orem, Utah, is most religious U.S. Metro Area. Gallup.com. Retrieved November 20, 2022, from https://news.gallup.com/poll/161543/provo-orem-utah-religious-metro-area.aspx

10. Ritchie, H., & Roser, M. (2019, December 5). Drug use. Our World in Data. Retrieved November 20, 2022, from https://ourworldindata.org/drug-use

11. Where families find answers. Partnership to End Addiction. (2022, November 16). Retrieved November 20, 2022, from https://centeronaddiction.org/

12. 2020 World Drug Report. America's need for and receipt of substance use treatment Retrieved November 18, 2022, from https://www.samhsa.gov/data/sites/default/files/report_2716/ShortReport-2716.html

13. Brook, D. W., Brook, J. S., Pahl, T., & Montoya, I. (2002). The longitudinal relationship between drug use and risky sexual behaviors among Colombian adolescents. Archives of Pediatrics & Adolescent Medicine, 156(11), 1101. https://doi.org/10.1001/archpedi.156.11.1101

14. Luk, Tracy. P.S. I love you. (n.d.). Retrieved November 19, 2022, from https://psiloveyou.xyz/what-happens-to-your-brain-after-having-too-much-casual-sex-41a206c7f303

15. Cochran, D. M., Fallon, D., Hill, M., & Frazier, J. A. (2013). The role of oxytocin in psychiatric disorders. Harvard Review of

Psychiatry, 21(5), 219–247.
https://doi.org/10.1097/hrp.0b013e3182a75b7d

16. Milenkovic, D. (2022, August 15). 24 harrowing drunk driving statistics. Carsurance. Retrieved November 20, 2022, from https://carsurance.net/insights/drunk-driving-statistics/#:~:text=1.,year%20due%20to%20drunk%20driving.&text=In%20other%20words%2C%2028%20people,driving%20accident%20in%20their%20life.

17. Drunk driving fatality statistics. Responsibility.org. (2022, March 2). Retrieved November 19, 2022, from https://www.responsibility.org/alcohol-statistics/drunk-driving-statistics/drunk-driving-fatality-statistics/

18. Substance Abuse and Mental Health Services Administration. SAMHSA.gov. (n.d.). Retrieved November 19, 2022, from https://www.samhsa.gov/data/

19. Fight the New Drug. (n.d.). 20 stats about the porn industry and its underage consumers. Fight the New Drug. Retrieved November 19, 2022, from https://fightthenewdrug.org/10-porn-stats-that-will-blow-your-mind/

20. Bell, S. (2019). "Testing the Historical Reliability of the New Testament." Josh McDowell Ministry. January 10, 2018. https://www.josh.org/historical-reliability-new-testament/ (Accessed November 21, 2022)

21. Armstrong, D. (2021, November 20). Manuscript evidence: New testament vs. Plato, etc.. Biblical Evidence for Catholicism. Retrieved November 20, 2022, from https://www.patheos.com/blogs/davearmstrong/2015/10/manuscript-evidence-nt-vs-plato-etc.html

22. McDowell , S. (2017, March 13). What is the most recent manuscript count for the new testament? Sean McDowell. Retrieved November 20, 2022, from https://seanmcdowell.org/blog/what-is-the-most-recent-manuscript-count-for-the-new-testament

23. Bancarz, S. (2017, May 17). A list of extra-biblical sources for the historical jesus. Reasons for Jesus. Retrieved November 21, 2022, from https://reasonsforjesus.com/a-list-of-extra-biblical-sources-for-the-historical-jesus/

24. WayofLeaf. (2020, September 3). The link between Marijuana & Dopamine. WayofLeaf. Retrieved November 21, 2022, from https://wayofleaf.com/cannabis/101/marijuana-dopamine

25. Center for Disease Control (2020) Marijuana and Public Health | Mental Health. Retrieved November 21. 2022, from https://www.cdc.gov/marijuana/health-effects/mental-health.html

26. Wald, George (n.d.). Revolution against evolution. Retrieved November 21, 2022, from https://www.rae.org/essay-links/quotes/

27. Intelligent Design Biology Essay Essay - Free College essays. An Essay. (2020, April 17). Retrieved November 21, 2022, from https://an-essay.com/intelligent-design-biology

28. Darwin, Charles, Leonard Kebler, and Joseph Meredith Toner Collection. The Descent of Man: And Selection in Relation to Sex . London: J. Murray, 1871

29. Smith, Wolfgang (n.d.) Retrieved November 21, 2022 from https://www.goodreads.com/author/quotes/254790.Wolfgang_S mith, Wolfgang Smith, Ph.D., physicist and mathematician

30. https://libquotes.com/ludwig-von-bertalanffy/works/general-system-theory

31. George Kocan, Evolution isn't Faith But Theory, Chicago Tribune, Monday, April 21, 1980.

32. https://nida.nih.gov/publications/drugfacts/cannabis-marijuana

33. Meier MH, Caspi A, Ambler A, et al. Persistent cannabis users show neuropsychological decline from childhood to midlife. Proc Natl Acad Sci U S A. 2012;109(40):E2657-E2664. doi:10.1073/pnas.1206820109.

34. Meier MH, Caspi A, Ambler A, et al. Persistent cannabis users show neuropsychological decline from childhood to midlife. Proc Natl Acad Sci U S A. 2012;109(40):E2657-E2664. doi:10.1073/pnas.1206820109.

35. [This is from page 75 of Blaise Pascal's Pensees (New York; Penguin Books, 1966)

36. 1954 Milner and Olds Rewards/Pleasure rat experiment (https://prezi.com/sbwnqfio9iip/milner-and-olds-rewardpleasure-experiment/)

37. Hay, P., Girosi, F., & Mond, J. (2015). Prevalence and sociodemographic correlates of DSM-5 eating disorders in the Australian population. Journal of eating disorders, 3(1

38. https://eating-disorders.org.uk/information/bulimia-nervosa-a-contemporary-analysis/

39. https://breakbingeeating.com/male-bulimia/

40. Byrne, R. (2006) *Secret.* Atria Books, Beyond Words Publishing

41. Tillich, P. (1948) *The Shaking of the Foundations.*186 pp. New York, Charles Scribner's Sons.

42. The National Society of Leadership and Success. (n.d.). NSLS | The National Society of Leadership and Success. https://www.nsls.org/

43. Lipson, H.S. Cosmology and Physics (n.d.). Retrieved November 21, 2022 http://www.ideacenter.org/contentmgr/showdetails.php/id/745

44. Hoyle, F (n.d.) *A quote from Evolution from Space.* Retrieved November 21, 2022 from https://www.goodreads.com/quotes/621156-once-we-see-however-that-the-probability-of-life-originating

45. Spurgeon, Charles (n.d.) AZQuotes.com. Retrieved November 21, 2022 from https://www.azquotes.com/quote/798497

46. Lewis, C. S. (2015). *The Great Divorce* (Revised ed.). HarperOne.

47. Aldous Huxley. (n.d.). AZQuotes.com. Retrieved November 19, 2022, from AZQuotes.com Web site: https://www.azquotes.com/quote/719861

48. The Ragamuffin Gospel by Brennan Manning (2005-06-01). (2022). Hovel Audio.

About Kharis Publishing

.

Kharis Publishing, an imprint of Kharis Media LLC, is a leading Christian and inspirational book publisher based in Aurora, Chicago metropolitan area, Illinois. Kharis' dual mission is to give voice to under-represented writers (including women and first-time authors) and equip orphans in developing countries with literacy tools. That is why, for each book sold, the publisher channels some of the proceeds into providing books and computers for orphanages in developing countries so that these kids may learn to read, dream, and grow. For a limited time, Kharis Publishing is accepting unsolicited queries for nonfiction (Christian, self-help, memoirs, business, health, and wellness) from qualified leaders, professionals, pastors, and ministers. Learn more at: About Us - Kharis Publishing - Accepting Manuscript

CPSIA information can be obtained
at www.ICGtesting.com
Printed in the USA
JSHW012042200323
39193JS00004B/11